Oxford Studies in European Law

General Editors: Paul Craig and Graínne de Búrca

THE EU PRINCIPLE OF SUBSIDIARITY AND ITS CRITIQUE

The EU Principle of
Subsidiarity and its Critique

ANTONIO ESTELLA

OXFORD
UNIVERSITY PRESS

OXFORD
UNIVERSITY PRESS

Great Clarendon Street, Oxford OX2 6DP

Oxford University Press is a department of the University of Oxford.
It furthers the University's objective of excellence in research, scholarship,
and education by publishing worldwide in

Oxford New York

Auckland Bangkok Buenos Aires Cape Town Chennai
Dar es Salaam Delhi Hong Kong Istanbul Karachi Kolkata
Kuala Lumpur Madrid Melbourne Mexico City Mumbai Nairobi
São Paulo Shanghai Singapore Taipei Tokyo Toronto

Oxford is a registered trade mark of Oxford University Press
in the UK and in certain other countries

Published in the United States
by Oxford University Press Inc., New York

© A Estella de Noriega 2002

The moral rights of the author have been asserted
Database right Oxford University Press (maker)

First published 2002

British Library Cataloguing in Publication Data
Data available

Library of Congress Cataloging in Publication Data
Estella de Noriega, Antonio.
The EU principle of subsidiarity and its critique / Antonio Estella.
p. cm.—(Oxford studies in European law)
Based on the author's thesis (doctoral)—European University Institute, 1997.
Includes bibliographical references.
1. Central-local government relations—European Union countries. 2. European federation.
3. Subsidiarity. 4. Court of Justice of the European Communities. I. Title. II. Series.
KJE5076 .E88 2002   341.242'2—dc21   2002028015
ISBN 0–19–924242–9 (hardback: alk. paper)

1 3 5 7 9 10 8 6 4 2

Typeset by Hope Services (Abingdon) Ltd.
Printed in Great Britain
on acid-free paper by
Biddles Ltd., Guildford and King's Lynn

GENERAL EDITORS' PREFACE

Subsidiarity is, as lawyers and politicians involved in European Union matters well know, a concept that is regularly invoked in the context of fundamental questions concerning the spheres of power of the Member States and the EC, and concerning the appropriate role of the EU. Although expressed in the EC Treaties as a legal principle, subsidiarity is a concept that is notoriously fluid and difficult to define, something which prompted many commentators to dismiss its legal relevance at the time of its introduction. However, as is evident from the debate currently taking place within the Convention on the future of Europe, the anxieties over 'creeping competences' which the subsidiarity principle was originally intended to address, and the search for specifically legal and constitutional solutions to the challenges of a divided-power system, continue with as much vigour today.

While the interest in the concept demonstrated by the initial outpouring of literature from lawyers and political scientists—and also from a number of economists—which followed the adoption of the Maastricht Treaty, in which subsidiarity was legally enshrined in a general way for the first time, has gradually abated, it is only in recent years that the first opportunities to assess some of the legal implications of subsidiarity have arisen. Thus the question of the justiciability of subsidiarity is no longer an entirely speculative question, as the first significant cases—on the working time directive, the deposit-guarantee directive, and very recently the biotechnology directive—in which the concept was addressed by the Court of Justice have been decided mainly in the past five years.

This book, which appears ten years after the Maastricht Treaty was signed, aims to provide a critique of the subsidiarity principle which goes beyond what is termed the 'classical' legal critique, and which at the same time engages fully with both the legal and the political dimensions of the concept. Distancing himself from some of the traditional methodologies underlying classical legal analysis, Antonio Estella's work provides an refreshing and critical account of the principle of subsidiarity and of the Court of Justice's response to it. He seeks to explain why the principle was introduced in the first place, why the Member States chose to give it legal form as a 'binding commitment', and why this attempt to secure a commitment has not been successful. His own critique of subsidiarity rests not on the argument that it runs counter to integration, but rather that the conception of integration on which it is founded is damaging to the more important task of finding solutions 'which combine integration and diversity'.

This is a book that should be of considerable interest to lawyers and political scientists alike, and to all those who are engaged in questions concerning the powers and competences of the EU.

P.P. Craig
G. de Búrca

PREFACE

This work is based on the Doctoral Thesis that I successfully submitted to the European University Institute in 1997. Many people have made important contributions, both while I carried out my research in Florence and afterwards, in the publishing of this work. Attempting to cite them all would be a daunting task and might be unjust, since someone is always involuntarily left out of lists of acknowledgements. So for the sake of brevity I cite only the indispensable people. First, of those who were most helpful during the course of my research in Florence, I must cite my supervisor, Renaud Dehouse, who had a significant input on the work submitted at the EUI, especially as far as method is concerned. I also wish to cite two of my friends, Juan Fernandez Martín and Alfredo González Diaz, and my parents and brothers. Though they were far from me physically, they were very close in spirit as I was drafting my thesis in Florence. Secondly, concerning those who were important in the publishing of this work, I wish to thank Tomás de la Quadra-Selcedo and the President of the Court of Justice, Gil Carlos Rodríguez Iglesias. Gráinne de Búrca and Paul Craig were crucial in supporting this work for publication. I also wish to thank Xabier Basozabal Arrue, of the Civil Law Department of the University Carlos III de Madrid, for his helpful advice. I wish to make a very special mention of Professor Martin Shapiro: our discussions at Berkeley University during the months of autumn 1999 were illuminating for me, and many of the ideas that emerged during those dialogues have improved this book greatly. Finally, I wish to thank the Instituto Pascual Madoz of the University Carlos III de Madrid for its generous financial contribution to the publication of this work.

Last but not least, I want to thank María Fernández Mellizo-Soto for her unfailing support, both during the elaboration of the thesis in Florence and during the publishing of this work. Without her help this would have remained a mere project.

Antonio Estella de Noriega
Madrid, August 2001

CONTENTS

TABLE OF CASES

European Community

Court of First Instance (numerical order)

European Court of Justice (alphabetical order)

European Court of Justice (numerical order)

Germany

United Kingdom *see* European Court of Justice (alphabetical order):

TABLE OF LEGISLATION

European Community

Commission Communications

Directives

Recommendations

Regulations

Treaties and Legislation

Germany

United Kingdom

Introduction

The aim of this work is twofold. First, it aims to construct an alternative and more complete legal critique of the principle of subsidiarity. Secondly, it attempts to analyse the problem of the implementation of subsidiarity by the European Court of Justice and to explain the Court's case-law on the principle.

The principle of subsidiarity has been examined at length in legal and political science literature over the past five years. The number of analyses of the subject since its introduction into the European Community Treaty (ECT) is so overwhelming that it is necessary to begin this essay by justifying the need for yet another work on subsidiarity. This Introduction is therefore intended to explain the relevance of this work.

A. The 'classical' legal critique on subsidiarity

Most legal analyses are critical of subsidiarity. Perhaps one of the clearest illustrations of this is an article published by Toth in 1992. According to this author:

> . . . the incorporation of the principle of subsidiarity in the Maastricht Treaty has been a retrograde step. Without providing any cure for any of the Community's ills, it threatens to destroy hard-won achievements. It will weaken the Community and slow down the integration process. It will suit those who would like to see the Community move not towards but away from a truly federal structure (Toth, 1992:1105).

This quotation shows that, for lawyers, subsidiarity is at best an exceptional, and at worst a pathological condition with which the European Union has to live. It is important for my purposes to disentangle this legal critique of the principle. What I shall call the 'classical' legal critique, for reasons explained below, makes at least two points.[1] The first point is that the principle is *a-legal*. In effect, due to its location between the sociological, philosophical, and political universes (more than in the legal one) it is difficult to deal with in strictly legal terms. This is problematic since the Member States made the 'juridification' of subsidiarity a matter of principle, resulting in the incorporation of the principle of subsidiarity into Article 3(b)2—now Article 5(2) of the ECT. Its legal implementation will involve many difficulties, not least of which will be the Court's application of the principle. The second point goes beyond mere technical aspects and reaches the normative. According to this second critique, the principle is detrimental to the continuation of the process of European integration. Subsidiarity is deemed to be an anti-integrationist principle, and therefore contrary to the 'integrationist' logic of the Treaties. This is considered to be unacceptable: 'a retrograde step', in Toth's words. In short, subsidiarity is criticized not only for technical, or functional, reasons (it does not work as a legal tool), but also for normative ones (it runs counter to the process of 'integration', and so is counter-productive).

It is therefore no exaggeration to say that subsidiarity has disappointed lawyers. But it has also confused them. This confusion explains why many lawyers have written and keep writing articles attempting to show not that subsidiarity is dangerous for integration, but that the principle will ultimately not be detrimental to the constitutionalism of the European Community. Lenaerts and Ypersele, in the concluding remarks of a lengthy article on the principle, state that:

The Member States have come full circle [with subsidiarity]: they have found a perfect equilibrium between, on one hand, their desire that decisions should be taken as closely as possible to the citizens [. . .] and, on the other, their desire that the integration process should continue its normal pace towards the establishment of an ever closer union among the peoples of Europe [. . .] *Conceived in this way, subsidiarity should even allow for new transfers of competences to the Community* (Lenaerts and Ypersele, 1994:83, my translation, my emphasis).

This last sentence is critical. As shown in this work, the Member States' fundamental objective when they decided to incorporate subsidiarity into the ECT was precisely to place another obstacle in the path of the transfer of sovereignty from Member States to the EC. To criticize subsidiarity on the basis that the principle apparently 'goes against integration' may be more or less

---

[1] Belonging to the classical legal approach on subsidiarity we may find the following: Bermann (1994); Basabe (2000); Cass (1992); Constantinesco (1991; 1992); Emiliou (1992; 1994); Fernández Esteban (1996); Gaudissart (1993); Goucha Soares (1998); Harrison (1996); Toth (1994a; 1994b); Vandersanden (1992).

appropriate, but at least that criticism is based on the very particular way of thinking about Europe in which lawyers have been educated. However, to say, as Leanerts and Ypersele do, that subsidiarity is a principle which may, under certain circumstances, allow for more (rather than less) competences for the Community is entirely to miss the point of the whole debate on this issue. That stance can be only understood as a reaction to the confusion which the insertion of subsidiarity into the ECT has caused lawyers.

B. The foundations of the 'classical' legal critique of subsidiarity

Subsidiarity therefore disappoints and confuses lawyers who, in turn, have directed their analyses towards criticism of the principle on both functional and normative grounds. This is here referred to as the 'classical critique' of subsidiarity. It is important to delve into the foundations of the classical critique on subsidiarity. In the first place, it is evident that the assumption underlying the first critique is that the principle of subsidiarity should be treated as a mere technical tool. In the second place, and maybe more importantly, the assumption underlying the second critique is that law and integration are synonymous terms in the Community context. Both assumptions are the result of very particular methodological and conceptual choices which traditionally classical legal analyses have made. I next examine in more detail what these choices are and where their limits may be found.

Foundation 1: The context

To start with, the classical legal approach to European *legal* integration has moved exclusively, at least until recent times, within a methodological framework of analysis that could be categorized, without wishing to be pejorative, as formalist. Traditionally, lawyers have tended to concentrate their analyses on the technical subtleties of EC positive law, focusing more often than not on microscopic details rather than on the macroscopic context in which legal phenomena came about. In so doing, other factors or variables (economic, political, etc.) were neglected. However, this approach to the study of law has its limits, not only because it does not integrate variables other than the legal ones (which is legitimate since this is a methodological choice) but also for the understanding of law itself. This point is hardly new. As early as 1980 Shapiro stated that in legal analyses of European integration:

The Community [is represented] as a juristic idea; the written constitution, as a sacred text; the professional commentary as a legal truth; the case law as the inevitable working out of the correct implications of the constitutional text; and the constitutional court as the disembodied voice of right reason and constitutional theology (1980:538).

Naturally, Shapiro's observations represent a response to a long-standing tradition of legal formalism which also evolved for a reason. This is, however, not the place to list the positive benefits that legal formalism has had overall for the development of law. Rather, the point here is that without the help of other instruments besides legal ones, legal analyses fail to provide answers to many juridical issues. Law should therefore attempt to develop a more sophisticated analytical apparatus to fill that gap. *Contextual law* (or *law in context*) is an answer to that methodological deficit. It attempts to integrate other perspectives with the legal one, in order to understand legal phenomena. This is an important point, about which there are many misunderstandings. In effect, *contextual law* does not attempt to focus on new and different dependent variables. As a legal theory, contextual analysis also focuses on law. However, the shift comes in relation to independent variables. Contextual law attempts to intertwine legal and other variables in order to better understand legal phenomena. However, the contextual law method has experienced a profound development in recent years, so it is difficult to speak of a unified contextual approach. That is, there are many different versions of contextual law. One version attempts to mix law and economics. The result has been labelled (maybe unsatisfactorily) as the economic analysis of law. Another attempts to integrate sociology and law. A third aims to combine political science and law. This last version of the contextual method has been chosen for this work.

The choice is not random. I am not only persuaded in general that legal analyses need more than legal input alone. Also, in particular, the dependent variable here is subsidiarity as a legal principle. Subsidiarity is very ambiguous in nature, and clearly goes beyond law and reaches, at the very least, political science issues. In these circumstances, the contextual method here chosen is especially appropriate. However, I wish to stress that the aim here is, as Weiler pointed out (1991), not to trespass beyond the limits of 'pure theory of law'. The following is a 'pure' legal analysis, although it has been enriched with a better understanding of the tools of legal analysis.

Foundation 2: The concept

Regarding the second assumption made by the classical reading on subsidiarity, it must be recalled that all analyses rest, either explicitly or implicitly, upon a set of conceptual or substantive premisses. This is also true of legal analyses of the EU. I suggested above that the second assumption made by the classical legal critique of subsidiarity is that law amounts to integration in the European context. Therefore, for the classical reading, EU 'integration' is the governing value for EC law. The point is not new either. Shaw has brilliantly argued that European lawyers have traditionally linked law with integration. According to this author:

In conventional wisdom, it is the process of integration which gave the EC legal order an impetus and purpose, and EC law, conversely, which structures, disciplines and pushes forward the process of integration. Law and integration—structural and socio-economic—exist in a cosy, intimate and entirely positive relation. Law is a useful form of glue for the supranational enterprise, as it brings with it an ideology of obedience, which substitutes the absence of force and violence within the EU legal order. Member States adhere to the rule of law within the EU legal sphere, the dominant narrative runs, because they adhere to it to a large extent within the domestic sphere. They are, simply put, liberal democratic states, whose basic instinct in relation to legal authority is one of compliance and obedience. When they do so, Member States also implicitly sign up for more integration because—in EC rhetoric—law (and obedience to law) has traditionally meant integration. In this way, two circles are squared through integration and through the rule of law. Integration is what is natural for the EU and equally what is natural for the law (1995a:7).

The law of the European Union has therefore been interpreted by classical legal analysts from the perspective of the sole normative criterion of integration. This is due to that confusion between law and integration at which Shaw points. From this perspective, it may be easier to understand why the insertion of subsidiarity into the ECT has been so coldly received in the legal world. In effect, the principle of subsidiarity implies, to start with, that central intervention (in this case, that of the European Community) must cede to intervention by Member States. This amounts to giving priority to 'autonomy' when the circumstances of the case recommend it. From this one can infer a shift in the hierarchy of values that presided over the process of integration. Before subsidiarity (though this reading is being increasingly questioned) it seemed clear that the aim of 'integration' was at the top of the Community's normative pyramid. After the insertion of the principle of subsidiarity into the ECT this can no longer be assumed. In fact different, and even contradictory values now have to coexist. This shift in values has thrown legal analysts into perplexity and even self-indulgence.

A twofold conclusion can be drawn from these introductory lines. On one hand, as far as the method is concerned, the perspective adopted here is contextual law, and in particular that version of contextual law which links political science and law. The use of this methodology is justified above all by the subject. The final objective is to make a legal analysis, although the legal independent variables will be intertwined with political ones. On the other hand, the normative perspective adopted here starts from the assumption that, in the present stage of European integration, both integration and diversity (or autonomy) are important values for the Union, and that one may not establish any normative preference between them. This perspective is, like any normative perspective, open to criticism, but I wish to avoid falling into the trap of many legal analyses, which do not explicitly show the normative perspective which they adopt.

C. Moving to content

Now that the method and the normative framework adopted for this analysis have been made explicit, I can turn to my argument. As stated above, the aim of this work is twofold. It attempts to set out a more sustained critique of the principle of subsidiarity and to analyse and explain the European Court of Justice's reaction to subsidiarity. First, I conceptualize subsidiarity as the Member States' reaction, or institutional response, to the growth of the Community's powers, both competentially and institutionally speaking. In particular, the idea is that subsidiarity was an attempt to react to the growth of the Community's powers in a procedural context dominated by majority voting. In this sense subsidiarity was a 'binding commitment' of Member States acting at the Community level, whereby the Community's intervention would be restricted to what was strictly necessary. In order to make this commitment credible, Member States converted subsidiarity into a legal principle, thus making it reviewable before the ECJ. This was a critical aspect in the negotiation of subsidiarity. As will be shown below, for the commitment to be credible, the involvement of the ECJ was an indispensable aspect. Secondly, I seek to show that subsidiarity is, from a functional perspective, devoid of clear legal content. Analysis of both Article 5(2) ECT and of Protocol Number 30 on subsidiarity supports that conclusion. This is the first indication that the commitment to subsidiarity will not work. Thirdly, I also argue that subsidiarity is problematic not only from a legal perspective, but also from a normative one.

Here the idea is that the principle is not against integration, but instead it includes a very particular view of integration which is detrimental to the search for solutions which combine integration and diversity. Fourthly, I analyse the legal implementation of the principle by the ECJ to show that the Court has adopted a very low profile towards the principle. The reasons why the ECJ has reacted with caution towards subsidiarity are also examined. In essence, these reasons have to do with the Court's legitimacy as a legal institution and with the fact that the implementation of subsidiarity was deemed by the Court to be counter to its own political agenda.

The outcome of this analysis may also be connected to a more theoretical discussion of the conditions under which binding commitments dependent on the delegation of power to independent agencies will work. In this sense, this work illustrates with a concrete example—the implementation of subsidiarity in the EU context—that the effectiveness of binding commitments is highly contingent on the nature of the commitment concerned and on the fact that independent agencies develop agendas that are not always in line with the principal's objectives.

I

Growth

A. Introduction

Current legitimacy problems affecting relations between the centre and the periphery in the European Community system are the result of the growth of the Community powers. At the higher level of abstraction, this may be defined as the degree or level of control that Community institutions have upon their environment. Such a definition suggests, more concretely, that the process of growth involves two different but related dimensions. On one hand, there is the vertical dimension of the growth process. By 'vertical growth' I mean the process through which sets of policies (entire or partial) move from being under the control of Member States' public authorities to being under the control of Community institutions. On the other hand there is the process of horizontal Community expansion. The expression 'horizontal growth' refers to *how* powers are managed and implemented by Community institutions. Horizontal growth involves not only the development of the Community institutions' respective powers, but also the evolution of voting procedures.

All analyses of the evolution of the Community system start from the distinction between vertical and horizontal expansion, either explicitly or implicitly. However, few of them combine both dimensions. That is, the evolution of the Community powers is usually seen as a problem relating to the protection of Member States' sovereignty, whereas the evolution of, say, the European Parliament's powers, is seen as part of another set of problems, for instance balancing the Community institutions. The intention here is not to deny the soundness of the previous link. Rather, the point is that there is a strong connection, often overlooked, between the vertical and the horizontal dimensions of the growth process. Therefore, not only does the vertical expansion of powers have consequences for the sovereignty of Member States, but the horizontal extension of the Community institutions' powers also has an impact on the Member States' spheres of sovereignty. The contrary is also true: the vertical evolution of the Community often involves a correlative reinforcement of the Community institutions' powers (Dehousse, 1994a).

The analysis of the process of growth of the Community's powers, to which this chapter is devoted, raises first a methodological issue: how can this process be described, or to be more exact, measured. That is, starting from the assumption that an analysis of the 'hard facts' that underlie the Community's legitimacy crisis should not be taken for granted, the issue of the ways in which such a process may be described must first be addressed. It is also important to note, as a preliminary remark, that although all the different aspects of the process of vertical expansion are described here, not all aspects of the process of horizontal expansion are measured. As stated above, horizontal expansion involves a set of different things: in particular, it involves the evolution of powers of the Community institutions, and the evolution of voting procedures. However, only one of these procedures, majority voting, is here considered. The reason for this choice is that the crux of the argument of this work is that subsidiarity was introduced into the Community as a consequence of the expansion of powers which the Community experienced in a procedural context dominated by majority voting. Therefore, although it must be clear from the outset that the evolution of the powers of the Community institutions is also a factor that explains the Community's legitimacy crisis, it is assumed that the explanatory relevance of this factor is less important than the emergence of majority voting. Therefore the description of the evolution of the powers of Community institutions has been omitted. Finally, it must be also noted that the time-frame starts at the moment of the enactment of the Treaty of the European Economic Community and extends to the period of operation of the Single European Act. The reason for this choice is that, as argued in Chapter II below, subsidiarity was introduced into the ECT as a result of the evolution of the Community powers which took place in the period before Maastricht. The Rome Treaty period has been included to enable comparison, and to provide a more dynamic picture of the whole process I seek to measure.

Measuring the process of the growth of the Community's powers provides answers to the following questions. The first question is whether Community growth may be depicted as a 'process of stops and goes' (Moravscik, 1993; 1998) during the periods under observation. This involves the analysis of three items: first, whether there is a general trend towards growth or not; secondly, whether, despite that general trend, there are concrete inflection points, or 'stops', within an overall process of increase; and thirdly, whether the process of growth involves paradoxes, or whether there are stops when there should have been starts, and starts when there should have been stops. The second question concerns more specifically the SEA period of development. Here the issue is whether, within the previous picture, the SEA period had marked peculiarities.

This Chapter is organized as follows. The next section is a preliminary discussion of the parameters used to measure the vertical and horizontal dimensions of the growth process. Here I explain why this work opts for quantitative parameters, instead of other alternatives. The following section includes a 'formal' analysis of the process of vertical expansion and of the evolution of majority voting, which is complemented by another section containing a 'material' analysis of both items. In the final section some conclusions are restated, and the questions posed in this Introduction are answered.

B. Measuring growth: the state of the question

What tends to be confusing when analysing the literature on growth, is the variety of the parameters employed to measure this process at the Community level. Parameters vary in nature from the formal, such as the simple comparison between the powers attributed to the Community under the different constitutional reforms of the Treaties (Tizzano, 1987; Louis, 1990; Lenaerts, 1988; Constantinesco, 1974) to the quantitative, such as the counting of the Council's and Commission's legislative outputs (Pryce, 1973; Krislov *et al.*, 1985) and the qualitative, such as the comprehensive character of a field of regulation (Majone, 1993). Or else the parameters involve a mix of legal and institutional criteria, such as the incidence of Community law in the national legal orders and the nature of decision-making processes (Dehousse and Weiler, 1992). The problem arising from using such different measures is that the various conclusions are often very different, if not contradictory. Another problem is that outcomes are difficult to compare. The overall result is a fragmented and chaotic picture of the Community's growth process.

Nevertheless, despite this diversity it is possible to say something about the above-mentioned literature. In the first place, there is a broader preference for quantitative methods. There are, however, exceptions to this rule: Majone, for example, in his latest works on this subject, seems to give more weight to qualitative parameters (Majone, 1994a). In the second place, among quantitative methods of measurement there is a preference for the use of the 'decisional' outputs of the Community organs (Council and Commission). Again there are exceptions, since some authors employ non-decisional quantitative parameters, such as budget appropriations (Pollack, 1994 and 1996). Furthermore, among the authors who employ decisional outputs, the majority use legally binding acts as a criterion for measurement, while some authors also include soft law in their analytical apparatus (Cram, 1993 and 1997).

The second factor that causes confusion is that, even when using roughly the same parameters, results may differ. Here it is useful to compare the work of Krislov *et al.* and that of Majone. According to the former, who draw from Pryce, 'in 1970, twenty-eight directives were in force. Ten years later, it would appear that within the legal order of the Community there were no less than 700 directives in force' (Krislov *et al.*, 1985:66). Majone states in a rather evasive way that: '. . . Concerning the phenomenon of over-regulation, one can mention the almost exponential growth of the number of directives and regulations produced, on average, each year: twenty-five directives and 600 regulations by 1970; fifty directives and 1,000 regulations by 1975; eighty directives and 1,500 regulations per year since 1985' (Majone, 1994a:4).

Naturally, the parameters used by these authors are not exactly the same: while Krislov *et al.* use as a parameter the total number of directives that were in force at two particular times (1970 and 1980), Majone employs as a parameter the average number of directives produced per year, in particular years (1970, 1975, and 1985). However, it is possible to compare at least some of the data offered by these authors. If, as a 'per year' average, twenty-five directives had been produced by 1970, this means that, according to Majone, around 300 directives were produced in the first twelve years of Community operation. However, according to Krislov *et al.*, only twenty-eight directives were in force by 1970. It is less than plausible to argue that this divergence could be explained by saying that the first author is referring to the number of acts *produced* (and not in force) and the second to the number of acts in *force*, since the difference between the two results is more than double. This divergence serves only to illustrate the difficulties inherent in the task of measuring a phenomenon as complex as the process of growth of the Community's powers.[1]

---

[1] Notice also the lack of rigour in the way in which some of these parameters are employed. To show 'an almost exponential growth' of the Community's regulatory activity, Majone (1994a) uses, as time references, 1970 and 1975, then jumping to 1985. This inconsistency in the time references that are used makes it more difficult to compare data and, therefore, to have the most reliable information about the reality one wants to measure.

A third and striking aspect is the lack of detailed discussion about the justification of the choices that are made as far as the selection of parameters is concerned. A good example of this general trend can be found in the work of Pollack, who reduces the previous discussion to the following lines:

In this study, we are seeking to measure policy outputs across a range of policy types, including both regulatory or legislative policies and spending policies. In these circumstances the best option seems to be a dual measure of policy output: EC legislation for regulatory policies, and budgetary appropriations for distributive and redistributive policies (Pollack, 1994:113).

There is no doubt that the parameters used by Pollack are innovative (especially the 'budgetary appropriations' parameter) and that they give a good indication of the process this author intends to measure. But taking into account the strong analytical implications that Pollack derives from this information,[2] it might have been helpful to include further remarks to justify the use of these—as opposed to other—parameters.

Can an explanation for these findings be unearthed? From the perspective of this work, the problem seems to lie in the fact that the methods of measurement are not sufficiently disentangled from the reality to be measured. In other words, a confusion exists between the *object* that is being measured—the process of growth of the Community powers—and the *infrastructure* used to this end—a different set of parameters. Both aspects need to be clearly separated so that (i) the choices made are sufficiently justified (and are not merely assumed as 'logical' ways to measure); (ii) results can be compared with each other; and (iii) the analytical conclusions that are drawn from measuring the process of growth can be subject to scientific challenge, and not simply to value-based analysis.

In this regard, a differentiation is made here between the process of growth of the Community's powers, defined as the process of vertical and horizontal expansion of the Community, and a set of quantitative parameters to be employed in order to measure the reality under examination. These parameters are twofold: first, 'formal growth', which entails comparing the formal attribution of powers to the Community by the different Treaty reforms,

---

[2] Pollack (1994:95) offers an eclectic explanation of the process of growth of the Community's powers in some areas, and concludes by arguing that '... (growth as regards) regulatory policies can be explained in terms of functional spill-over from the Internal Market, while redistributive policies can be understood as side payments in larger intergovernmental bargains, and distributive policies are the result of the Commission's policy entrepreneurship and log-rolling Council bargaining'.

as regards both competence and the horizontal dimension; and secondly 'material growth', which attempts to measure the process of growth of the Community's powers from the perspective of the *de facto* developments that have occurred. Finally, as mentioned in the Introduction to this Chapter, two time references have been selected: the dates when the Treaty of the European Economic Community (hereinafter the TEEC) and the Single European Act came into force, respectively.

The use of other parameters, such as qualitative parameters, was also envisaged for measuring the process of vertical and horizontal growth. However, this was discarded for several reasons. The first is that qualitative parameters are difficult to elaborate. As opposed to quantitative parameters, whose content is more visible, qualitative parameters would have required me to engage in a difficult discussion about their exact profile. The second reason is that the benefits arising from the use of qualitative parameters are not certain, since the results they offer add little to the general argument. Thirdly, quantitative analysis seems a safer method to pursue the previously stated objective of disentangling the process under examination and the methods of measurement. Had qualitative methods of measurement been used, the risk of failing to meet this objective would be too great. Notwithstanding, it should be pointed out that the parameters established here are not totally pure; therefore it would be more exact to say that, although quantitative methods dominate the following analysis, qualitative tools are used in certain parts of it. Prominent examples of this are the references to the Transport Policy and Environmental Policy when measuring material vertical growth.

C. Formal growth

1. *Formal Vertical Growth*

From a quantitative perspective, the first way of measuring whether there has been an increase in Community powers is to take into account its formal growth. Applied to the field of competence there is formal growth whenever a new competence is expressly attributed to the Community by Member States through reform of the Treaties. The use of the parameter 'formal growth' is justified because a new attribution of competence to the Community indicates, at least in theory, a correlative restriction of Member States' sovereignty (Dehousse, 1994a:103).

With regard to the attribution of competence, the Treaty of Rome conferred the Community eleven subject-matters or fields of competence. These were the three common policies (transport,[3] agricultural policy,[4] and commercial policy),[5] competition,[6] taxation,[7] free movement of goods,[8] persons (including provisions relating to the right of establishment),[9] capital[10] and services,[11] worker protection policy,[12] and economic policy[13] (although limited to co-ordination between Member States).

In turn, the Single European Act (hereinafter the SEA) extended the scope of Community competence by, first, complementing some of the Treaty of Rome fields of competence, and secondly, by attributing new powers. Concerning the first aspect, Articles 118a and 118b complemented the old provisions relating to worker protection, whereas Article 102a complements the Treaty of Rome provisions on economic policy by introducing co-operation in economic and monetary policy. Though this provision simply provided for co-operation between Member States, the inclusion of Article 102a in the Community pillar was important at a symbolic level because it indicated the political commitment not to leave any Member State outside of future developments, especially the monetary union (De Ruyt, 1987:187).

Concerning the second aspect, the SEA attributed three new fields of competence to the Community. These were: economic and social cohesion;[14] research and technological development;[15] and environmental policy.[16] With regard to the last, it is important to note that the introduction of this subject-matter constituted the formalization of a policy developed by the Community since 1970, as shall be seen in the analysis of the Community's material growth.

Table I.1 summarizes the process of formal growth in the periods here examined.

2. *Formal Majority Voting*

The Treaty of Rome established at least twenty-five cases in which resort to voting was foreseen.[17] Yet, as will be seen in our analysis of material majority

---

[3] Treaty of Rome, Arts. 74–84.   [4] Arts. 38–47.   [5] Arts. 110–16.
[6] Arts. 85–94.   [7] Arts. 95–9.   [8] Arts. 9–37.   [9] Arts. 48–58.
[10] Arts. 67–73.   [11] Arts. 59–66.   [12] Arts. 48–51.   [13] Arts. 103–9.
[14] Arts. 130a–e.   [15] Arts. 130f–q.   [16] Arts. 130r–t.
[17] Art. 7; Art. 8; Art. 20; Art. 21.1°; Art. 22.2°; Art. 25; Art. 43.2° (third paragraph); Art. 43.3°; Art. 44.4°; Art 44.5°; Art. 55; Art. 63.2°; Art. 69; Art. 70.2° (second paragraph); Art. 75; Art. 79.3°; Art. 87; Art. 94; Art. 111.3°; Art 112; Art. 113; Art. 114; Art. 116. Further, in 1977, the Treaty amending certain financial provisions of the European Economic Community Treaty (OJEC L 359 of 31 December 1977) established two more cases in which resort to a majority vote was foreseen: these were Arts. 203 and 204 of the Treaty of Rome.

Table I.1: Attribution of new powers to the European Community

Powers from the TEEC (1958–87)	Powers from the SEA (1987–92)
1. Transport	1. Regional Policy
2. CAP	2. Technological Research and Development
3. Competition	3. The Environment
4. Commercial Policy	4. Co-operation in economic and monetary policy
5. Taxation	
6. Free Movement of Goods	
7. Free Movement of Persons and the Right of Establishment	
8. Free Movement of Services	
9. Free Movement of Capital	
10. Worker Protection	
11. Economic Policy (co-ordination only)	

voting, in 1966 Member States would sign the 'Luxembourg Compromise', which overruled in practice the possibility of resorting to a vote in those cases provided by the Treaty of Rome.

In turn, the SEA established thirteen more cases in which resort to a vote was foreseen.[18] These findings are summarized in Table I.2.

Table I.2: Formal majority voting

Parameters	TEEC	SEA
Majority voting	25	25+13

[18] The list is the following: Art. 49; Art. 56.2°; Art. 57.1; Art. 57.2°; Art. 86; Art. 28; Art. 59 (second paragraph); Art. 70.1°; Art. 84.2°; Art. 100a; Art. 118a 2°; Art. 130e; Art. 130q.

D. Material growth

1. *Vertical Material Growth*

Formal growth gives a first indication of the increase of the Community's powers. However, this parameter is limited in that it is essentially static. It does not give any information concerning real developments in Community competence. Therefore it has to be complemented with a more dynamic parameter. The analysis of material growth has been conducted by obtaining information about the actual development of Community policies during the periods of operation of the European Economic Community Treaty and the SEA, using two measures. First, the number of legally binding acts (regulatory output) produced in these two periods are counted. This shows how policies were developed and the rhythm of the growth process in the two periods (acceleration). Secondly, budget expenditure is examined.

The rationale that underlies the choice of the above parameters is the following: the Community may intervene through two means: regulation and financial spending. These two basic ways of intervention give rise, subsequently, to two different policy types: regulatory policies and spending policies. Therefore it is appropriate to use the Community's legislative output as a marker of the growth of regulatory policies. To complement the previous information, budget appropriations for measuring the growth of Community spending policies have been included.[19]

(1) Regulatory Output

Concerning the first parameter, Community regulatory output, it is necessary to start by considering several factors to interpret the data obtained. First, as mentioned above, only legally binding acts have been taken into account. This is because the adoption of legally binding acts and the ECJ doctrines of direct effect and, above all, supremacy, produce a visible and direct impact on Member States' sovereignty. Soft law has been therefore excluded. Soft law *does impinge in practice* upon Member States' sovereignty,

---

[19] It is preferable to characterize regulatory and spending polices according to the instrument, not its objective. An opposing view is that of Majone, who orders his typology according to the objective being pursued (Majone, 1994a:10). In the opinion of that author, spending policies are those that pursue redistributive and distributive objectives. However, this differentiation according to objective is unclear, since both regulatory and spending policies may pursue redistributive and distributive objectives.

but only under certain conditions.[20] This peculiarity implies that, in order to identify those categories of soft law acts that would have an impact on Member States' sovereignty, one must first distinguish between the various soft law acts that the Community institutions adopt.

Secondly, concerning legally binding acts, the following have been taken into account: Council and Commission regulations; directives; decisions; and international agreements signed by the Community. Legally binding acts affecting the functioning of the Community institutions (such as regulations regarding the Community's civil servants) have not been taken into account, since they do not have an impact on Member States. Financial and budgetary provisions have also been disregarded to avoid duplication, since everything concerning Community spending policies has been included within the parameter 'budget appropriations'. Furthermore, it must be pointed out that the distinction between 'legislative' and 'administrative' (rule making and adjudication) acts is of no interest here, and therefore has not been used in this analysis. The reason for this is that in terms of the impact of Community intervention upon the Member States' sovereignty, both a decision adopted by a commitology committee and a decision adopted by the Council have an equivalent meaning.[21] Thirdly, concerning sources, I have used the *Directory of Community Legislation in Force* as of 1 June 1995.[22] It is necessary to note that this source is, to some extent, problematic. In effect, the *Directory* does not reflect the number of acts adopted each year, but only those that, having been adopted in a particular year, are still in force in 1995. For a complete picture of the number of acts produced each year, the *Directory* should be cross-checked with another source, such as the *General Report of the Activities of the European Union*,[23] which is published on an annual basis. However, that task would go beyond the scope of this work, and therefore the data concerning the number of acts produced by year should be interpreted with this qualification in mind.

[20] According to Snyder (1993:2), soft law is defined as 'those rules of conduct which, in principle, have no legally binding force but which nevertheless *may* have practical effects' (my emphasis).

[21] Though, admittedly, legitimacy problems are not the same (if not in nature, at least in intensity) in the legislative and administrative processes: for example, commitology has transparency problems that are not present (at least as fully) in the Community legislative process.

[22] Luxembourg: Office for Official Publications of the EC, 1995. The year 1995 has been retained as it is approximately since this year that the community institutions started implementing subsidiarity. Since, in principle, this may imply the abrogation of some of the old legislation, to use sources later than 1995 may disrupt the final picture on material growth both under the Rome Treaty and SEA.

[23] Luxembourg: Office for Official Publications of the EC (Annual).

Fourthly, I have followed the categorization of acts established in the *Directory*. Again, this classification is not ideal, being in some cases arbitrary. For example, as far as state aids are concerned, some Commission decisions are placed under the corresponding sectoral heading (for example, transport) whereas others, which could be placed under such a particular heading, are situated under the general one of 'state aids'. Nevertheless, the *Directory* categorization has been respected.[24] Fifthly, and this applies also to the 'budget appropriations' parameter, as shown below, only acts produced in the framework of the European Community have been taken into account. Therefore, those acts enacted in the framework of EURATOM or the European Coal and Steel Community have been excluded, for the sake of simplifying the task of measurement. Sixthly, I have also excluded those acts adopted within the framework of the European Co-operation Policy (as such, an intergovernmental institution) for they have a different regime than acts adopted in the Community framework.

The results of the survey are summarized in Tables I.3 and I.4. Table I.3 shows the number of legally binding acts adopted in each of the periods under survey, by year. Table I.4 lists the number of acts adopted by policy.

In global terms, the first aspect of interest is the important development of Community regulatory activities that took place during the SEA period. This is all the more striking if the 'policy of Community regulatory restriction' introduced by the Commission's *White Paper* of 1985[25] is taken into account. The tendency towards over-regulation is illustrated by the fact that in the SEA period the total number of legally binding acts that were adopted (2,809) amounted to approximately three-quarters of the total number of acts adopted under the preceding period (3,734). Furthermore, under the SEA the Community experienced an important acceleration of its regulatory activities. Whereas the Community's rhythm of growth was of 270 legally binding acts per year in the six years before the SEA,[26] this grew to the considerable figure of 468 legally binding acts per year under the SEA.

[24] Despite the shortcomings that have been noted, the *Directory of Community Legislation in Force* has been retained as a major source of information since it remains, at present, the most reliable public source of information concerning the regulatory expansion of the Community.

[25] *Completing the Internal Market: White Paper from the Commission to the European Parliament*, COM(85) 310 final. By 'regulatory restriction' I mean the emphasis of the White Paper on minimal harmonization and mutual recognition. In principle, legislative intervention would be used as a last resort alternative. This explains why some institutions, like the Commission, trace back the 'spirit' of subsidiarity to White Paper 85. See, for instance, Communication of the Commission to the Council and the European Parliament on the Principle of Subsidiarity, SEC (92) 1992 final of 27 Oct. 1992.

[26] These were the years of the period under the Treaty of Rome that experienced the major growth. See Table I.2 above.

Table I.3: The number of legally binding acts adopted, by year

TEEC (1958–1987)	SEA (1987–1992)
1958: 3	1987: 345
1959: 2	1988: 270
1960: 7	1989: 423
1961: 4	1990: 490
1962: 19	1991: 531
1963: 13	1992: 752
1964: 35	
1965: 14	
1966: 27	
1967: 49	
1968: 76	
1969: 69	
1970: 91	
1971: 79	
1972: 121	
1973: 112	
1974: 112	
1975: 157	
1976: 200	
1977: 213	
1978: 210	
1979: 247	
1980: 252	
1981: 261	
1982: 255	
1983: 231	
1984: 254	
1985: 309	
1986: 311	
Total: 3,734	Total: 2,809

Source: Directory of Community Legislation in Force as of 1 June 1995.

The data in Table I.3 enable more specific analysis. First, Table I.3 helps to establish three different phases of evolution in the Treaty of Rome period. The first phase runs from 1958 to 1971. In this phase the Community was able to enact only around 600 measures, at an average rate of forty-two acts

Table I.4: The number of legally binding acts adopted, by policy

Subject-matter	TEEC 1958–87	SEA 1987–92
Transport	111	89
Competition	216	123
State Aids	94	91
CAP	1,672	1,138
Fisheries	111	106
External Relations	455	543
Taxation	37	24
Free Movement of Persons[a]	61	53
Free Movement of Goods+Customs Union	411	273
Free Movement of Services+Right of Establishment	93	43
Free Movement of Capital+Economic/ Monetary Policy	34	10
Energy	31	10
Environment	99	74
Consumer Protection+Health	15	53
Science and Information	9	19
Education and Vocational Training	24	16
Industrial Policy[b]	57	46
Regional Policy	24	17
Internal Market	180	81

[a] The *Directory* includes worker protection within the heading 'free movement of persons'.
[b] Law relating to undertakings has been included under 'industrial policy'.
Source: Directory of Community Legislation in Force as of 1 June 1995.

per year. The first four years of Community history were particularly low in quantitative output, with an outcome of only sixteen acts. This might be explained by the 'the Commission build-up' in the formative years (Krislov *et al.*, 1985:36); however, the fact that the situation did not get much better in the later years of this period (1967 being the most prolific year, with forty-nine measures) probably obscures the previous explanation. The second phase begins in 1972 (in which the barrier of 100 acts is passed) and ends at the end of 1984. In this second phase the Community experienced significant regulatory growth, the majority of the measures under the Treaty of Rome being enacted in this time (2,625 measures). In terms of the rhythm of growth, the Community grew at an average speed of 219 acts per year. These achievements are paradoxical if we take into account that they were made under the shadow of the Luxembourg compromise. One would have expected that unanimity, instead of fostering Community regulatory growth, would have stifled growth, or at least kept the rhythm at the same pace. The latter figure seems also to call into question (Golub, 1999), at least during the second phase of the Rome Treaty, the classical contention that unanimity brought about (or increased) the lack of effectiveness (*lourdeur*) in Community decision-making[27] (Winscott, 1995:304). The third wave of evolution of the TEEC period is represented by the years 1985 and 1986. Though this phase is constituted by only two years, and therefore could have been assimilated to the second TEEC period, it seems useful to distinguish it since it was a period of transition between the end of the TEEC and beginning of the SEA periods. In 1985 the Community adopted more than 300 acts, and even more in the subsequent year (311 acts). This development may be considered as heralding the impressive development in the Community's regulatory activity that would take place during the SEA period.

Secondly, Table I.3 allows the general finding as regards regulatory growth in the SEA period to be qualified. As remarked above, Table I.3 shows that the Community experienced an exponential growth during these years. However, in 1988 this impressive rhythm of regulatory growth decreased by seventy-five measures with respect to the previous year. It is also interesting to note the grand regulatory effort made in 1992, in which the number of measures enacted (752) was double the number enacted at the beginning of the SEA period, in 1986 (345), and exceeded by approximately 200 those enacted in 1991 (531).

The comparison of formal growth (Table I.1) with material growth (Table I.4) shows that the Community had difficulty in developing some of the policies which it was formally entitled to pursue during both the TEEC and SEA periods. Table I.4 is somewhat misleading in this respect. In the case of transport, for example, Table I.4 seems to indicate an acceptable record (111

---

[27] This finding apparently corroborates the preliminary conclusions that were obtained by the seminal study on quantitative growth of the Community competences undertaken by Krislov *et al.* (1985:57). Note the following passage: 'Given the preliminary nature of this Pilot Project any conclusions may be drawn with caution (. . .). However, at the level of management of existing Community policies, despite the fact that this activity engages the full Community apparatus, burdened by the well known Member State controls, the emerging picture is not what one would have expected at the commencement of the study. In quantitative terms, the Commission proposal rate has been steady and the capacity of the Council and the COREPER to deal with the Commission output does not seem to be overly handicapped'. Note, however, that here I am concerned with effectiveness, and not so much with efficiency problems, since my focus is on the impact of community intervention upon the Member States' sovereignty. On the efficiency of the EC decision-making during both the Rome Treaty and SEA periods see Golub (1999).

measures), although compared to the rest of the common policies perform-ance was somewhat poor during the TEEC period. Yet the common trans-port policy remained almost stagnant at least for the first sixteen years of Community history (twenty-one measures adopted before 1974). In the remaining years up to the SEA the average improved, but no important meas-ure regarding the liberalization of the sector was enacted until the SEA entered into force. Although improvements were made during the SEA period (above all in the field of air transport liberalization) some sectors, such as rail transport, experienced only limited development (Megret, 1990:214). Transport is therefore a good example of a Community regulatory paradox.

In effect, the relative lack of development of a common transport policy dur-ing the Rome Treaty and SEA periods is a good illustration of the failure of a policy which the Community had formal powers to pursue, or of material growth being less important than the formal growth would suggest. Certainly, one should start by saying that national preferences have traditionally diverged widely between Member States as regards transport policy. This is the result of three main factors. First, transport policy is greatly determined by the geo-graphical characteristics of a country and, in particular, by distance. Thus, in principle, a rail-oriented transport policy makes sense from an economic per-spective in countries where distances are great. Therefore France and Germany have traditionally relied heavily on this mode of transport, whereas road and inland waterway transport have dominated in Belgium, the Netherlands, and Luxembourg. The UK has traditionally maintained a mid-dle-way approach between rail and road transport. Nevertheless, it has in gen-eral supported pro-liberal measures in this sector at the Community level (Erdmenger, 1983:1–5). Secondly, different modes of transport compete with each other. Therefore to make a policy choice in favour of one particular mode of transport usually has direct consequences for the others. For instance, coun-tries like France and Germany have traditionally adopted measures oriented to protect their rail transport industry, mainly due to the heavy losses which they had incurred. In turn, the development of their other transport industries has been considerably slower (Erdmenger, 1983). Finally, within the transport market, there has historically been a division between small transport firms and large ones, the latter being traditionally more successful in obtaining market share. Thus the well organized Dutch road transport industry expected to make significant gains from liberalization of the transport sector at Community level, while the smaller German and Italian transport industries feared a loss of market share and therefore put pressure on their governments to block Community liberalization measures (Héritier, 1996:6).

It was in these circumstances that the Commission implemented its First Action programme for Transport Policy on 23 May 1962. The action programme was of a comprehensive character. It detailed a series of measures concerning: first, the elimination of bilateral quotas and the establishment of a Community quota in road freight; secondly, the introduction of bracket tariffs for all modes of transport (as a compromise solution between total liberalization of tariffs and state-imposed ones); and finally, the harmonization of conditions of competition in the fields of taxation, state aids, protection of workers' safety, etc. The measures proposed were to be implemented by 1970, the end of the transitional period.

The outcome was rather disappointing: no more than fourteen measures had been adopted by 1970 (up to 1974: twenty-one measures). Subsequently, the Commission changed its approach to the Common Transport Policy and, as explained in a 1973 communication,[28] implemented a 'pragmatic' approach. This consisted of the development of each transport sector 'on its own merits', therefore each independent from the other sectors. The idea was to avoid the Member States' traditional approach to transport policy, in which, as the Commission communication of 1973 said, assistance for one mode of transport was achieved by imposing undue restrictions on another. Although the Community's transport policy gained some impetus with the new approach, the results were few: from 1973 to 1983 no more than fifty measures were adopted. From 1983 to 1986, the period in which the Commission tried to give new momentum to Community transport policy through another communication of 1983,[29] only forty more measures were adopted. More importantly, from a qualitative point of view, many restrictions on the creation of a common transport market existed even after the SEA was implemented, above all in the road and railway sectors[30] (Megret, 1990:323; Whitelegg, 1988). Given the importance that the Member States accorded to the development of a Common Transport Policy in the TEEC, the failure to implement the policy during this period emerges as a paradox of the Community's growth process.[31]

---

[28] Published in *Bulletin CEE*, suppl. 16/73.

[29] Communication of the Commission to the Council 'Towards a Common Inland Transport Policy', OJEC C 154/9 of 13 June 1983.

[30] This was acknowledged by the ECJ in the case 13/83 *European Parliament v Council* [1985] ECR 1513, for the Rome Treaty period.

[31] Another case that is of particular interest in this regard is the field of state aids. Again, Table I.3 is misleading in this respect. It seems to imply that the Community (Council and Commission) was active in the field of state aids. Instead, all the decisions taken were adopted by the Commission, the Council being unable to enact any single measure under the Treaty of Rome. This situation did

Turning again to my general analysis of the Community's regulatory growth, it is noticeable that in the SEA period all new competences were significantly developed, above all if taking into account the short period of time which had elapsed (six years). The measures adopted for the new competences were: regional policy, seventeen measures; research and development, nineteen measures; economic and monetary policy, ten measures; and environmental policy, seventy-four measures. The important development experienced in the field of social regulation, understood as regulation against risks (consumer protection, worker health and safety protection, environmental protection) during the SEA period is notable. That development has prompted authors to state that, in general terms, Community regulation experienced a shift in its focus towards social regulation during the SEA period.[32]

Some of these policies had already been significantly developed under the Treaty of Rome, which illustrates again the important contrast between formal and material growth during this period (though in the opposite direction to what was examined above). In fact, during the period before the SEA, there was a widespread phenomenon of policy development under the shadow of catch-all provisions, such as, notably, Articles 100 and 235 of the EEC Treaty (Megret et Teitgen, 1987). Therefore fields such as regional policy (twenty-four measures), education (twenty-four measures), industrial policy (fifty-seven measures), research and development (nine measures), and consumer protection (fifteen measures) had already experienced significant growth without a clear legal base in the EEC Treaty. A typical example of this trend is environmental protection policy, which merits closer examination for this reason.

The development of environmental policy before the SEA is a good illustration of material growth breaking through the limits of formal growth. Given that environmental policy was only formally introduced by the SEA, its earlier significant growth emerges as another paradox of the growth process. An illustration of this important growth before the SEA is the nearly 100 legally binding environmental measures that were adopted during the TEEC period. Moreover, some of these measures were also important from a qualitative perspective, since they introduced an intense degree of policy innovation. The following are examples. First is Directive 76/769,[33] the 'PCB directive'. This Directive was concerned with the harmonization of Member State legislation relating to the marketing and use of certain dangerous

---

not improve under the SEA. Only one directive taken by the Council during this period has been traced (Council Directive 90/684 EEC of 21 December 1990, on aid for shipbuilding: OJEC L 380/27 of 31 December 1990).

[32]   Dehousse, 1993: 29, at footnote 55.   [33]   OJEC L 262/201 of 27 September 1976.

substances, such as, notably, polychlorinated biphenyl (PCB) and polychlorinated terphenyl (PCT). Referring to the innovative character of this measure, some authors have pointed out that Directive 76/769 'had no parallel in existing Member States' (Rehbinder and Stewart, 1985:214). Secondly, Directive 80/779[34] concerned the establishment at Community level of air quality standards to control the emission of sulphur dioxide and suspended particles into the atmosphere. The innovative character of this measure is shown by the fact that most of the Member States did not use quality standards as a control strategy before the Directive was enacted (Majone, 1994:8). A final example is Directive 79/831,[35] concerning the free movement of dangerous substances within the Community. This Directive established an innovative procedure to provide for the mutual recognition of authorizations given by the Member State authority in which the dangerous substance was marketed. In particular, it established a series of procedural safeguards according to which other Member States' authorities would take part in the national administrative procedure leading to the authorization of the substance. To conclude, from a quantitative viewpoint (but, as we see, also from a qualitative perspective) the development of the Community's environmental policy was already substantial before the start of the SEA period.

More generally the phenomenon of material vertical growth breaking the limits of formal vertical growth was reproduced, although to a lesser extent, under the SEA. Examples of this trend are, notably, education policy (sixteen measures) and industrial policy[36] (forty-six measures).

(2) Budget Expenditure

The second parameter used to measure material growth is Community budget expenditure. The use of this parameter complements the information on regulatory growth given in the previous section. This parameter was chosen because the Community, as well as national states, makes use of financial instruments to intervene. In this sense, it may be said that budget expenditure is the other side of the coin of modern public intervention. However, the Community's budgetary intervention is smaller than that of Member States in relative terms. Therefore, this parameter is only of complementary importance with regard to regulation, which is the preferred intervention instrument of the Community.

---

[34] OJEC L 229/30 of 30 August 1980.   [35] OJEC L 259/10 of 15 October 1979.
[36] Within this field, one could think for instance of telecommunications policy.

The increase in the Community's budget expenditure therefore gives an additional indication of the general process of material vertical growth of the Community. In effect, although the Community's monies are redistributed between the Member States, the point is that the decision to redistribute is adopted by the Community, not by single Member States. From that perspective, any increase in the Community's budget means a decrease in Member States' budgetary sovereignty, irrespective of whether a particular Member States is a net recipient or a net payer.

Yet before entering into the analysis of the growth of the Community's budget, it is necessary to give some preliminary explanations in order to interpret correctly the data obtained. Three points must be noted in this regard. First, the sources of the data are the 1995 *Vade-Mecum Budgetaire des Communautées* for the data concerning budget expenditure by year, and the *Official Journal of the European Communities* for the data concerning budget expenditure by policy. Secondly, I have taken into account only budget expenditure or outturn and not budget appropriations. The reason is that budget expenditure or outturn gives a better indication of the Community's real growth, for these variables reflect what the Community has actually spent in a certain period and on a particular policy.[37] Finally, I have excluded, as I did in the regulatory growth parameter, budget expenditure in the framework of the ECSC and EURATOM. However the *Vade-Mecum* specifies that the EURATOM budget was integrated into the EEC budget from 1969. Therefore, data concerning the evolution of Community expenditure by year must be interpreted with this qualification in mind. The data obtained are summarized in Tables I.5 and I.6.

It can be seen from Table I.5 that the general tendency is one of steady growth of expenditure under both the TEEC and the SEA. In the Treaty of Rome period we can, however, differentiate three different phases of budget growth, marked by 'budgetary booms'. The first phase is from 1958 to 1967, in which budget growth was relatively small, the average rate of growth being 47 million ECUs per year. The first budgetary boom was in 1968 in which 476 million ECUs in 1967 grew to 1,487 million in the following year, an increase of approximately 1,000 million ECUs. The second phase of Community budgetary growth started in 1968 and ended in 1977. The average rate of growth during this phase was roughly 725 million ECUs per year.

---

[37] A further reason is that the first Community budgets are expressed in terms of 'appropriations' and also in terms of 'expenditure/outturn', whereas later ones are expressed simply in terms of 'expenditure/outturn'. The selection of the latter variables therefore allows for comparison between all years.

Table I.5: European Community budget expenditure, by year (in millions of ECUs)

TEEC	SEA
1958: 7.3	1987: 35088.0
1959: 18.1	1988: 41021.7
1960: 21.2	1989: 40757.1
1961: 34.0	1990: 44062.9
1962: 41.5	1991: 53650.2
1963: 39.8	1992: 57946.0
1964: 46.8	
1965: 76.6	
1966: 125.2	
1967: 476.1	
1968: 1487.9	
1969: 1904.8	
1970: 3385.2	
1971: 2207.1	
1972: 3122.3	
1973: 4505.2	
1974: 4826.4	
1975: 5816.9	
1976: 7562.8	
1977: 8735.9	
1978: 12041.8	
1979: 14220.7	
1980: 15857.3	
1981: 17726.0	
1982: 20469.6	
1983: 24506.0	
1984: 27081.4	
1985: 27867.3	
1986: 34675.4	

Source: Vade-Mecum Budgetaire des Communautés (1995).

The third significant phase was from 1978 to 1986. At both the beginning and the end of this phase the Community experienced impressive booms. In 1978 the Community budget increased by 4,000 million ECUs from 8,735 million ECUs in 1977 to 12,041 ECUs in 1978. Subsequently, before the enactment of the SEA, the Community budget grew from 27,867 million ECUs in 1985 to 34,675 million ECUs in 1986 (an increase of 7,000 million ECUs). The average rate of growth during the third phase was 2,265 million ECUs per year, that is an acceleration of approximately 1,500 million ECUs per year with respect to the previous period.

It is also interesting to note that, within this general trend of growth in Community expenditure under the TEEC, some periods saw a budgetary decrease. The clearest occurred during the second phase (1968–77). The Community's expenditure increased in 1970 to 3,385 million ECUs, only to decrease to 2,207 and 3,122 million ECUs in the two following years.

It is also worth comparing budget booms and legislative booms. In general, budget booms have preceded legislative ones. Thus, for example, during the TEEC period, regulatory growth passed the psychological barrier of 100 legally binding acts per year in 1972, whereas the first budget boom had taken place some years earlier, in 1968. In 1985 the Community exceeded the barrier of 300 legally binding measures per year, whereas the Community budget had experienced another significant boom some seven years earlier, in 1978.

As in the case of regulatory growth, the effects of the political convulsions which occurred under the TEEC, such as the shift towards unanimity from 1966 onwards, do not seem to have had a negative impact on Community growth. On the contrary, two years after the signing of the Luxembourg compromise, the Community experienced the first significant boom: an increse of 1,000 million ECUs in 1968.

Regarding the data for the SEA period, it is interesting to note, first, that the enactment of the new Treaty did not immediately translate to a large increase in Community expenditure. From 1986 to 1987 the Community budget experienced a growth of only 300 million ECUs. Only in 1988 did the Community budget grow considerably (by 6,000 million ECUs with respect to 1987). This may be understood as a consequence of the implementation of the *First Delors Package*.[38] From 1990 to 1991 the Community experienced another boom of approximately 8,000 million ECUs. Growth was also significant in 1992, but not as important as in previous years (3,000 million ECUs more, compared with 1991 figures). Secondly, in general terms, the average rate of growth in the SEA period was 3,833 million per year, which

---

[38] The *First Delors Package* was proposed by the Commission in February 1987 (COM(87) 376 final, note EC Bull 7/8-1987 at 9) and approved by the European Council one year later, in February 1988 (European Council of Brussels; 11, 12, 13 February 1988, note EC Bull 2-1988 at 8) for the period 1988–92. The *First Delors Package* was intended to be the financial complement of the achievement of the single market objective.

implies an acceleration of 1,000 million ECUs per year with respect to the last six years of the pre-SEA period (2,800 million growth per year from 1981 to 1986).

Table I.6 complements the previous analysis by offering an overview of the budget expenditure on particular Community policies in specific years (1980, 1986, 1987, and 1992). It is important to note that the time references have not been randomly selected. On the contrary, they have been selected to illustrate general tendencies with regard to the evolution of each of the policies examined.[39] Nor is the selection of policies to be examined random. Thus regional policy, research and development, and the CAP have been selected because, first, they are the most important Community spending policies, and secondly, they are clear examples of distributive (research and development and the CAP to a certain extent) and redistributive (regional policy and the CAP) Community budgetary interventions.[40] The choice of environment and consumer protection is explained by the fact that they are good examples of Community 'social regulation' policies.[41] Transport has been selected to complement the data on regulatory growth in this policy which demonstrated a case of policy failure irrespective of its status as a common policy. The same can also be said of environmental policy.

The first point to note is the dominance of the expenditure on the Common Agricultural Policy by comparison with the other policies, in all the time references examined. However, it is interesting to note that CAP budgetary intervention has decreased through the years. Whereas in 1980 CAP expenditure represented as much as 73.2 per cent of the total Community budget, in 1992 it had decreased considerably to 58.8 per cent. This may be the result of the reform of the CAP, which was initiated in the SEA period and still continues, intended to downsize the overall importance of this policy within the total Community budget.

[39] A complete table with the evolution, year by year, of the set of policies that are analysed has not been included here for technical reasons. For further information, see the *Vade-Mecum Budgétaire*, cited above, as well as the budgets for each year, in which the reader will find confirmation of the tendencies which are illustrated here by the data on budgetary growth in particular years.

[40] Majone's (1994a:10) definition of redistributive and distributive policies is followed here. Majone argues that redistributive policies are those in which a transfer of resources is made from one group of individuals, regions, or countries to another group. Distributive policies are those in which a transfer of resources is made in favour of different economic activities.

[41] Joerges' (1994:44) definition of 'social regulation' is followed here. According to this author, 'social regulation' is understood as regulation of risks produced to the environment, workers at the workplace, and consumers.

In general, all policies experienced growth, including transport policy. Therefore the findings regarding the difficulties encountered in the implementation of this policy at a regulatory level are counterbalanced, to a certain extent, by these data on its financial aspect. Notwithstanding, Community financial expenditure in this field was and still is scant, in both relative and absolute terms.[42]

Expenditure on regional policy also shows a significant general trend. This also applies to the Treaty of Rome period, in which regional policy was not, formally speaking, a Community field of interest (14 per cent of the total budget in 1986, which reflects the trend of the years before the SEA was enacted). The same growth trend before the formal enactment of the SEA is also visible in the financial development of research and development. Though less significant than regional policy, expenditure on Research and Development (R and D) had already experienced some growth before its formal introduction as a Community policy under the SEA (by 1.6 per cent in 1980 and 2 per cent in 1986). Therefore we are confronted with two cases of budgetary paradox, or cases in which material development anticipated formal growth. Further, the introduction of R and D through the SEA was not directly supported by a major budgetary expansion of this policy (in 1992: 3.7%). Instead, there was a major development of regional policy expenditure in the SEA years (in 1992: 22.1 per cent, an increase of nearly 8 per cent in five years).

Although the preferred instrument of Community intervention in the field of consumer and environmental protection has been regulation, there has also been intervention through financial means. The patterns of budgetary growth of some of the policies examined above (e.g. R and D) are also visible in consumer protection and environmental policy, though expenditure is much more limited in this latter case due to its marked regulatory profile. The general tendency has been of steady but gradual growth in both fields of action. Findings regarding budgetary expenditure by policy are summarized in Table I.6 on p. 32.

2. *Material Majority Voting*

The question that a material analysis of majority voting must answer is whether or not in the different periods of Community evolution this rule applied *de facto* in those cases for which it was formally provided by the Treaties.

---

[42] Note 1995 *Vade-Mecum budgétaire*, cited above, at p. 28.

Table I.6: European budget expenditure, by policy

Policies	1980	1986	1987	1992
CAP[a]	73.2%	66%	67.6%	58.8%
Regional policy[b]	9.4%	14%	14.4%	22.1%
Transport	0.006%	0.1%	0.07%	0.015%
Consumers/environmental policy	0.02%	0.04%	0.07%	0.12%
Research and development	1.6%	2%	2.12%	3.7%

[a] Includes both sections of the European Agricultural Funds, (guarantee and guidance).
[b] Includes the European Regional Development Fund and the European Social Fund.
Sources: Community budgets (OJEC, 1979, 1985, 1986, 1991).

First, as regards the Treaty of Rome period, the answer is probably negative. Unanimity became the *de facto* voting procedure through the adoption by the Member States of the legally dubious Luxembourg compromise (Weiler, 1991a; Hartley, 1994:21). The Luxembourg compromise was adopted in an extraordinary session of the European Council held in Luxembourg on 28 and 29 January 1966. It was the Member States' reaction to the *'chaise vide'* crisis that, from 30 June 1965, set France against its Community partners regarding the establishment of new agricultural prices (Gerbet, 1999: 274). France demanded that the adoption of the new prices be made by unanimity, and not by majority voting as the TEEC foresaw for the third transitional period. The way out of the crisis was the Luxembourg compromise, which affected all cases in which majority voting was foreseen (not only for agricultural prices). Its final text[43] read as follows:

I. Where, in the case of decisions which may be taken by majority vote on a proposal of the Commission, very important interests of one or more partners are at stake, the Members of the Council will endeavour, within a reasonable time, to reach solutions which can be adopted by all Members of the Council while respecting their mutual interests and those of the Community, in accordance with article 2 of the Treaty.

II. With regard to the preceding paragraph, the French delegation considers that where very important interests are at stake the discussion must be continued until unanimous agreement is reached.

III. The six delegations note that there is a divergence of views on what should be done in the event of a failure to reach a complete agreement.

[43] Reprinted in EEC Bull. 3-1966, at p. 9.

IV. The six delegations nevertheless consider that this divergence does not prevent the Community's work being resumed in accordance with the normal procedure.

Further, the text of the Luxembourg agreement incorporated a set of decisions that should be adopted by a unanimous vote:

The Members of the Council agreed that decisions on the following should be adopted by common consent:
   a) The financial regulation for agriculture;
   b) Extensions to the market organisation for fruit and vegetables;
   c) The regulation on the organisation of sugar markets;
   d) The fixing of common prices for milk, beef and veal, rice, sugar, olive and oil seeds.

Thus the Luxembourg compromise meant that all decisions were to be adopted unanimously during the whole TEEC period. Although there is no direct evidence showing whether unanimity was *de facto* applied, most observers agree that this was the case (De Ruyt, 1987). Although unanimity was, from the Luxembourg compromise onwards, the *de facto* voting rule, there are indications that the majority principle did not totally disappear from the Community institutional map. For instance, De Ruyt remarks that during the period 1966 to 1974, at least 'six to ten decisions were adopted by resorting to a vote'. Further, he states, 'from 1974 to 1979 at least thirty decisions' were adopted by majority vote (1987:116). De Ruyt also notes that in the years before the adoption of the SEA there was already an increasing tendency to adopt decisions by vote. From 1980 to 1984 majority voting was used in around ninety cases. More importantly, some of the decisions taken by majority votes were of great importance, such as the budgets after 1982 and the agricultural prices for 1982–83. This latter decision was adopted by a majority vote despite the fact that the United Kingdom invoked the application of the Luxembourg compromise. This case was by no means unique. Other decisions were made by majority vote in spite of explicit invocation of the Luxembourg compromise by some Member States. For instance, in December 1982 Denmark opposed several Council regulations for fisheries by invoking the Luxembourg compromise. In June 1983 it invoked the Luxembourg compromise to oppose a Council decision regarding the 'Hareng' issue. Denmark's demands were rejected by the other Member States, and decisions were adopted by majority vote in both cases (De Ruyt, 1987:117; Hartley, 1994:21–3).

Secondly, the SEA formally introduced majority voting for the adoption of important decisions regarding, notably, the completion of the internal market.[44] From a material perspective, there is no direct evidence showing to what extent majority voting was implemented. In effect, unlike the present procedure under the Amsterdam Treaty,[45] the votes of the Council were not published in the SEA period, despite the formal adoption of the majority principle. Therefore, we need to turn here to indirect indications and the testimony of observers. Regarding the first, one indication at least of the political will to implement majority voting was that Member States expressed their commitment to implement it once the SEA was enacted. This compromise was illustrated, in particular, by the reform of the Rules of Procedure of the Council in October 1987.[46] The new Article 5 of the Council Rules of Procedure established that a majority of the Member States was sufficient to proceed to a vote, on the request of a Member State or the Commission (Dehousse, 1994a:103). Regarding the second, some observers have pointed out that many decisions were still being adopted by unanimity in the SEA period (Weiler, 1991a). Therefore, the conclusion for the SEA period may be that although in general resorting to a vote was rare, Member States could use majority voting as a threat. As is argued below, more important than the fact of implementing majority voting was the firm commitment of Member States to resort to voting in cases of need. In other words, it seems clear that policy-making developed during the SEA period under the shadow of majority voting (Weiler, 1991a; 1999).[47]

E. Conclusions

1. *Community Growth: 'Stops and Goes'?*

The first question posed at the beginning of this Chapter was whether the growth of the Community powers during both periods under examination could be described as a process of 'stops and goes'. Generally speaking, it is clear that the growth of the Community, both vertical and horizontal, had much more to do with 'goes' than with 'stops'. Formally speaking, the TEEC and SEA periods saw both vertical and horizontal growth. Materially speak-

---

[44] Art. 100a TEEC.

[45] Note Art. 7 of the Council internal rules (Decision 1999/385, OJEC L 147 of 12 June 1999).

[46] Council Rules of Procedure, OJEC L 291 of 15 October 1987.

[47] This does not mean that majority voting was the factor explaining the acceleration of community regulatory growth during this period. Naturally, a complex mix of factors accounts for this. My argument is that, irrespective of how this growth can be explained, it happened under a different institutional setting, majority voting. See, however, Golub (1999).

ing, the aggregated numbers also speak in favour of this conclusion, especially at the regulatory level, but also at the budgetary level. Further, although from a material perspective we lack information about whether majority voting was implemented during the SEA period, it seems that Member States were willing to act by majority during this period when the need arose. This may be interpreted also as a confirmation of growth at this level.

The general trend was therefore one of growth both at the formal and material levels, and in both vertical and horizontal dimensions. However, within this broad picture particular inflection points are discernible, concrete cases of 'stops' within the general context of growth. Materially speaking, there were inflection points in specific periods of time (for example 1971) for both regulation and budget intervention. Moreover, from the perspective of majority voting, the clearest example was provided by the shift to unanimity through the Luxembourg compromise. Although the Luxembourg compromise was made outside the Treaties, and setting aside the question of its probable illegality, the fact that it was implemented amounts to a counter-tendency or inflection point, that is, a *de facto* or material stop within a general trend of growth in the horizontal dimension.

Also from a concrete perspective, it must be pointed out that the process of Community growth involved paradoxes during this period. Paradoxes emerge if formal and material growth are compared. An example is the non-development of transport policy in both periods. Though ample powers were given here to the Community, this policy showed no notable development in any of the periods under survey (though this was even more evident in the Rome Treaty period). Another case, this time of a contrary nature to that of transport, was environmental policy before the SEA. Given that the Rome Treaty established no competence in this field for the Community, its extensive development during this period is astonishing. From a budgetary perspective, it is also interesting to note that some policies were funded well before they were established within the Treaties. Here the example was regional policy.

Therefore, the general conclusion is that the process of Community growth during the periods under survey was one of generalized 'goes' and specific 'stops', mixed with the emergence of a number of paradoxes. It seems then that the process of growth of the Community powers was, in general, quite linear. Competences were granted to the Community and then implemented. However, there were exceptions to this rule, whose importance, in both qualitative and quantitative terms, prevents us from making broad generalizations on the issue.

2. *The Single European Act period: not only* European *and* Act, *but also* Single

How does the SEA period compare with the previous description? The answer to this question also has several parts. To start with, it is important to point out that the SEA period was also one in which generalized growth, particular 'stops', and a number of paradoxes may be found. The general trend was of growth during the SEA, at both the formal and material levels and in the vertical and horizontal dimensions. Formally speaking, the number of Community powers were increased and majority voting was expanded. From a material point of view, during the SEA period most policies developed, and the budget expanded. While there is no direct evidence of how majority voting was employed, the Member States' seem to have employed this new instrument in case of need. However, there were cases of 'stop', in terms of both regulatory output and budgetary output (i.e. 1988 for regulatory output, and 1989 for budgetary output). There were also paradoxes, like transport policy (which continued to stagnate) or education (a case of material growth breaking the limits of formal growth—though less evidently than in the case of environmental policy during the Rome Treaty period—since education was formally introduced as a Community competence only in Maastricht).

However, there is one feature that makes the SEA phase a distinctive period in the growth process of the Community: the exponential growth of regulatory intervention. The figures in this regard are impressive: more than three-quarters of the measures adopted during the twenty-nine years of the Rome Treaty period were adopted in the six years of the SEA period. To this finding one must add majority voting. Majority voting was formally re-introduced (and extended) with the SEA, but more importantly from a material perspective Member States were willing to implement this institutional shift during this period. The combination of these facts meant that the Community experienced one of the greatest regulatory efforts of its history under a procedural context *dominated by the threat of voting*. This particular outcome is what makes the SEA a rather unusual period. The consequences of this outcome, from a legitimacy perspective, are examined in the next Chapter.

II

Legitimacy

A. Introduction

The principle of subsidiarity was incorporated into the ECT through the Maastricht Treaty, signed by the representatives of the Member States on 7 February 1992. The incorporation of subsidiarity within the Treaty followed the debate on the Community's legitimacy between the Member States from the end of the 1980s onwards. This debate was prompted by the overall awareness of the dimensions that the process of growth had by then taken place. As shown in the previous Chapter, the Community experienced a dramatic expansion of its regulatory activities during the SEA period. By itself, this fact would be almost irrelevant. However, as noted above, this expansion took place in a procedural context dominated, if not by the reality of majority voting, then at least by the real threats by Member States to implement the principle. In the period prior to the SEA, Member States had the guarantee that Community powers would not develop if a single Member State opposed it. Before 1966, unanimity was established by the Treaty for almost all cases of Community intervention. After 1966, the Luxembourg compromise came to mean that this institutional status quo was to be maintained. However, the Single European Act dramatically changed this state of affairs. Member States, prompted by the European Commission,[1] decided to re-incorporate and even extend majority voting. This procedure was established for the adoption of important Community decisions and, notably, for the adoption of all decisions concerning the establishment of the internal market,[2] the backbone of Community intervention. The expansion of the Community powers during the SEA was dramatic. The Community expanded its regulatory activities exponentially. In just six years the Community

[1] See Estella (1999d).   [2] Art. 100a ECT (now Art. 95 ECT).

adopted more than three-quarters of all the measures in the whole of the Rome Treaty period (almost thirty years). Institutionally speaking, the shift to majority voting meant that Member States could no longer seek shelter under the procedural safeguard of unanimity to defend their national interest. Policy-making therefore developed during the SEA period under the shadow of majority voting. Member States could appeal to the new procedure to increase their leverage; in extreme cases, they could even resort to voting. Consequently, the shift to majority voting profoundly changed the institutional rules of the Community game.

Member States' reactions to this shift were soon noted. The most notable expression of Member States' rage against the Community's machine was the Danish, and to a certain extent the French, referenda on the Maastricht Treaty. As often happens, the theoretical interpretations of these facts have had more impact than their actual emergence. According to some authors (Weiler, 1991a; 1999; 2002; Dehousse, 1995; 2002) the Community is experiencing a legitimacy crisis as a consequence of the competential and institutional developments that took place during the SEA period. This stance has almost become the new dogma in many, if not all, analyses of the Community's *political* integration. All authors accept this point at present, with some exceptions that only confirm the rule (Moravscik, 1993; 1998). However, the debate on legitimacy is far from being exhausted. On the contrary, the contours of this debate seem in many cases to be blurred, if not incoherent. In fact, the expression 'the Community's legitimacy crisis' evokes many different things in many different people. For some, it implies that the Community suffers from a lack of democratic legitimacy; expansion of the powers of the European Parliament would be the antidote to this ill. For others, the expression denotes a lack of efficiency in the Community's decision-making process. What the Community needs, according to this second view, is more, rather than less, majority voting. For yet other authors, majority voting is the source of the Community's legitimacy problems. The solution would be, not to eliminate majority voting, but rather to stress the positive benefits of a consensual decision-making style for the Community. The debate on the Community's legitimacy is further complicated by the fact that not all analysts seem to give the same meaning to the concept of legitimacy. This comes as no surprise, for the concept of legitimacy is, in reality, elusive. It is used, time and again, in many different senses to indicate many different things. However, this is never made explicit. Rather than specifying the difficulties and the limits of the concept, or the sense in which it is used, authors simply employ the term, probably thinking that it is better to be partially understood than to risk engaging in an endless and complex discussion on the precise contours of the concept. As a result of both trends, the current debate on the Community's legitimacy is chaotic and ill structured.

The next section of this Chapter considers the nature of the concept of legitimacy, and both the potential and the limits of the concept of legitimacy, as well as the problems inherent in its use. The following section describes the basic traits of three models of legitimacy that can be found in the litera-ture on the Community's legitimacy crisis. This *post-hoc* reconstruction is an attempt to systematize present debates on the Community's legitimacy since, as previously suggested, most authors employ a particular model in an unex-plained—if not unconscious—way. These models are the following: the 'democratic' legitimacy model; the 'formal' legitimacy model; and the 'feder-al' (for lack of a better expression) legitimacy model. I advocate the validity of the third model. From this perspective, the 'federal' legitimacy model is the theoretical paradigm which best captures the problems caused by the growth of Community regulation in a procedural context dominated by majority voting for Member States. The fourth section of this Chapter illustrates how the model operates with a concrete example. One of the deficiencies encoun-tered in the literature on the Community's legitimacy is that the problems arising from the implementation of majority voting are always assumed, but never demonstrated. I attempt to fill that lacuna with a concrete example of the meaning that the implementation of environmental policy had for one Member State, the UK, before and after the SEA reform changed the insti-tutional rules of the Community. Finally, the last section of this Chapter pre-sents some conclusions.

B. Legitimacy: an elusive concept

The concept of legitimacy is present—omnipresent, one is tempted to say—in almost every analysis of modern political science and sociology. It is less well known in the legal universe, although in some European Union lan-guages—such as Spanish—the concept is used to refer to a radically different set of problems—those derived from standing in a legal process.[3] The elusive character of the term legitimacy has not impeded its extensive use in political science and sociology. This overuse of the expression notwithstanding, the

---

[3] In Spanish legal jargon, 'legitimacy' means *locus standi*.

question emerges: what is indeed to be understood by legitimacy? And further, how is it to be understood—if at all—in the legal world?

Hyde, in a well known essay, illustrates the dramatic dimension of the previous questions with the following story:

Late at night, at a clear intersection with no drivers to be seen on any side, Joe Driver stopped at a stop sign. Why? His stop, after all, delayed his return home, cost him gasoline and wear on his breaks [*sic*], and denied him some psychic gratification in driving fast. There is, social science would hold, no single reason why this Joe, or other Joes, stopped at the stop sign. Partly it was unthinking habit, the reflex on seeing a red octagon. Partly it was fear of a police cruiser lurking unseen. Partly it was fear of other hazards, cars or pedestrians, that might not be visible. Partly it was a desire to avoid the disapproval of passengers, a disapproval that might stem from their fear or sense of the rightness of stopping at stop signs. Partly it was an obscure sense in Joe or his passengers that everyone is better off if everybody stops at stop signs. The question is whether there are additional motives in Joe's action. Those who believe that there are call these 'legitimacy' (1983:386).

There could be, as Hyde points out, a number of explanations for the protagonist's attitude. One of them is that Joe Driver stopped at the stop sign because he understood that the legal order was legitimate. Legitimacy in this sense would be the acceptance of a norm or a set of norms for the mere reason of its or their existence. From the moment a norm is enacted, its validity would therefore generate a presumption of legitimacy.

It is also possible to find other explanations for the driver's conduct: for example, fear of coercion by the State. This underlies many constructions of the law's legitimacy which basically understand law as the legitimate instrumentation of force. Perhaps the driver decided to stop out of fear of the police. Another explanation rests on the idea of interest: perhaps his action was prompted by his interest in avoiding the costs that might arise from not stopping. Habit is another possible explanation: perhaps the driver stopped due to his ingrained habit of stopping at every stop sign.

It is also possible that the concept of legitimacy extends beyond the pure assumption of the validity of norms to include at least some of the explanations outlined above. Would it be possible to construe a concept of legitimacy that integrates all of them? Or are we speaking of something else when we use the term legitimacy? More subversively, it could be even asked whether the concept of legitimacy is a subterfuge, a kind of default procedure that social sciences use when other explanations do not seem entirely convincing. In that case the concept of legitimacy would have to be considered as a prescientific tool. From a methodological viewpoint the most sensible thing would be to abandon this concept, and try alternative explanations. Scepticism is, for example, Hyde's stance towards the concept of legitimacy, as the above quotation suggests.[4]

Turning now to the studies of European integration, the relevance of this debate about the exact profile of the concept of legitimacy becomes apparent when one compares the different analytical (and even normative) perspectives that authors adopt on the issue of the Community's legitimacy. For example, if the positions of Weiler and Przeworski are compared, we find that:

[Weiler's] answer is connected to the idea of legitimacy. However, as A. Przewoski (1991) has shown, there is no need to employ the concept of legitimacy in order to understand the fulfilment of the rules of the system. To accept democratic results which are unfavourable may be an equilibrium in the sense of game theory. The key is that the political forces involved in the democratic game have a probability high enough to be on the winner's side. Therefore, the idea is to obtain more utility in the long run by playing 'democracy' than by breaking the rules of the game or not participating in the system. A democracy in equilibrium does not presuppose anything on the homogeneity or heterogeneity of the demos. Identity conflicts must therefore be understood as endogenous to the political system and not, as proposed by Dahl and Weiler, as exogenous parameters that pre-exist and predetermine democracy. If a minority does not believe in the compromise of the majority that the latter will respect the former's rights, it is possible to think that a problem of demos or nationalism may arise. However, this will be a consequence of a democracy not truly being in equilibrium (Sanchez-Cuenca, 1997a:44, my translation).

Here we have two different readings of the Community's legitimacy problems which start from different premises concerning the concept of legitimacy. For Weiler, the concept of legitimacy has an inherently embedded social connotation. The key to understanding the degree of legitimacy of a given *polis* is not the way its institutions function, but rather the way in which the decisional output is accepted. The notion of legitimacy that Weiler employs is therefore connected to the concept of the *demos*, in an historic and organic sense of the word. Weiler's point of departure in approaching the legitimacy problems of the Union can be found in authors like Carl Schmitt. Therefore, for Weiler, the concept of the *demos* has both an objective and a subjective aspect. The objective side encompasses things such as a common language and a common history. The subjective aspect is the interpretation of the objective side: a sort of spiritual union of the people linked by a common

---

[4] In the conclusions of the work cited, Hyde admits, this time explicitly, that social sciences would be better off if the concept were abandoned (1983:426).

history and a common language that serves to identify those who are *inside* and to exclude those who are *outside* of the *demos*. However, for Weiler, the solutions to the legitimacy problems of the Union do not necessarily lead to the adoption of a historic-organic view of a supposed European *demos*. On the contrary, the European *demos* would have to be designed differently. It would be a *demos* built upon rational premisses, and in particular, upon a certain vision of the individual and his or her values that could be vaguely termed as *neo-Kantian*. It would be in this common space of rationalist-shared values where citizens of different Member States could identify with each other. This rational concept of the *demos* would complement the (national) historic-organic concept of the *demos*, but would not replace it.

Contrary to Weiler, Przewoski seems to deny the relevance of the idea of legitimacy in order to explain issues like the Community's uneasiness. However, one could argue that Przewoski in fact adopts an instrumental, or functional, view of the concept of legitimacy, using the tools of rational choice. For Przewoski the point of departure is not how a *demos* is or should be, but the institutional arrangements that are adopted by a *polis*. There would be a legitimacy problem when those arrangements are sub-optimal, for example, from the Pareto's optimum perspective. Therefore, if in the long run institutional arrangements do not create a positive-sum game situation, then one should expect legitimacy problems (demands to change the rules of the game, or simply exit). The fact that in the Community such demands are the exception, and that no Member State has left the Union, seem to indicate that, at least in the long run, there is institutional equilibrium. Therefore the emphasis of some authors on the legitimacy problems of the Community are not entirely justified.

We see, therefore, that the definition of legitimacy adopted determines the view of the problem and that, consequently, the conclusions that are reached are very different, or even contradictory. The concept of legitimacy is diffuse and abstract and this explains why some authors place themselves at one extreme of the intellectual spectrum and others at the contrary one. This open-ended nature of legitimacy allows definitions which are highly contingent on the methodological perspective adopted. Rather than negating the utility of the concept—as Hyde strongly advocates—this means that the model of legitimacy employed must be explained before engaging in any discussion on the Community's legitimacy. I address this in the following section.

C. Europe as a legitimacy problem

Theoretically speaking, it is possible to distinguish between two categories of legitimacy: *input legitimacy* and *output legitimacy* (Dehousse, 1995). In general terms, it could be said that input legitimacy puts the focus on *process*, whereas output legitimacy looks at *results*. Starting from this basic format, different models of legitimacy have developed. All of them can be connected with one of these categories, and some with both. While acknowledging the extensive attention that this matter has attracted in literature, I describe here only the main aspects of three models of legitimacy: 'formal legitimacy', 'democratic legitimacy', and 'federal legitimacy'. All offer different interpretations of the consequences that derive, from a legitimacy viewpoint, from the adoption of majority voting in the Community setting. However, only the first and the second can be categorized as 'input legitimacy' models. The third one lies somewhere in between the input and output legitimacy models. The model I support is the third one. It is also important to stress that these models are not always defended explicitly by specific authors or by well defined doctrinal currents; rather, the contrary is true, with some exceptions. Therefore, the advocacy elsewhere of these models (at least of some of them) is made in a discrete, almost imperceptible way, and it is found dispersed in many different writings. The analysis presented below attempts to systematize and organize the main arguments of these writings. In many cases the arguments are not directly attributed to specific authors, but this is irrelevant for my present purposes.

1. *Formal Legitimacy*

Formal legitimacy offers an interpretation of the consequences of the majoritarian principle for Member States, and consists mainly of approaching this problem from the perspective of formal validity. According to this model, the adoption of decisions by majority voting ceases to be a legitimacy problem when the Member States decide to adopt this institutional shift following the procedures established by the ECT for 'constitutional' reform. In effect, the majority rule, as shown in the previous Chapter, was introduced (or re-introduced) by the SEA in 1987. This reform was made following Article 313 of the ECT (ex Article 247). This means that it was formally accepted by all Member States of the European Community at that time. New Members have not made exceptions (as public international law permits) to the implementation of this procedure. Therefore, for both new and old Member States, the shift to majority voting has been accepted, as the Treaty indicates, according to their respective 'constitutional requirements' of Treaty reform or approval.[5] Member States may agree to a lesser or greater extent with the impact that a particular Community measure can have on their legal order and sovereignty, when they are outvoted. What is not acceptable is for Member States to attack that measure from the perspective of its legitimacy, when the norm was adopted in accordance with procedures that they themselves freely adopted (Louis, 1990).

To better illustrate this model, the example of the Luxembourg compromise may also be adduced. According to the formal view of legitimacy, the material shift from majority to unanimity brought about by the Luxembourg compromise was clearly illegitimate. In effect, the Luxembourg compromise constituted a modification of certain procedural aspects of the Rome Treaty which was *not* made in accordance with the Treaty reform provisions. However, as seen in the previous Chapter, the Community's procedural panorama was *de facto* changed as a consequence of this compromise. It is important to understand this point. From a formal legitimacy viewpoint, the argument is not only that the Luxembourg compromise was illegal: no author claims that it was legal. In this, there is a broad doctrinal agreement. The point that formal analyses wish to make is that, besides its illegality, the Luxembourg compromise was illegitimate. Therefore, formal analyses directly link the legality (or illegality) of a decision with its legitimacy (or illegitimacy). What is legal is legitimate; what is illegal is illegitimate.

The formal legitimacy model advocates the spread of majority voting in the context of the Community, which is the consequence of its analytical point of departure. In effect: for formal analysts, the Community's legitimacy problems are the result of lack of efficiency in the Community's decision-making process. The problem for them is not so much that the Community acts too much, but that having decided to act it takes so long to reach a decision. This creates an impression of stagnation, that the Community is not doing its work properly, which in turn explains the public's rejection (in some periods at least). The cure for this ill is more—not less—majority voting. Majority voting would, on this view, increase the efficiency of the Community's decision-making process. The argument has come full circle with the prospect of enlargement: in an enlarged Community, the expansion

---

[5] Art. 313 establishes the following: 'This Treaty shall be ratified by the High Contracting Parties in accordance with their respective constitutional requirements'.

of majority voting is seen to be not only a normative stance, but an objective need if the Community is to work.

2. *Democratic Legitimacy*

The shift from unanimity to majority voting has been interpreted by an important doctrinal sector as a democracy deficit. In turn, this reading has had a great impact upon legal scholars (for example Mangas and Liñan, 1996). At first glance, this may seem normal: after all, the lawyer's first instinct when the word legitimacy appears is to link it with the word democracy. Democracy and legitimacy amount to the same thing from a lawyer's perspective. It is difficult to explain why this is the case in the legal world and not—or not so much—in other disciplines. The reason is probably linked to education (though this is very tentative): lawyers—at least continental lawyers—are taught about legitimacy in law school when they learn about the foundations of the parliamentary system.

Be that as it may, the point is that democratic legitimacy is a model frequently employed by lawyers. The core of this model is the following: the concept of legitimacy refers to the *democratic quality* of a particular *polis*. Such democratic quality is measured primarily by the degree and intensity of involvement of democratic institutions in the political life of the *polis*. Applied to the Community context, the democratic legitimacy model assumes that under the unanimity rule Community decisions were indirectly legitimized by national parliaments through the decisive role that national governments played in the Community's decision-making process. The legitimation of Community decisions was indirect since, if governments adopted a decision at Community level, they could be controlled by their parliament at home. Each government knew that it could not adopt a decision at Community level that would not be accepted at the national level by the national parliament. In such a case, that government could oppose its veto to the adoption of the decision. Thus unanimity at Community level ensured (albeit indirectly) the involvement of *all* national parliaments in the Community's decision-making process and therefore the democratic quality of the Community's decisional output.

This system of indirect democratic legitimacy was upset when majority voting came to the fore. In effect, if a decision was adopted by majority voting (and therefore a national government was outvoted) domestic political control by national parliaments lost all significance. The adoption of decisions without the indirect participation of *all* national parliaments amounted to a democratic deficit. The system therefore had to be reformed. The only solution to this problem was to substitute the indirect system of democratic legitimation—no longer valid after majority voting was introduced—for a system of direct legitimation. This amounted to an outpouring of support for the emergence of the European Parliament as a key player in the Community legislative process, which it had not been before the SEA.

Although this thesis acknowledges the progress that has been made in this area, it argues that many decisions are still adopted without the intervention of the European Parliament. Until the European Parliament is placed at the centre of the Community's legislative process, the democratic legitimacy model maintains that the Community suffers from a democratic deficit (Corbett *et al.*, 2000).

3. *A Critique*

None of the models presented above seems adequately to capture the issue that emerges as a consequence for Member States' sovereignty of the shift from unanimity to majority voting. The first model described, the formal legitimacy model, is clearly insufficient to explain the problem. In fact, rather than attempting to explain the problem, it represents an attempt to negate its existence. From the moment when the Member States formally adopted the majority principle into the EC legal order, no legitimacy problem can arise from that reform. Majority voting was formally and freely accepted by all Member States. There would have been a problem if the principle had been introduced into the EC legal order through the back door, as was the case with unanimity and the Luxembourg compromise.

Notwithstanding its apparent intellectual elegance, this reading of the Community legitimacy crisis presents more questions than answers. One of the questions that emerges from the viewpoint of formal legitimacy drives the point home. If, as this model suggests, Community intervention under majority voting is legitimate, how can the introduction of mechanisms for the Community's growth, such as the subsidiarity principle, be understood? Clearly, this perspective simply shifts the analysis on legitimacy back to its starting point.

On the other hand, the second thesis, the democratic legitimacy model, argues that the adoption of majority voting has produced a democratic deficit whose resolution could only be achieved through a definitive expansion of the powers of the European Parliament. A critique of this thesis merits more attention. This is not only because it has been very successful among legal academics, but also because any criticism of the democratic model may be interpreted as a defence of an undemocratic Community. This is a very common counter-criticism made by the advocates of the democratic legitimacy model: 'Why is democracy good for the Member States but not for the Community?' However, the advocacy of a non-democratic model for the Community is not the issue at hand. The point is, rather, that not all legitimacy problems of the European Community have to be interpreted in terms of a democratic deficit, at least in the sense in which 'democratic' is used in this model. Put in positive terms, the idea is that the 'deficit' arising from the switch to majority voting would be different from the one that arises from the limited role that the European Parliament still plays at present.

To point out the problems that this model presents for understanding the consequences of the shift to majority voting for Member States, let us imagine that the European Parliament had powers similar to those of national parliaments in parliamentary systems. Let us even imagine that the European Parliament had supremacy over the Council, in the sense that it could veto all its proposals and even adopt alternative ones under certain conditions. In other words, let us assume that the European Parliament had the final say regarding the adoption of all Community legislation. If this were the case, could it be seriously claimed that when the European Parliament adopted a decision that affected, for example, British interests, the United Kingdom would be reassured by the fact that it was the European Parliament, and not the Council, who adopted the measure? The answer to this question is so clearly negative that it does not merit empirical testing.[6] On the contrary, it could be argued that the reaction of British citizens would be even more negative if, instead of being adopted by an inter-governmental organ (though with supranational elements) like the Council, the measure was adopted by a fully supranational and remote institution like the European Parliament. Thus we see that the legitimacy problems of the EC are not limited to questions of parliamentary democratization.

4. *Federal Legitimacy*

The issue that emerged as a result of the adoption of the majority principle in the EC, after the SEA came into force, is better captured from the perspective

[6] However, I offer some empirical support to my argument. According to a survey made by the Taylor-Nelson-Sofres group in 11 Member States (which included the UK) 46% of people surveyed said they had 'little or no' confidence in the EP, against 39% who said they had 'quite a lot or a lot' of confidence in this institution. Note *El País*, 9 November 1998 (page 7). See, in general, on the issue of Europe and public opinion, Niedermayer and Sinnott (1998).

of the 'federal' legitimacy model (Bellamy *et al.*, 1995:61). The first thing to point out is that the term *federal* should not confuse the reader. This model does not advocate federalism as a political model in the Community. Rather, by *federal*, I wish to point out not so much the solutions, but rather the problems. Federal arrangements are an attempt to establish equilibrium between a majority and a minority. This implies that the tensions between the majority and the minority are even more pronounced in federal systems. Thus, the word *federal* is used in this work to describe the nature of the problem that the majority principle introduced into the European Community. The aim is not to support a 'federal solution' for the Community in the sense of a political union that would adopt the form of the federal state. Although, as will be seen in the following, the solutions proposed are not necessarily contradictory to a federal logic, it must be clear from the outset that the model proposed here does not prejudge anything from the perspective of the political destiny of the European Community.

The starting point for the federal legitimacy model is that any process of integration among states is characterized by the surrender of part of their sovereignty, with the aim that decisions affecting those areas are taken in common (Dahl, 1986:114). Therefore, in those areas that are now shared, the societies of the different states will have to accept, overnight, that decisions previously adopted by them alone are now adopted collectively. The implications of integration are dramatic for each *demos* involved in the new entity. On one hand, from the moment the new entity is born there would be, from a formal legal standpoint, a reconversion of old *poli* in a new, more inclusive, *polis*. On the other hand, the emergence of a new *polis* would not necessarily imply the emergence of a new *demos*, which would represent the addition of old *demoi*. Therefore, in the new *polis* the old *demoi* will continue to think in terms of 'us and them'. The process through which old *demoi* start to think simply in terms of 'us' will take longer. There will therefore be an interim situation in which the old dichotomy 'us and them' continues to be valid, though within an overall process of transition towards a new situation in which social borders will be reconfigured. Until this process comes about, when decisions are adopted by a majority, thus forcing one of the outvoted *demos* to implement it, this latter *demos* will interpret that decision in terms of imposition from outside, and not in terms of acceptance from inside. It will still be 'them' who forced 'us' to follow a particular path which is perceived by the outvoted *demos* to be contrary to its interests. Therefore, if the new situation (the emergence of a new *polis*) does not correspond with the emergence of a new *demos*, it will be important that decisions are adopted according to institutional mechanisms that foster the incorporation of all interests at stake, and aiming adequately to protect minorities in particular. In other words, unless the social situation does not match the new formal situation, majority voting will create tensions. The risks that arise from the adoption of decisions by majority, which exist in any political context, are even higher when the social substratum of a given *polis* lacks the necessary degree of unity and cohesion (Weiler, 1995; 1999).

The importance of procedures and decisional institutions must therefore be emphasized in this situation of social fragmentation which the new *polis* will have to confront. The question that emerges at this point is obvious: what are these procedures and decisional institutions? From a normative viewpoint, they must have a certain deliberative potential. Decisions should have to be adopted on the basis of argumentation and conviction, rather than on the basis of the force of the votes. A majoritarian democracy should leave a wider margin, in the absence of social cohesion, for a deliberative democracy. Procedures and decisional institutions in a deliberative democracy should foster the development of a communicative action (Habermas, 1984) among the different players of the political game.[7]

If we turn now to the European Community, we can understand better, from the perspective of a 'federal' legitimacy model, the consequences of majority voting for Member States' sovereignty and interests. To start with, it is clear that the EC is not now a *demos* in its social and organic sense. Data in this regard seem to support that conclusion.[8] Therefore, the transference of loyalties predicted by Haas (1958/68) does not seem to have occurred. On the basis of this evidence, it is likewise apparent that the British, for example, will feel, if outvoted in the Council, that the Member States which voted in favour of the measure forced the UK to adopt a measure against its will. Their perception will be that the measure is, consequently, illegitimate. The conclusion is that the European Community suffers at present from a 'federal' legitimacy problem which stems from the expansion of majority voting in the institutional structure of the Community. This problem has been further aggravated by recent Treaty reforms, which have extended the majority principle in the Community even more. Furthermore, there are data that seem to indicate that majority voting is becoming not only a threat, but a solid reality

---

[7] Føllesdal argues that subsidiarity and democratic deliberation are compatible among each other. I offer a contrary interpretation in Chapter IV of this book (point F).

[8] According to the survey cited in the previous footnote, 60% of people surveyed felt 'no or very little' concern by European integration, as opposed to 33% who felt 'very much or quite' concerned by European integration. Note *El País*, 9 November 1998 (page 7). See Niedermayer and Sinnott (1998).

Table II.1: Member States outvoted in the period 6 December 1993 to 1 September 1995

Member State	Number of times outvoted
UK	16
Germany	14
Netherlands	15
Denmark	15
Spain	4
Portugal	6
Italy	5
France	2
Greece	6
Luxembourg	5
Ireland	3
Belgium	2

Source: *European Voice* 2–8 November 1995 (Vol. 1, no. 5), page 2. However, the figures have to be interpreted with caution, since in Maastricht not all votes taken by the Council had to be published.

in Community decision-making. Table II.1 shows the frequency of Member States being outvoted during a certain period of time. Since the expansion of majority voting has not been compensated through the introduction of efficient correction mechanisms, the legitimacy gap that first opened in the SEA seems to have widened in recent years.[9]

The thesis that is being defended here, that the EC suffers from a legitimacy deficit as a consequence of the expansion of majority voting, might be attacked from a number of angles. The argument is clearly open to criticism from the perspective of efficiency. The classical contention is to say that a 'federal' model of legitimacy establishes a trade-off between legitimacy and effectiveness. The 'federal' legitimacy model appears to say that costs in terms of inefficiency would be out-weighed by the benefits in terms of legitimacy. Therefore, consensus-prone solutions should be preferred in a case like the EC, since the costs in inefficiency that this kind of solution would produce would be the price to pay.

However, this is not the case. It is not certain that such a huge trade-off between legitimacy and effectiveness must exist in a 'federal' legitimacy model. It is clear that consensus-prone solutions are costly from the efficien-

---

[9] This explains expressions of anti-communitarism, such as the Danish referendum on Maastricht.

cy viewpoint. However, the efficiency costs that this kind of solution may produce have been overestimated in the classical literature (Louis, 1990). Some of the data that emerged in Chapter I of this work may be adduced to support this argument. For instance, conventional wisdom states that one of the worst periods in terms of efficiency was the time between the enactment of the Luxembourg compromise and the adoption of the SEA (Barón, 1996). The Community manifested a clear *lourdeur*, if not complete stagnation, during this phase. The Community also manifested *lourdeur* in the period prior to the adoption of the Luxembourg compromise. However, the adoption of the Luxembourg compromise resulted in the number of acts that were adopted almost doubling over the previous year (fourteen measures in 1965; twenty-seven measures in 1966). The figures rise constantly after 1966, to reach the psychological barrier of 100 measures adopted in 1972. The remaining period (from 1972 to 1987) was of sustained and constant growth: in 1986, the year before the SEA was enacted, the Community adopted 300 legally binding acts. All this was achieved through unanimity.

The evidence presented here seems to contradict the conventional perception that consensus-prone institutional and decisional mechanisms constitute an important break in the regulatory activities of the EC. This is not to say that the solution which the 'federal' legitimacy model advocates is without cost; clearly, majority voting produces fewer costs from the efficiency perspective. The idea is, rather, that consensus-prone solutions do not necessarily entail massive costs in terms of efficiency, as is usually assumed. Further, they establish a better equilibrium between legitimacy and efficiency, at least in the Community.

Another way to approach criticism is, not from the perspective of efficiency, but from that of the interests that a consensus-prone solution better advances. It has been argued that, since a system based on majority has a majoritarian bias, a system based on consensual solutions would produce a minoritarian bias. Therefore, minoritarian interests would be over-represented in a system based on consensus. This has clear implications, for regulatory outputs, for example. As intergovernmentalists assume (Garrett, 1992 and 1997; Moravscik, 1992; 1993 and 1998) the minoritarian bias of a consensual system means that regulation will usually be ordered around the least forthcoming Member S tate (the minimum common denominator). Thus the Member State least interested in 'integration' will finally win. Innovation would be almost impossible in Community regulation, since policies would tend to incorporate those solutions that already exist in the least forthcoming Member State.

It is true that there is very little evidence of the Community's regulatory outputs to contradict the previous conclusion. However, the small amount of evidence that is emerging seems to be pointing in the opposite direction. This evidence shows that Community regulatory outputs do not reflect the preference of the least forthcoming Member State, but that, on the contrary, Community regulation incorporates an important degree of innovation. The examples, although specific, are sufficiently important to cast doubt on inter-governmentalist theses. For example, Directive 76/769[10] is a good example of regulatory innovation. This Directive was adopted with the aim of harmonizing Member States' legislation relating to the marketing and use of certain dangerous substances (PCBs and PCTs). As Rehbinder and Stewart point out (1985:214), the Directive 'had no parallel in existing Member States'. Another example is Directive 80/779.[11] The aim of this Directive was to establish qualitative Community standards in order to reduce and control sulphur dioxide (and other suspended particles) in the air. The innovative character of the measure is shown by the fact that most Member States did not use qualitative standards before the Directive was implemented (Majone, 1994a:8). A further example is Directive 79/831[12] relating to the free movement of dangerous substances in the Community. This Directive established an innovative procedure of mutual recognition of authorizations granted by the Member State in which the substance was marketed, a procedure not followed in all Member States until its implementation. A final example is Directive 79/409,[13] the famous 'Birds' Directive. This introduced protection mechanisms for certain migratory species that went far beyond what had previously been implemented by Member States' legislation on birds. The innovation is all the more remarkable if one takes into account that the Community had no powers for animal and environmental protection at that time (before the SEA). If one considers that all these decisions were adopted by unanimity, the conclusion seems to be that consensual decision-making mechanisms do not *necessarily* involve a 'race to the bottom'.[14] The idea is not that unanimity is cost-free from the perspective of a race to the bottom, but rather that this effect has been greatly exaggerated by intergovernmentalism. In some instances a race to the bottom will come about, and in others the outcome will be the opposite one.

To conclude, there are sufficient indications to support the idea that consensus-prone decisional mechanisms do not necessarily involve a high cost in

10 OJEC L 262/201 of 27 September 1976.   11 OJEC L 229/30 of 30 August 1980.
12 OJEC L 259/10, of 15 October 1979.   13 OJEC L 103/1 of 25 April 1979.
14 Eichener (1992) gives further evidence in support of this conclusion.

terms of efficiency, on one hand, and that these mechanisms do not necessarily mean that integration (in terms of regulatory innovation) will be stifled. However important this conclusion may be for the federal legitimacy model, it is necessary to note that the pure and simple return to unanimity is not advocated from the perspective of 'federal' legitimacy, above all in the perspective of enlargement. More than unanimity, I am thinking of the establishment of mechanisms aimed at correcting the majoritarian bias involved in a majoritarian system.[15] In this sense, subsidiarity may be better examined or understood as precisely one of those mechanisms.

D. The United Kingdom and the Community's environmental policy as an example of the impact of the majority principle upon the sovereignty and interests of Member States

The following case study, concerning the Community's environmental policy and the UK, illustrates the theoretical discussion presented above. However, before beginning the discussion, it is necessary to make the following comment. In order to ascertain the extent to which the implementation of the majority principle has been problematic for the Member States, it is not sufficient to speak about sovereignty in general terms. Naturally, when a Member State is overruled, its sovereignty is curtailed and therefore its capacity to pursue its own policy preferences is undermined. However, this cannot simply be assumed: it must be demonstrated. Therefore, it is necessary to spell out the particular policy preferences that were maintained by a particular Member State as regards a given policy, and then analyse how the majority principle has entailed a modification of previous policy preferences. The following analysis of the Community's environmental policy begins with some remarks on the UK's policy preferences before the majority principle applied in the Community system. I then demonstrate how the UK was, on the whole, able to protect its sovereignty and interests under unanimity. Finally, I examine the impact of the adoption of the majority principle on the UK's environmental policy preferences.

---

[15] Dehousse (1993) proposed a number of them.

1. *The Distinctive British Approach to Environmental Protection*

The UK is said to be one of the earliest European countries to become aware of environmental concerns. The oldest conservation movement was British;[16] the first agency for environmental matters was also British;[17] and the first comprehensive air pollution control act was enacted in Britain.[18] Nevertheless, its traditional approach to environmental matters has, in general, differed widely from continental approaches, and also from the environmental philosophy of other Anglo-Saxon countries, such as the USA (Vogel, 1986:21[19]). Thus the British approach to pollution control has been constructed on an inductive, flexible, case-by-case, and non-legalistic basis, whereas continental approaches have traditionally relied on the establishment of uniform standards and general principles encapsulated in law. With regard to enforcement, Britain has relied on voluntary and co-operative enforcement, whereas other countries, such as Germany, have relied on the more traditional method of sanctions and fines (Vogel, 1986:106).

The singular British approach to environmental matters is most noticeable in the area of water quality protection. The following remarks must be taken as an illustration of a more general point, which is the unique character that has traditionally characterized the British regulatory approach to environmental matters.[20]

---

[16] Led by philosophers such as John Ruskin, John Stuart Mill, and William Morris. It dates back to the last two decades of the nineteenth century. See Vogel (1986:33).

[17] Known as the Alkali Inspectorate, created in 1863. See my remarks below.

[18] The Clean Air Act 1956. See Golub (1994:3).

[19] Vogel (1986) asserts: 'On balance, the American approach to environmental regulation is the most rigid and rule-oriented to be found in any industrial society; the British, the most flexible and informal'.

[20] The characteristics that define the British approach to environmental matters as 'unique' are also present as regards other important fields of action within the environmental domain, such as air and waste. Here I shall briefly outline them.

First, the British approach in the field of air quality protection has traditionally pivoted around two axes: 1) the practice of setting 'presumptive limits'; and 2) the principle of 'best practicable means'. As regards presumptive limits, it is normally assumed that firms which comply with those limits exercise correct control over their emissions. If, on the contrary, presumptive limits are violated, this does not involve direct sanctions, but is considered a matter of fact that may be used against a firm in court. Note therefore that quantitative control of emissions is an *ex post* control, exercised once it is understood that the quality of the air in a determined area does not reach a minimum standard. Note also that emission limits are not legally binding, but only general guidelines. The uniqueness of the British approach to environmental protection is best illustrated, however, with regard to the BPM principle. According to British environmental protection authorities (Alkali Inspectorate, 1957, cited by Vogel, 1986:79), the 'best practicable means' philosophy constitutes a compromise between 'the natural desire of the public to have pure air', and 'the legitimate

Before any legislation was implemented in the UK, private individuals relied on the common law to protect against water pollution. The first public actions regarding water protection date from 1876, when Parliament passed the Rivers (Prevention of Pollution) Act. This established new regulation of sewage and industrial emissions. The Act established that sewage could only be discharged by polluters if the best available means were used. Industrial emissions were prohibited, as a general rule. However, the Act limited to a considerable extent the circumstances under which the latter aspect of law could be implemented (Haigh, 1987:25).

More recent legislation started with the Rivers (Prevention of Pollution) Act 1951. This Act gave the river boards (regional water authorities) two kinds of power: the power to grant authorizations for discharges, subject to conditions; and the power to prescribe emission standards within the authorizations. Concerning the first power, the river boards were only obliged to ensure the 'wholesomeness' of rivers. In fact the river authorities enjoyed a wide margin to manoeuvre, which allowed them to pursue an individual, case-by-case approach. The second power would have enabled, as Haigh notes, standards to be made uniform. But as the author remarks, this power was hardly ever used and was finally repealed in 1961 (Haigh, 1987:25).

At the time of the UK's entry into the EEC the matter was regulated by the Water Act 1973 and the Control of Pollution Act 1974. However, neither of those Acts established a specific duty on local or central authorities to impose

desire of manufacturers to meet competition by producing their goods cheaply and therefore to avoid unremunerative expenses'. In British practice, however, the term 'practicable' has never been defined and it has been for the Alkali Inspectorate to make a case-by-case judgement of whether the technique used by a firm under scrutiny meets the requirements of the BPM principle or not. In this sense, Vogel (1986:79–80) contends that the term has come to encompass 'local conditions and local circumstances, the state of technological knowledge, and, above all, the costs of pollution control in relation to the economic size of the particular firm', which has allowed, according to the same author, 'a very flexible application of the requirements of air pollution control in the UK'.

Secondly, with regard to waste control, Haigh asserts that before the Control of Pollution Act of 1974 (which was the major effort of the 70s regarding environmental protection, due to its comprehensive character, and due to the fact that it established a number of concrete measures that were unknown until that date not only of waste control but also of other fields, such as the setting of a series of obligations upon the waste disposal authorities and a licensing system for the disposal of waste) the matter was regulated in a piecemeal fashion, mainly in laws designed to protect public health, rather than being environmentally oriented. Further, the Public Health Act 1936, which consolidated earlier legislation, gave local authorities the power to remove domestic and trade refuse and to require the removal of 'any accumulation of noxious matter'. It also placed on them a duty to inspect the areas for which they were responsible. As Haigh comments, these inspection powers could not prevent nuisances arising, but should have ensured that they were recognized. The discovery made during the 60s and the 70s of major toxic deposits in Britain gives an idea of how strictly the existing regulation was implemented (Haigh, 1987:127).

specified standards. Therefore, before the Community directives on water protection were applied, the UK still relied on its old approach based on consent given by the regional authorities. Vogel remarks that the granting of consent was in fact a matter of negotiation between the water authorities and the polluters. While the conditions of consent tended on the whole not to vary greatly, in practice their enforcement depended heavily on the absorption capacity of the receiving environment (Vogel, 1986:78). In this respect, regional authorities usually followed as a guide the non-binding quality standards set by the central administrative authorities (Haigh, 1987:27).

The rationale underlying this flexible approach to pollution control, not only for water but also for other sectors,[21] lay both in the UK's unique conception of pollution, and in its special geographical conditions. Regarding the first aspect, Haigh notes that the notion of pollution has been defined in Britain with reference to the target. According to this author, pollutants are 'substances causing damage to targets in the environment' (1987:13). It follows from this definition that if the pollutant reaches no target in damaging quantities because it has been rendered harmless, either by being transformed into another substance or into a form where it cannot affect the target, or because it has been diluted to harmless levels, then 'there has been no pollution' (ibid.:13). Haigh contrasts this approach with the German one, which has been based primarily on the control of emissions with reference to quantitative standards. As he notes, 'For those who believe that man should emit the least possible quantity of pollutant, even if it is having no known effect—an approach being developed in Germany under the name of Vorsorgeprinzip, the principle of anticipation or foresight—then the point of emission is the logical point to set the controls' (ibid.:21).

Concerning the second point (the particular geographical conditions of the UK), Golub explains that Britain has a uniquely favourable ecosystem characterized by the existence of tidal sea waters, the greater absorption capacity of rivers, the resilience of soil, and strong winds. The British approach has therefore taken advantage of an ecosystem which is able to absorb or remove greater quantities of pollutants (Golub, 1994:5).

To sum up, since the inception of its efforts against pollution Britain has developed a distinct approach to environmental protection, characterized by its informality and flexibility. This was translated into a *preference* for individual rather than uniform regulation; for quality rather than quantity standards; and for co-operative rather than hierarchical enforcement styles. The

---

[21] Note the previous footnote.

reasons that justify this approach lay, according to British observers, in a different concept of pollution and in the special geographical characteristics of this country. This was the situation, with regard to environmental policy, before the UK entered the EEC.[22]

2. *The Impact of Community Environmental Policy on the UK under Unanimity*

Environmental policy was introduced into the Community system at the Paris Summit of 1972. Although Britain formally entered the Community on 1 January 1973, it also participated in the deliberations that took place in Paris (Hildebrand, 1993:20). The British position was one of reluctance to endorse the changes that would be introduced by the Paris Summit (Golub, 1994:6). A new increase of Community powers would imply a correlative curtailing of British sovereignty. However, the fact that decisions concerning the environment were to be taken by unanimity played an essential role in the final British acceptance. Although British autonomy in the field of environmental protection would be curtailed by Community action, British preferences in environmental policy should not be put in danger. A review of some of the most important measures adopted in the period from 1972 to the enactment of the SEA, presented in Table II.1, seems to confirm that, on balance, the British prediction would prove correct.

From the nine cases presented in Table II.2, only six may be catalogued as 'curtailing' British sovereignty. These are Directive 80/779[23] ('sulphur dioxide'), Directive 83/351[24] ('emissions from vehicles'), Directive 84/360[25] ('emissions from industrial plants'), and the Directives on water protection (75/440,[26] 'drinking water'; 76/160,[27] 'bathing water'; and 76/464,[28] 'dangerous substances in water'). In all these cases there was some curtailment of British sovereignty since Community directives impose legally binding standards. However, the types of standard that the directives impose are generally qualitative, so that there is no major reversal of Britain's previous

---

[22] However, the question of the extent to which this approach constituted a policy is discussed in the British context. Note for instance the remarks of MacCormick (1991:9) arguing that before the British entry into the EEC there was virtually no environmental protection in that country. Golub (1994:5) argues that, although environmental protection was never high enough on the government's agenda, one may trace (as I have done) the existence of fundamental views regarding environmental policy that may be described as a policy.

[23] OJEC L 229/30, 30 August 1980.   [24] OJEC L 197/1, 20 July 1983.

[25] OJEC L 188/20, 16 July 1984.   [26] OJEC L 194/26, 25 July 1975.

[27] OJEC L 31/1, 5 February 1976.   [28] OJEC L 129/23, 18 May 1976.

approach. The only exceptions to this trend may be found in Directive 84/360, which gives the Council powers to impose quantitative limits on emissions into air by industrial plants, and in Directive 83/351, which imposes quantitative limits on emissions from vehicles. As for Directive 84/360, the UK succeeded in introducing unanimity for the establishment by the Council of emission standards; and in the case of Directive 83/351 one cannot speak of the existence of an obligation, since the mode of harmonization used by the Directive is 'optional'. The remaining three cases may be described as 'highly consistent' with British interests. These are Directive 78/611[29] ('lead content in petrol'), Directive 75/442[30] ('on waste'), and Directive 78/176[31] ('titanium dioxide'). In all these cases the final outcome was in line with British policy preferences. Therefore, none of the nine cases constitutes a clear case of impact such that not only British sovereignty but also its policy preferences were affected by the enactment of Community legislation.

Further, in some of the cases examined the threat of a veto played a considerable role in the protection of British policy preferences. Notable examples are Directive 84/360, 'emissions from industrial plants', Directive 76/464, 'dangerous substances in water', and Directive 78/176, 'titanium dioxide'.

As regards Directive 84/360, the initial Commission proposal was to impose an obligation on polluters to apply 'state of the art' technology and provided for the setting of emission standards by a qualified majority of the Council. Britain succeeded in replacing the expression 'state of the art' technology, which could have been interpreted as imposing on firms an obligation to establish the most recent technology available in the market, with the expression 'best available means not entailing excessive costs' (BAT-NEC) which was more closely in line with the British 'best practicable means' air protection philosophy. Secondly, British negotiators also succeeded in changing the procedural rule for the Council's adoption of emission standards from qualified majority voting to unanimity (Haigh, 1987:226). Naturally, the extent to which Britain could use the threat of vetoing the proposal was not absolute; the Directive produced an impact on British preferences insofar as it introduced the possibility for the Council to set quantitative standards, which was contrary to the common British practice in the field of air pollution.

A second example of how British preferences were protected by the veto power is provided, as indicated above, by Directive 76/464, on 'dangerous

---

[29] OJEC L 197/19, 22 July 1978.   [30] OJEC L 194/39, 25 July 1975.
[31] OJEC L 54/19 of 25 February 1978.

substances in water'. This represents a better example of the protection of British policy preferences by veto. The initial Commission proposal provided for the setting of quantitative (emission) standards to control the deposit of dangerous substances into water. The Commission proposal was widely supported by other countries, such as Germany, which had traditionally relied on this means of control. Moreover, the establishment of qualitative standards would involve a disadvantage for Germany's strong chemical industry. Britain threatened to veto the proposal if amendments were not introduced. The final result was the setting up of two lists of substances, one for which quality standards would be applied (List II) and the other for which a system of quantitative and alternative qualitative standards would apply (List I). In the Council meeting of 4 May 1976, all Member States except Britain decided to apply the preferred standards (quantitative standards) for List I (Haigh, 1987:71–4). This shows that Britain was the only country interested in the implementation of qualitative standards and demonstrates the effectiveness of the veto threat as exerted by this Member State.

A final example of this trend is given by Directive 78/176, on 'titanium dioxide'. The initial Commission text proposed the establishment of uniform emission standards for the industrial emission of pollution from TiO_2. Haigh notes that it was not only Britain which opposed this measure. However, Britain was the major Community producer and exporter of titanium dioxide, and so had the greatest incentive to water down the Directive in order to prevent an excessive burden on its industry, and therefore it led the opposition to the Commission proposal. Again, the veto power resulted in a very general obligation upon Member States to periodically control TiO_2 emissions and to send the Commission details of programmes for the elimination and reduction of such emissions (Haigh, 1987:113–17).

To sum up, the period prior to the SEA was characterized by the curtailment, to some extent, of British sovereignty by Community action. Nevertheless, as we have seen, the UK was able to avoid, on balance, the enactment of Community measures contrary to long-standing British preferences (Golub, 1994:7).

3. *The impact of Community Environmental Policy on the UK under Majority Voting*

As has been seen, prior to the enactment of the Single European Act, all measures related to environmental protection were adopted by unanimity. The SEA was to alter the nature of EC environmental policy-making. Article 100a

Table II.2: Review of environmental measures adopted under the SEA[a]

Field	Legislation	Commission proposal	UK position	Outcome
A	Dir. 80/779 'sulphur dioxide'	Set air quality standards for sulphur dioxide.	Initial opposition to legally binding standards.	Quality standards for s.d. set.
I				
R				
A	Dir. 78/611 'lead in petrol'	Set 0'40 g/l in first stage and 0'15 g/l in second stage. Second stage to be implemented on 1 Jan 78.	Favourable to Dir. But wanted establishment of both max. (0'40) and min. limits (0'15). Pushed for implementation of Dir. in 1981.	Sets max.(0'40) as well as min. (0'15) limits. Implemented in 1981.
I				
R				
A	Dir. 83/351 'emissions from petrol engine vehicles'	Set (quantitative) emission standards.	Opposed to Com. proposal.	Adoption of 'optional' standards based on ECE standards
I				
R				
A	Dir. 84/360 'emissions from industrial plants'	Set a system of prior authorization of plants; imposes on plants 'state of the art' technology; imposes emission standards to be set by Council by QM.[b]	Above all, opposed to the setting of uniform standards by QM and 'state of the art' technology.	Replaces 'state of the art' with the 'BAT-NEC'[c] notion. Emission limits by unanimity.
I				
R				

W A T E R	Dir. 75/440 'quality of surface water for drinking'	Set quality standards.	Opposed to the setting of uniform standards.	Sets quality standards.
W A T E R	Dir. 76/160 'bathing water'	Quality standards; imposes obligation on water authorities to monitor quality of water.	Favourable to Com. proposal.	Sets minimal quality standards.
W A T E R	Dir. 76/464 'dangerous substances in water'	Set (quantitative) emission standards.	Opposed to quantitative standards; pushed for qualitative standards.	Alternative approach for List I substances (quantitative or qualitative standards) and qualitative standards for List II substances.

over./

Table II.2: (*cont.*)

Field	Legislation	Commission proposal	UK position	Outcome
W A S T E	Dir. 75/442 'on waste'	Appointment of authorities responsible for waste; waste disposal plans; authorization system; polluter pays principle.	Favourable to the Com. proposal.	Member State must appoint competent authorities responsible for waste; waste disposal plans are to be prepared by them; authorization system for polluters; polluter pays principle.
W A S T E	Dir. 78/176 'titanium dioxide'	Set quantitative standards; authorizations system; programmes.	Opposed to the setting of emission stds.; favourable to the rest.	General obligation upon Member States to present to the Com. programmes for the elimination and reduction of emissions of TiO_2.

[a] The nine measures reviewed here are selected from Hildenbrand and Weizsäcker's list of the 20 most important environmental measures adopted by the Community prior to the SEA. See Hildebrand (1993:27) and Weizsäcker (1989:42).

[b] Qualified majority.

[c] Best available technology not entailing excessive costs.

introduced majority voting for the harmonization of Member State legislation affecting the establishment of the internal market. In turn, the SEA introduced a new provision for Community environmental action. Article 130s provided for unanimity in Community regulatory intervention related to the environmental field. Given the dangers that the shift to majority voting posed for British sovereignty and preferences it is important to understand, before examining the extent to which the new provisions altered the *status quo*, why the UK accepted that institutional switch.

When negotiations to reform the Treaty of Rome started, Britain—which from the outset had opposed any reform of the Treaty of Rome (Moravcsik, 1991:49)—was against the extension of majority voting. Why did this country finally accept Article 100a? To answer this question, it is sufficient to mention the following two-fold point:[32] first, the focus of the *White Paper* on the achievement of the internal market; and secondly, the *White Paper*'s preference for a regulatory approach based on mutual recognition. These were the essential elements that explain the final British acceptance of majority voting. Majority voting was interpreted by Britain as the logical continuation of the *White Paper*'s objective to implement the internal market. It represented a minor effort from the perspective of sovereignty that could be afforded in exchange for market integration. Further, in those cases in which, according to the new strategy, mutual recognition of environmental standards was not possible, Article 130s provided the locus for future Community action regarding environmental protection. Consequently, Community action in this field would continue to be ruled by unanimity. Therefore, for British negotiators, the SEA outcome was highly consistent with British interests and changed 'virtually nothing'[33] with regard to the Treaty of Rome.

Existing evidence seems to confirm the view that from the British perception the SEA outcome was in line with UK interests. In this connection, Golub reports that Lynda Chalker, Minister for Foreign and Commonwealth Affairs at the time, assured the House of Commons that: 'our special interests are fully safeguarded . . . There has been no change whatsoever in the so-called Luxembourg compromise. It remains open to us, where necessary, to invoke that compromise to protect a very important national interest' (Golub, 1994:13).

---

[32] For extensive discussion on the matter, see Dehousse and Majone (1994).
[33] This sentence is attributed to the then British Prime Minister, Margaret Thatcher. See Sked and Cook (1990:498).

Concerning Article 130s, the Minister asserted that: 'What we have done is to establish criteria for [environmental] activities [. . .] We will be able to ensure that, where we wish, decisions continue to be taken by unanimity' (Golub, 1994:15–16).

In short, it can be inferred from the above that, according to the British view: first, majority voting would be circumscribed to the area of market integration; secondly, environmental policy would develop through Article 130s, that is by unanimity; and finally, even in the context of Article 100a, when the UK disliked a measure it could invoke the Luxembourg compromise as a last resort.[34]

However, during the era of the SEA, Community environmental action developed, at least in part, contrary to British expectations. Although Article 130s was employed to enact measures in the environmental field, Article 100a was also used to this end. In support of this finding, Table II.3 reviews the measures adopted under Articles 130s and 100a.

Table II.3: Measures adopted under Articles 130s and 100a of the Single European Act

Adopted under Article 130s	Adopted under Article 100a
Dir. 87/416 (amends 85/210) lead in petrol	Dir. 88/76 (amends 70/220) vehicle emissions
Dir. 88/346 (amends 86/85) sea spillage	Dir. 88/77: gas pollutants from diesel engines
Dir. 88/347 (amends 86/280) dangerous substances	Dir. 88/180 (amends 84/538) lawnmower noise
Reg. 1734/88: dangerous chemicals (export/import)	Dir. 88/181: as above
Dir. 88/381: Rhine Protocol	Dir. 88/182 (amends 75/442) on waste
Dir. 88/540: ozone layer	Dir. 88/436: German transitional measures
Dir. 88/609: large combustion plants	Dir. 89/458: as above
Dir. 88/610 (amends 82/501) major industrial accidents	Dir. 90/660: as above
	Dir. 91/441: as above

[34] According to Golub (1994), the British government also placed important emphasis on subsidiarity, as introduced by Article 130s. For this author, the perception of the UK government was that the principle of subsidiarity would limit Community environmental action to those areas in which Community intervention was strictly necessary. In other words, the British government viewed subsidiarity as a further safeguard of UK sovereignty in the field of environmental protection. This complementary element explains the British acceptance of the switch to majority voting in the SEA reform.

Dir. 89/369: municipal waste
incineration

Dir 89/427 (amends 80/779) air
quality and nitrous oxides

Dir. 90/170: acceptance of OECD
decision on transboundary
hazardous waste

Dir. 90/219: genetically modified
micro-organisms

Reg. 1210/90: European
Environmental Agency

Dir. 90/313: free access to
information on the environment

Dir. 90/956: German transitional
measures

Dir. 91/271: urban waste water
treatment

Reg. 594/91: ozone layer

Reg. 563/91: protection of
environment in the
Mediterranean Sea

Dir. 91/598: Protection of the River
Elbe

Reg. 3907/91: nature conservation

Reg 3908/91: coastal areas

Dir. 91/676: nitrates

Dir. 91/689: hazardous waste

Dir. 91/90: ozone

Dir. 91/629: implementation reports

Dir. 89/235 (amends 78/1015) motor-
cycle noise

Dir. 89/677 (amends 76/769) marketing
use of dangerous substances

Dir. 89/678: as above

Dir. 91/173: as above

Dir. 91/338: as above

Dir. 90/220: genetically modified
organisms

Dir. 91/157: batteries containing
dangerous substances

Dir. 91/542: diesel emissions

Source: Golub (1994:22–5).

As can be seen from Table II.3, at least nineteen measures were enacted under Article 100a, as opposed to at least twenty-five measures adopted under Article 130s, during the SEA period. Whether Britain was in fact out-voted in cases where a measure was adopted under Article 100a cannot be ascertained since votes were not published under the SEA. Nevertheless, it is apparent that the Member States' power to veto proposals, and therefore Britain's ability to protect its sovereignty and preferences, were considerably weakened under this period. Furthermore, the possibility of using the veto depended entirely on the legal basis on which the proposal rested. Thus the crucial point in this situation of choice between legal bases (with different procedural rules) was whether the Community supranational institutions or the Member States had the power to determine the appropriate legal basis of a particular proposal. That this power did not always lie with the Member States is well illustrated by the *Titanium Dioxide* case.[35]

On 18 April 1983 the Commission issued a proposal concerning the amendment of Directive 78/716 (as last amended by Directive 83/29) which dealt with the establishment of an obligation upon Member States to draw up programmes designed to reduce or eliminate waste from the titanium dioxide industry.[36] Article 9.3 of that Directive established that, once Member States had submitted the reduction/elimination programmes to the Commission, the latter would make proposals for the harmonization of those programmes. As described above, the titanium dioxide Directive 78/716 was one in which the UK, with other Member States, succeeded in introducing substantial modifications to the original Commission proposal. As a matter of fact, Directive 78/716 imposed very loose obligations upon Member States. The only way for the Commission to impose more stringent control of pollution from titanium dioxide was through the indirect means of harmonizing Member States' programmes. The Commission proposal of 18 April 1983 was intended to achieve this goal.

Therefore the Commission proposed: first, the reduction and eventual elimination of certain kinds of discharge from the titanium dioxide industry; secondly, the establishment of time limits within which Member States were to implement the Directive (Article 7.3 of the proposed measure established that Member States could depart from the timetable set by the Directive, although extensions could only be granted for twelve months); and finally, quantitative limits for the reduction of discharges into water and air.

Following the enactment of the SEA, the Commission changed the legal basis of the proposal and based it on the new Article 100a. Although the more stringent proposal offered by the Commission might have inflicted serious burdens on some Member States, there was a real possibility that it would have been agreed by a majority in the Council (Golub, 1994:28). However, in a meeting held on 24 and 25 November 1988 the Council arrived at a common position whereby the Directive would be based on Article 130s of the

---

[35] Case C-300/89, *Commission v Council* (*Titanium Dioxide*) [1991] ECR I-2867.

[36] Proposal for a Council directive on procedure for harmonizing the programmes for the reduction and eventual elimination of pollution caused by waste from the titanium dioxide industry, OJEC C 138/5 of 26 May 1983.

EC Treaty. Subsequently, the proposal was adopted by unanimity and became Directive 89/428.[37]

The Directive eventually adopted substantially modified the original Commission proposal. There were two main changes: first, the possibility for Member States to 'defer' the implementation of the Directive for two or three more years, depending on the provision;[38] and secondly, for the reduction of discharges into water, Article 8 provided for alternative harmonization, whereby Member States could use either quantitative or qualitative standards. The spirit of the British approach to water quality control may be traced back to this Article of the Directive. In general, the Directive was considerably more lax than the original Commission proposal (Golub, 1994:28).

Following the adoption of Directive 89/428 by the Council, the Commission, supported by the European Parliament, brought an action before the ECJ for its annulment. The main charge of the Commission and Parliament was that the Directive should have been based on Article 100a, instead of on Article 130s. Arguments concerning the more democratic character of Article 100a and the aim and content of the Directive were used to uphold their position. The Directive was, according to the applicant and supporter, primarily designed to harmonize the conditions of competition in the titanium dioxide market.

In its ruling, the Court started by repeating the principle that the choice of legal basis cannot depend on an institution's conviction as to the objective pursued but should be based on objective factors 'which are amenable to judicial review'.[39] It then analysed the content and aim of Directive 89/428, and concluded that it was intended to protect the environment and promote market integration.[40] Thus the analysis of the aim and content of the Directive could not determine which legal basis should take priority. Next, the Court went on to analyse Articles 100a and 130s of the EC Treaty. The ECJ rejected the possibility that *both* Articles could serve as the legal basis of the Directive, since the 'use of both provisions as legal basis would divest the co-operation procedure of its very substance',[41] which is 'to increase the involvement of the

---

[37] Council Directive 89/428 on procedures for harmonizing the programmes for the reduction and eventual elimination of pollution caused by waste from the titanium dioxide industry, OJEC L 201/56 of 14 July 1989.

[38] Note in this respect Arts. 5 and 7 of the Directive.

[39] Para. 10 of the ruling. This principle was set for the first time in Case 45/86 *Commission v Council* [1987] ECR 1493, para. 11.

[40] Ibid. para. 13.   [41] Ibid. para. 18.

European Parliament in the legislative process', and which in turn reflects 'a fundamental democratic principle that the people should take part in the exercise of power through the intermediary of a representative assembly'.[42] As a conclusion of its reasoning, the Court stated that Article 100a should constitute the legal basis of the directive in question, because an 'action intended to approximate national rules concerning production conditions in a given industrial sector with the aim of eliminating distortions of competition in that sector is conducive to the attainment of the internal market and thus falls within the scope of Article 100a'.[43] It added that the objectives of environmental protection could also be effectively pursued by means of Article 100a.[44] Consequently, the ECJ annulled the Council Directive. In short, the *Titanium Dioxide* case demonstrates that, during the SEA period, the Member States lost their control over the decision as to which voting procedures should be implemented in the field of the environment.

4. *Conclusion*

To sum up, the evidence from the evolution of Community environmental policy before and after the SEA enactment points to the following conclusions. First, the UK was able, on balance, to protect its sovereignty and its distinct approach to environmental protection in the period prior to the SEA due to its exercise of the power of veto. Secondly, this situation was modified in the period that followed the enactment of the SEA. Under the SEA, environmental policy developed, at least in part, contrary to British expectations. Article 100a was in fact used for the adoption of Community measures affecting pollution control. This weakened the previous position whereby the UK could exercise its power of veto in order to protect sovereignty and national preferences. Finally, the choice between the legal bases (Articles 100a and 130s) was a battle whose final arbiter was not the Member States, but the Court of Justice. Not only did the Member States lose their power over the decision concerning legal basis, but also the ECJ was likely to support the use of Article 100a for the implementation of environmental policy, as the *Titanium Dioxide* case demonstrates. This element further weakened the UK control of Community environmental policy.[45] As a result of the combined

---

[42]   Case 45/86 *Commission v Council* [1987] ECR 1493, para. 20.

[43]   Ibid. para. 23.   [44]   Ibid. para. 24.

[45]   It must be noted that the Court reached the contrary solution in Case C-155/91, ECJ [1993] I-939 (known as *Waste*). However, one may not extract consequences from this judgment since in *Waste* the environmental aspects of the measure in question were more than evident. It must be added that the ECJ case-law on legal basis has been addressed to expand the powers of the

effect of the introduction of majority voting and the shift of the decision regarding legal basis to the legal arena, one may conclude that, during the SEA period, British sovereignty and preferences lost some of their protection against the impact of the evolution of the Community's powers in the field of environment.

E. Conclusions

This Chapter started with a number of observations on the complex nature of the concept of legitimacy. My intention was not to develop fully a debate that is wider than can be dealt with here. Instead, I wanted to show the potential as well as the limits of the concept of legitimacy. I attempted to show that it is not sufficient to speak of legitimacy when analysing the Community's legitimacy deficit. Taking into account the inherent difficulties associated with the concept, a better approach seems to be first to define what different authors understand by legitimacy, and then to check which model of legitimacy is better suited for the Community. By so doing I identified three models: 'formal' legitimacy, 'democratic' legitimacy, and 'federal' legitimacy. I then analysed the alternative explanations offered by the first two models and explained why the model of 'federal' legitimacy deals more adequately with the issue of majority voting. In the following I present a summary of the whole discussion.

The 'formal' model of legitimacy approaches the matter of the Community's legitimacy as an issue of formal validity. Therefore the insertion of the principle of majority voting would have been problematic from a legitimacy perspective if it had not respected the EC Treaty provisions on the Treaty's reform. The only modifications that may be criticized from this model's perspective are those which are produced *de facto*, that is, outside the constitutional legality that the ECT establishes. From this somewhat top-down approach, in order to discern whether the majority principle constitutes a problem for the Community's *constitutionalism*,[46] it is sufficient to ask about the origin of such reform. As the reform was introduced (or re-introduced, but

European Parliament in the Community's legislative process, more than to expand majority voting. However, due to the institutional structure of the Community's decision-making process, the first expansion has, in general brought about the second one. In effect, in the EC Treaty those procedures that grant a wider say to the European Parliament are usually combined with majority voting at the Council level. A recent example illustrating again this trend in ECJ case-law is Joined Cases C-164 and 165/97, [1999] ECJ I-1139. Note also my comments in Estella (1999b).

[46] On the notion of European constitutionalism, see Dehousse (2002).

also expanded) by the SEA through legal means, it must be concluded that the use of majority voting in the Community is legitimate. This conclusion is not contingent on actual results. Therefore, a Member State may agree to a lesser or greater extent when it is outvoted, but it cannot criticize the Community for having acted in an illegitimate way.

The 'formal' legitimacy model contains no possibility of a legitimacy problem, given the introduction of majority voting into the ECT. However, in denying the relevance of legitimacy to such an institutional shift, the 'formal' legitimacy model provokes more questions than it answers. For example, it is not possible to understand from this perspective why, if Member States are comfortable with majority voting and with the process of competential growth associated with it, they fought for the introduction of subsidiarity into the ECT. On the contrary, subsidiarity seems to be a response to competential growth and to majority voting. However, formal legitimacy does not account for this. The problem seems to lie in the fact that, for formal legitimacy, legality amounts to legitimacy. Therefore the model may not explain developments that, although formally correct, produce opposition in Member States.

From 'formal' legitimacy I proceeded to analyse 'democratic' legitimacy. This model emphasizes the absence of an adequate development of the democratic structures in the EC institutional setting. The interpretation of the Community's legitimacy deficit, which is offered by this model, has been very successful, above all among lawyers. Its exposition, and its criticism, are therefore of great relevance here. According to this model, the concept of legitimacy essentially equates to that of democracy. In turn, the idea of democracy evokes that of 'parliamentarism'. If this model is applied to the EC, the outcome is that the Community suffers from a democratic deficit, due to the fact that the European Parliament does not occupy a central role in the Community's decision-making process, even after the Amsterdam and Nice Treaties and despite recent progress in this area. The example of the Community's external policy, or of the free movement of persons (new Title IV[47]) illustrates the democratic limitations of the EC. The only way to solve the Community's democratic deficit would be to invert the roles of the Council and the European Parliament as legislators. The Parliament should occupy the central position in the Community's decision-making process (overall), whereas the Council should become the equivalent of chambers of territorial representation (as happens in federal states such as Germany)

---

[47] Note, in particular, Art. 67 ECT (ex Art. 73o).

holding important powers but limited to representing the particular interests of Member States.

The majority principle is problematic from the perspective of the democratic legitimacy model since the system of *indirect* democratic legitimacy, on which the Community was previously based, was invalidated by the introduction of majority voting. The adoption of decisions by unanimity implied in essence that, when each and every national government adopted a decision, this decision was supported by their respective national parliaments. In effect, the accountability mechanisms at national level allowed censure of the government if it adopted a decision contrary to the national parliament's majoritarian stance. This equilibrium was not perfect but it was at least sufficient to legitimize the Community before the SEA was adopted. However, after the enactment of the SEA this equilibrium was distorted, since the mechanisms of national accountability were no longer effective when a national government was outvoted at the Community level. In this situation, a decision could be adopted in the EC without the intervention of the European Parliament and without the indirect backing of all national parliaments. This implies a decline in the democratic quality of Community outputs.

The implicit assumption of the democratic legitimacy model seems to be that all (democratic) political systems have the same legitimacy source: the people. The European Parliament would therefore be the recipient of popular legitimacy in the Community context. However, a question emerges at this point of the democratic legitimacy narrative: who are the people that the European Parliament would be representing? It is clear that the European Parliament would not be representing a hypothetical European *demos.* This is not only because the data available in this regard seem to deny the existence of a European people, but also because it is probable that the aim of the European Parliament is not that of representing the European people, but that of representing the European *peoples.* It is not pure formalism to recall that the ECT itself establishes this point with total clarity.[48] The answer to the question of *who is represented by the European Parliament* thus seems to be more complex than the answer that could be given to the same query at the national level. Proponents of the 'democratic' legitimacy model should be aware of this structural limitation, in order to avoid mapping the national democratic logic onto the European arena with no corrections.

It is also useful to recall that the process of European integration rests, in reality, upon a balance between two kinds of legitimacy (Dehousse, 1995). On

---

[48] In Art. 189 ECT (ex Art. 137).

one hand, advocates of the democratic legitimacy model argue that there is a kind of legitimacy that may be termed popular legitimacy, though with the implications that are derived from the fact that the European Parliament represents many peoples and not one people. On the other hand, there is a second kind of legitimacy that may be termed national or state legitimacy. Each national government represents, particularly in the Council, the interests of its own State. The point is to achieve equilibrium between national legitimacy and popular legitimacy, between *polis* and *demoi*. This demand for equilibrium was not invented by the Community: it is present in all federal systems. However, in the Community context the need for equilibrium between these two poles is more evident, since the degree of diversity between the peoples and the States is even greater than in other federal arrangements.

Given the above, it must be argued that the democratic legitimacy model makes the mistake of forgetting the second (State) pillar of legitimacy on which the Community rests. The model advocated here, the 'federal' legitimacy model, does not deny the existence of a popular pillar of legitimacy, rather it serves to remind us that the second pillar must not be forgotten. Both types of legitimacy are equally important, and any analysis of majority voting has to start from this premise.

The 'federal' legitimacy model has the idea of double legitimacies as its main foundation. This starting point allows a better understanding of the significance of the shift to majority voting for Member States. The absence of a European *demos* implies that only the *demoi* of different Member States can be talked about. Each *demos* would be represented by one national government at the Council level. The adoption of a decision by majority voting in the Council implies that some Member States may be outvoted. The *demos* of the outvoted Member State, however, would have to implement within its legal order the decision that it opposed. The problem here is that unless the different Member States' *demoi* do not develop in a single *demos*, the *demos* of the outvoted Member State will understand that decision in terms of imposition 'from outside'. Therefore, unless this process comes about, the majority principle will be particularly problematic in the European setting. On the other hand, the emergence of the European Parliament as a decisional arbiter would only add more distrust to this situation. The *demos* of the outvoted Member State would not necessarily be relieved if it were the European Parliament, instead of the Council, which took the contested decision. Rather, the contrary could be even argued.

That the implementation of majority voting in the Community has an impact on the sovereignty and interests of Member States is illustrated by the case study earlier in this Chapter. By doing empirical work I attempted to fill a common lacuna in conventional literature on the issue of legitimacy, which is that the Community's legitimacy deficit is assumed but never demonstrated. The analysis presented above shows that the United Kingdom had to modify its traditional approach to environmental protection once the SEA introduced majority voting. The analysis of the expectations of this Member State on the development of environmental policy confirms this point. The UK thought that after the SEA was implemented all decisions concerning the environment would be taken under Article 130s. This turned out not to be the case, or at least not entirely: many decisions were adopted under Article 100a. Whether this Member State was outvoted or not is irrelevant. What is relevant is that the evidence shows that an important part of environmental policy developed under the shadow of majority voting during this period. This must have restricted the margin for manoeuvring of this Member State, if we take into account that Member States were willing to implement majority voting. Furthermore, during the SEA period the European Court of Justice was an important player regarding the discussion on legal bases. The ECJ clearly preferred to give more room to the European Parliament in the Community's decision-making process. This meant that, in many cases, majority voting was preferred to unanimity by the ECJ. This curtailed the United Kingdom's preferences in the field of environment even further, as the analysis of the *Titanium Dioxide* case demonstrates. In summary, the above case study illustrates how the shift from unanimity to majority voting had very real consequences for Member States' sovereignty. In the next Chapter the introduction of the subsidiarity principle into the ECT is analysed, precisely as a tool employed to circumvent or correct the majoritarian bias that the Community system experienced from the SEA years onwards.

III

Subsidiarity in Maastricht

A. Introduction

In the reform of the Treaties that took place in Maastricht, the Member States decided to introduce into the Community legal order a new Article (Article 3b, now Article 5) of the ECT, whose second paragraph reads as follows:

In areas which do not fall within its exclusive competence, the Community shall take action, in accordance with the principle of subsidiarity, only if and in so far as the objectives of the proposed action cannot be sufficiently achieved by the Member States and can therefore, by reason of the scale or effects of the proposed action, be better achieved by the Community.

The incorporation of subsidiarity in the Treaties has been interpreted (Dehousse, 1995; 1997) as a political message from the Member States indicating that the legitimacy problems affecting the Union should be solved promptly. However, it is clear that the introduction of the principle has opened up more questions than it has answered. The text of Article 5(2) will not be seen by posterity as an example of legal transparency. The reason for this obscurity is probably to be found in the concept of subsidiarity itself, not just in the Community principle of subsidiarity as articulated by Article 5(2). Although it is usually assumed that there is a well established definition of subsidiarity in the socio-political literature dealing with the term, we will see that there is no such a thing as a single concept of subsidiarity. Maybe, as Weiler (1995) once suggested, one should find the beauty of the notion precisely in its radical and profound ambiguity. Leaving aside matters of definition, which are often elusive, it is also evident that it is difficult to make subsidiarity operational in legal terms. In effect, and contrary to what happens with other concepts (such as proportionality) subsidiarity is a tool that has been used only very rarely with a legal purpose in those constitutional systems in which the principle is formally recognized. Therefore, in the absence of any solid legal tradition on subsidiarity, comparative analysis is unfortunately of no use here. So the few indications given by Article 5(2) are of very little use for deciphering a legal principle that could be functional before the Community Courts.

In order to clarify this vagueness, Member States reopened the Pandora's box of negotiation on subsidiarity in the penultimate reform of the EC Treaty, in Amsterdam. The result was new Protocol No. 30 of the ECT on subsidiarity.[1] With the introduction of this Protocol Member States almost enter the area of constitutional obsession; however, the aim of this work is not to put Member States onto the psychiatrist's couch,[2] but to get at the meaning of this principle and its implications for the Community. The main arguments here are that subsidiarity is devoid of any clear substance from a legal perspective, and that the principle is not value-neutral, as is often assumed, nor that it goes against integration, as the classical legal vision claims. The idea is that subsidiarity involves a very concrete vision of integration, which is detrimental to the search for solutions to the *federal* deficit based on a consensual logic: a point that is often overlooked.

For the sake of clarity I have divided this analysis of subsidiarity into two Chapters. In this Chapter I analyse subsidiarity in Maastricht; in the next Chapter I analyse subsidiarity in Amsterdam. This Chapter presents a number of reflections on the theoretical and historical background upon which the Community principle of subsidiarity is built. This is not an end in itself, but a means to understanding, first, why Article 5(2) is so obscure, and secondly, why subsidiarity was chosen as a remedy to the Community's federal deficit. Section C of this Chapter is devoted to the analysis of the process of negotiation of the principle into the Maastricht Treaty. I argue that Member States were seeking to tie their own hands when introducing subsidiarity. In Section D I focus on the analysis of Article 5(2), and in the final section some conclusions are restated.

---

[1] Protocol No. 30 'on the application of the principles of subsidiarity and proportionality'. In the following text I refer to it as 'the Protocol on subsidiarity'.

[2] I attempted such an exercise in Estella (1999f), which resulted in some nice paradoxes.

B. The foundations of the Community principle of subsidiarity

The following is an analysis of the foundations that constituted the basis for the shaping of the Community principle of subsidiarity. Reference is made to the philosophical and political foundations of the concept of subsidiarity, and to the historical and constitutional ones. The objective is two-fold. The first is to show that subsidiarity has a multi-faceted character. This implies mainly that the principle has been developed in different contexts not only as a regulative principle of the relations between the public sphere and the private, but also as a regulative principle of the different layers of which both the public and the private sphere are composed. The second objective is to show that the principle contains, both in its conceptual construction and in its practical application, an essentially negative bias. This provides the main clue to understanding why subsidiarity, and not other instruments or techniques, was chosen in order to give an overall answer to the legitimacy problems derived from the expansion of the majority principle in the Community.

Although works on the origins of subsidiarity abound, the most systematic ones are those of Wilke and Wallace (1990) and Millon-Delsol (1992; 1993).[3] In their respective analyses of subsidiarity, these authors establish a link between Greek philosophy (and in particular the *Politics* of Aristotle), the writings of Saint Thomas Aquinas, the German corporatists of the seventeenth century and the 'social doctrine' of the Catholic church. Apparently it is in the last of these that the term subsidiarity was coined. Though Millon-Delsol does not deny that link, she points out that other lines of thinking influenced the shaping of the concept. This author refers, in particular, to the liberalism of John Stuart Mill (1975), and to what she calls the *philosphies de la troisième voie* (philosophies of the third way).[4] Of the latter ones, Millon-Delsol underlines the importance for the development of subsidiarity of the *personalist* movement, whose main leader was Utz (1976).

Such diversity of perspectives makes it difficult to refer to a single notion of subsidiarity. Its vague and complex character, not without ambiguities and

---

[3] For a recent survey on the origins of the principle, which summarises previous works on the topic, see Endo (2001).

[4] Not to be confused with Guiden's third way. Millon-Delsol uses the term 'third way' to refer to those currents of political and philosophical thought that, during the twentieth century, had as their main scientific aim the search for a middle ground between methodological individualism and the idea of 'common good' as justification for State intervention in society.

contradictions, explains in part the debate that took place in the Community over the precise meaning of the principle, even before the principle was introduced into the Treaties. In other words, in the shaping of the Community principle of subsidiarity not only questions related to the different national interests and visions of European integration (Dehousse, 1993), but also the lack of definition of the meta-Community concept of subsidiarity, added to the general confusion.

A brief examination of the literature cited above illustrates this point. As suggested above, the agreed point of departure for tracing the origins of subsidiarity is Aristotle. Aristotle's *Politics* depicted a society structured on the lines of an organic model, in which individuals belonged to groups and groups formed the organs of the larger social body. Each group, and each individual within the group, was called upon to accomplish a particular task which was to be performed autonomously. Each group's autonomy must be respected; a group was only allowed to interfere with the autonomy of other groups in cases of absolute need. Further, the Thomist perspective developed by Saint Thomas Aquinas connected the previous ideas with the notion of human dignity. Human dignity was understood by Aquinas as the recognition of a sphere of freedom for the individual that must be respected by both larger social groups and the State. However, the sphere of freedom that human beings should enjoy was far from absolute. As Aristotle concluded, human beings, and finally human dignity, were both driven by the search for the common good. For Aquinas, personal ends and personal interests were relegated to second place when they conflicted with the common good. Thomism acknowledged a certain degree of action for individuals, but always within the framework of the ends of society at large.

The exercise of power was articulated by Saint Thomas Aquinas in relation to the concepts of human dignity and the common good. For Aquinas, the intervention of public authorities was legitimate in so far as it was necessary for the attainment of society's common good. The limit of the exercise of power was found precisely in respect for human dignity. The exercise of power must respect human dignity as this is conceived from the perspective of natural law. Therefore any interference with an individual's person was unacceptable unless justified by the search of the common good.

In the seventeenth century, German corporatism solidified the organic vision of society and the concept of human dignity proposed by Thomist scholars.[5] For German corporatists, the point of departure was the recognition of the existence of society prior to the existence of the State. The emphasis was

[5] The main proponent of this trend was Althusius (1995).

therefore placed not only on the concept of human dignity, but above all on the autonomy of the social groupings. German corporatism advocated the establishment of a degree of autonomy and independence for the various groups comprising society. The relationships between the groups that comprise society and individuals revolved around the idea of *amititia*. *Amititia* was understood as the composite of natural links between individuals and between social groups when they interact with each other. Besides *amititia*, social groups and individuals within social groups were also bound to the attainment of the common good, even when there was no interaction between them. Ideally, from that moral tie to the common good, society should flow into a state of 'symbiotic co-operation' (Althusius, 1995).

The idea of contract is another foundation stone of German corporatism. The corporatist idea of contract was based on a model that was closer to the Lockian vision of 'ideal society' that to the Hobbesian idea of the 'state of nature'. For corporatists, a social contract was needed to limit the exercise of public power, with the aim of protecting the autonomy of social groups. Public power intervention would be justified for the attainment of public good, and therefore would find its limits in the autonomy of social groups. It is precisely in the context of the relationships between public power and social groups that the corporatist idea of 'supplementarity' arose. Supplementarity meant that the role of the State was essentially limited to complementing or supplementing social groups' activity where social groups were not efficient enough to fulfil their own social responsibilities. Thus, Althusius argued in his *Politics* (1995) that the legislature should adopt the smallest possible number of laws.

In the nineteenth century Ketteler[6] brought together the scholastic and corporatist traditions in order to form the basis of a new political and social movement that would be named 'Social Catholicism'. Social Catholicism was part of the origin of the 'social doctrine' of the Catholic Church. The movement led by Ketteler was founded on two main elements: the notions of 'intermediate groups' and of 'subsidiarity'. Ketteler may therefore be considered as the father of the concept of 'subsidiarity', according to Millon-Delsol. However, that author points out that the exact term used by Ketteler was *droit subsidiare*; the term subsidiarity would appear later, within the social doctrine of the Catholic Church.

Ketteler began by observing of the paradoxical nature of the relationship between the State and society. On one hand, Ketteler pointed out that society

[6] Quoted by Millon-Delsol (1992; 1993).

needs State intervention, since society was often unable to attain its own ends. On the other hand, Ketteler believed that State intervention should be limited to cases of real need since excessive State intervention would lead to a correlative weakening of society and individual potential in the long run. The resolution of this paradox would come from the development of what the author called 'intermediate groups'. Strong intermediate groups (associations of individuals whose function would be that of mediating between State authorities and individuals) were for Ketteler the only means of effectively limiting excessive State intervention.

The concept of subsidiarity governed the network of relationships that would be established between different social groups and the State authorities. The concept would be founded on the notions of human dignity and the common good, and would have an essentially negative facet. Subsidiarity would therefore be an obstacle to State intervention, and would foster the autonomy of social groups. In turn, human dignity would legitimate State intervention within the ambit of the autonomy of social groups, even against the will of the latter. Further, the common good would justify State intervention in general terms.

This ensemble of concepts, such as human dignity, the common good, social group autonomy, and limited intervention by public authorities formed the background for what by the end of the nineteenth century became known as the 'social doctrine' of the Catholic Church. It was within the social doctrine of the Catholic Church that the character of modern subsidiarity was formed. The birthplace of the social doctrine of the Catholic Church was probably the Encyclical letter, *Rerum Novarum*.[7] In the *Rerum Novarum* Pope Leon XIII pointed out the need for the Catholic Church to adopt a more active role in the debate over the resolution of social problems in modern societies. This was an initial reaction to the criticisms of ambiguity against the Catholic Church (and even within the Catholic Church itself) regarding the so-called social question, at a time when the economic changes resulting from the Industrial Revolution were starting to be felt. In the *Rerum Novarum* the Catholic Church began to draw the lines of an official version of the relationships between men and public power, whose nucleus was the role attributed to the State for the structuring of society.

The *Rerum Novarum* was followed by the *Quadragessimo Anno, Mater et Magistra, Centesimus Annus*, and others.[8] Each deals with one specific issue.

---

[7] See *Once Grandes Mensajes*, published by BAC (1991), p. 13.
[8] Ibid, pp. 57, 123, 712.

Thus while the *Rerum Novarum* was mostly concerned with class war, the *Centesimus Annus* attempted to formulate a response to the problem of the internationalization of the social question, in particular the issue of the domination of the Third World by the First World. One finds some common points in the social doctrine of the Catholic Church, such as the idea of the common good which governs social groups and State actions; or the importance of social groups for the structuring of society. One of these common points was subsidiarity. Perhaps the best formulation of the principle is found in the *Quadragessimo Anno*. In this Encyclical Letter, Pius XI said:

Just as it is wrong to withdraw from the individual and commit to a group what private enterprise and industry can accomplish, so too it is an injustice, a grave evil and a disturbance of the right order, for a larger and a higher association to arrogate to itself functions which can be performed efficiently by smaller and lower societies. This is a *fundamental principle of social philosophy*, unshaken and unchangeable. Of its very nature the true aim of all social activity should be to help members of the social body, but never to destroy them or absorb them (Pius XI, 1936:31, emphasis added).

Some conclusions may be drawn from my brief account of the origins of subsidiarity. In the first place, it is evident that subsidiarity, and the ensemble of notions and concepts that serve as the basis of the principle, such as human dignity or the common good, have an important degree of indeterminacy. Its contours are not clearly defined, to say the least. In the second place, as far as the working of subsidiarity and its background are concerned, the principle finds application not only in relationships between the public and the private spheres, but also within each of these spheres. In the third place, one may note that the ethos underlying subsidiarity is the protection of the autonomy of smaller entities (and in the last instance, the individual) against intervention by larger entities. This is irrespective of whether we speak of the public–public level, the public–private, or the private–private one. The starting point is mistrust in those entities which are larger, since it is assumed that boundary abuse is inherent. Boundary abuse is deemed to be a negative evolution since it may frustrate individual development, which is seen as the seed of social progress.

Subsidiarity apparently involves ambivalence. In principle it serves to justify the autonomy of smaller entities (both private and public). It therefore implies an obstacle to the expansion of larger entities' (both private and public) respective spheres of action. Once the hurdle of subsidiarity is cleared, then larger entities may act. This is what provokes confusion as to the ethos of the principle. When it is said that larger entities may act when this is in accordance with subsidiarity, in reality this does not mean that subsidiarity is justifying (supporting) larger entities' actions. The idea is rather that, when larger entities act, this is possible because subsidiarity does not impede it. Therefore claims that subsidiarity is value-neutral, or a Janus-faced concept (Golub, 1996) are not justified. As suggested above, the primary aim of subsidiarity is to stop undue interference by larger entities with smaller entities or individuals. The philosophy of subsidiarity thus involves a negative bias. From the perspective of subsidiarity, the ideal is to determine an appropriate separation of tasks between smaller and larger entities. In this ideal situation, recourse to larger entities for implementing smaller entities' tasks would not be necessary. Therefore recourse to larger entities is seen from the perspective of subsidiarity as a symptom of system malfunction: an indication that the division of tasks which subsidiarity advocates has not been attained.

As for the practical application of subsidiarity in a constitutional setting, the clearest example in the EC context is Germany. According to Schwarze (1993) the philosophy of subsidiarity governs relationships between the *Bund* and the *Länder* in this Member State. Article 72.2° of the German Basic Law is a constitutional provision which incorporates that philosophy clearly. One should speak of the 'philosophy or spirit of subsidiarity' rather than of 'subsidiarity' *tout court*, since the term is not expressly mentioned in Article 72.2°.[9] In particular, Article 72.2° reads as follows:

In this field the *Bund* will have the right to legislate if federal legal regulation is needed:
1) because a matter could not be settled effectively by the legislation of the various *Länder*, or
2) because the regulation of a matter by the law of a *Land* could affect the interests of other or all *Länder*, or
3) to safeguard the legal or economic unity, and in particular, to safeguard the homogeneity of the living conditions beyond the territory of a *Land*.

As Schwarze (1993) has noted there is a parallel between Article 72.2° and Article 5(2) of the EC Treaty. For instance, both in the Community context and in the German one, subsidiarity is applied to concurrent competences, and not to exclusive ones. Although the mechanical translation from the German text to the Community one is, as shall be seen, far from appropriate, it may be of interest to give some idea of the German constitutional experience of subsidiarity. In this regard, Constantinesco points out that although

---

[9] Neverthless, Article 23 of the German Basic Law was reformed in order to allow German ratification of the Maastricht Treaty, thus incorporating for the first time into the German Basic Law the term 'subsidiarity'.

the philosophy of subsidiarity seems to govern many of the decisions adopt-ed by the German Constitutional Court, the principle has never been used explicitly to restrain intervention by the *Bund*. On those rare occasions in which the German Constitutional Court has ruled on Article 72.2°, the Court referred to causes such as *ultra vires* actions and manifest error (but not subsidiarity) to strike down *Bund* measures (Constantinesco, 1992:10).[10]

   In conclusion of this section I wish to highlight the ambiguous character of subsidiarity. From a theoretical perspective, subsidiarity is so undefined that the concept amounts, at best, to a common sense principle of good govern-ment or a political objective. Subsidiarity therefore constitutes a very elastic notion, and this explains why, in the Community debate on the principle, visions as different as those of the German *Länder* and those of the UK were able to embrace subsidiarity.[11] From a more practical perspective, the German experience seems to give an initial indication that the principle is difficult to manage in strictly legal terms. These practical and theoretical constrictions influenced the shaping of the Community principle of sub-sidiarity. Despite comments in the next section, the success of subsidiarity in the Community is surprising given the limits of the principle in both content and concept. Only the negative bias of the principle can account for Member States' support of it.

C. Binding commitments: the introduction of subsidiarity into the EC Treaty by the Maastricht Treaty

The above outline of the concept of subsidiarity allows me to delve into the analysis of the process through which subsidiarity was incorporated into the EC Treaty as a general clause. As stated above, there is a direct connection between the introduction of subsidiarity into the EC Treaty and the legit-imacy crisis that has affected the Community since the inclusion of the majority principle in its institutional structure. The clearest expression of Member States' discontent with the process of European integration were the words pronounced by UK Prime Minister Margaret Thatcher in 1988, in the opening ceremony at the College of Europe (Bruges). On that occasion, Thatcher said that:

---

[10] See in the same vein Schwarze (1993:617).   [11] See the following section of this Chapter.

Closer co-operation requires neither centralisation of power in Brussels nor that decisions shall be taken by a bureaucratic apparatus which is not accountable before the electorate . . . We have not successfully reduced the State to its just terms in order that the State re-establishes its old borders at European level, constituting a super-European State that exerts a new power from Brussels.[12]

Harsh as they were, these words were not the only sign of Member States' unease with European integration. Another manifestation of that attitude was the Danish referendum in 1992, resulting in a vote against ratification of the Maastricht Treaty.[13] The Danes ratified the Maastricht Treaty a year later. However, four things had to happen to attain that objective: first, the conservative government of Schlüter fell;[14] secondly, the social democrat Paul Nyrup Rasmussen came to power; thirdly, the Danish compromises signed by the conservative government of Schlüter in the city of Maastricht were revised;[15] and finally, a second referendum took place in the spring of 1993.

The first Danish referendum on Maastricht was followed by a referendum in France on the same issue in September 1992. This was the third sign that is traditionally cited as evidence that European integration suffered crisis that began before the Maastricht negotiations. Even though the French finally backed ratification of the Maastricht Treaty, the majority was extremely narrow.[16] Considering France's historical support of European integration, this result is probably more relevant than the Danish one.[17] Although national circumstances certainly influenced both the Danish and the French referendums[18] it is clear that these national variables are not enough to explain the outcome.

A final indication of the view in most European capitals on European integration is the *Maastricht* judgment of the German Constitutional Court. The German Constitutional Court found no contradiction between the Basic

[12]   The text is reproduced by Areilza (1995a: 53).

[13]   The referendum took place on 2 June 1992, with the following result: 50.7% of people voted against Maastricht and 49.3% in favour of it. For data and post-hoc public reactions see *El País*, 3 June 1992, p. 1.

[14]   In January 1993.

[15]   See Part B of the Conclusions of the Presidency at the European Council of Edinburgh (Bull. EC, 12-1992).

[16]   The French referendum took place on 20 September 1992; only 50.8% of the votes went in favour of ratification.

[17]   Note the Eurobarometer (*Trends*, 1974–92). For example, in 1988 21% of the British (Britain was at the time the most anti-European Member State) thought that the Community was 'a bad thing'; at the same time, only 5% of the French thought in the same way.

[18]   See Sánchez-Cuenca (1997a).

Law and the Maastricht Treaty. However, the *Bundesverfassungsgericht* said, *obiter dicta*, that it had the *Kompetenz-Kompetenz*, since it explicitly reserved to itself the possibility of patrolling the limits of the competences granted by the German law of ratification of the Maastricht Treaty. The German Constitutional Court *Maastricht* judgment not only has legal relevance: from a sociological point of view it is also of interest since the judgment coincided with an important sector of German public opinion whose discomfort with European integration was growing.[19]

Clearly, the combination of these elements may have a number of interpretations.[20] One possible interpretation is, as argued in Chapter II above, that the circumstances referred to above are indicators of the existence, starting in the period preceding the Maastricht Treaty negotiations, of a widely shared perception among Member States of pure and simple defencelessness in the process of Community intervention backed by Brussels.[21] This overall perception was the main reason why Member States pushed for the introduction of the principle of subsidiarity into the Treaties (Dehousse, 1993; 1997).

The story of the incorporation of subsidiarity into the Treaty is illustrative of the link between the Community's federal deficit and the principle. As Wilke and Wallace (1990) point out, Delors, the President of the Commission at the time, had a meeting with some German *Länder* representatives in November 1988 in Bonn. The latter expressed their concern to him about the Community's advances into realms such as broadcasting and education, which were traditionally considered to fall within the *Länder*'s exclusive competence. The word subsidiarity was suggested by the *Länder* to President Delors as constituting a useful and flexible means of establishing limits on Community intervention (Wilke and Wallace, 1990:3). The idea of approaching the debate on the limits to Community intervention from the angle of the subsidiarity principle roused the interest of the President of the Commission. This is illustrated by Delors' response to Thatcher a year later when she initially queried the excesses of Community intervention. At the inauguration of the 1989 academic year at Bruges, Delors stated:

---

[19] See Eurobarometer (*Trends*, 1973–94, p. 75) which shows a progressive fall in German support for European integration since 1990.

[20] Sánchez-Cuenca (1997a) gives an alternative interpretation.

[21] Eurobarometer supports this conclusion: in 1990 8% of Europeans thought that the Community was something 'bad' and 19% thought that the Community was 'neither good nor bad', while in 1994 the figures had already risen to 13% and 19%, respectively.

I often have the opportunity to resort to federalism as a method, including the principle of subsidiarity. I see therein the inspiration for reconciling what appears to be irreconcilable: the emergence of a united Europe and loyalty to our nation, to our motherland; the need of a European power adapted to the problems of our times plus the vital imperative of preserving our nations and regions (Delors, 1989,[22] my translation).

Furthermore, the concept of subsidiarity was not unknown in the Community context. The first important references to the principle were made in the mid-seventies, in the Tindemans Report on the European Union[23] and in the MacDougall Report on fiscal federalism[24] (Wilke and Wallace, 1990:23). The European Parliament draft treaty on the European Union also made an implicit reference to subsidiarity in its Article 12.2°. In addition to this, in 1987 the SEA incorporated subsidiarity (without mentioning the term) in Article 130r.4° of the EC Treaty, relating the principle to environmental protection (Lenaerts and Ypersele, 1994).

The fact that the principle was not a new concept for the Community, the connection of its social Christian flavour with the intellectual origins of President Delors, and the fact that the principle had been used historically in various contexts as an argument for restraining State intervention all ensured that subsidiarity moved smoothly onto the agenda for institutional reform of the European Communities. Therefore, when the two intergovernmental conferences on monetary and political union were officially opened in December 1990 to reform the Rome Treaty, the representatives of the Member States backed subsidiarity as an important element of the future Community constitutional architecture. In particular, the European Council of Rome established that: '*Le Conseil Européen reconnaît l'importance que revêt le principe de subsidiarité, non seulement lorsqu'il s'agit d'étendre les compétences de l'Union, mais aussi pour la mise en oeuvre des politiques et des décisions de l'Union*'. (European Council of Rome, 1990).[25]

Following the European Council of Rome, a debate took place between different players regarding the place that the principle of subsidiarity should have in the Treaty. Two camps emerged (Elorza, 1992:126). Some Member States advocated a mere mention of subsidiarity in the Preambles of the Treaties. This political position was maintained by Spain, France, and Italy, among others. Another set of players favoured the inclusion of the principle

---

[22] Extracted from Wilke and Wallace (1990).   [23] Supplement 1/76, Bull. EC.
[24] 'Report of the Study Group on the Role of Public Finance in European Integration' (1977).
[25] Bull. CE 12-1990, p. 11.

of subsidiarity in the operative part of the Treaty. This legal stance was defended by the Commission, the European Parliament, and among Member States by the UK and Germany, though for different reasons.[26]

However, even in the camp that defended the legal profile of the principle, there were important divergences in the concrete formulation of subsidiarity and its exact location within the Treaties. At one extreme, the Commission[27] proposed the inclusion of the principle of subsidiarity within the framework of old Article 235 of the EC Treaty. The Commission therefore appeared to propose that subsidiarity should be applied only to cases in which the Community lacked sufficient means for action and therefore needed to enact new powers. At the other extreme, the UK and Germany advocated a text that highlighted the negative aspect of the principle, and supported the establishment of subsidiarity as a broader principle of Community law (Cloos *et al.*, 1993:149).

The European Parliament maintained an intermediate position between these extremes. It advocated the introduction of subsidiarity as a general legal principle, but also the limitation of its scope of application to the exercise of concurrent Community competences. Moreover, the European Parliament Report on the principle of subsidiarity advocated an *ex ante* subsidiarity control of Community legislation before the Court of Justice. Legally binding acts adopted by Community institutions could be scrutinized by the Court before they entered into force. The Council, the Commission, the European Parliament, and Member States were accorded *locus standi*. In the case of a negative opinion of the Court, the European Parliament Report suggested the procedure of treaty revision (Article 236 of the EC Treaty) for the adoption of the act in question.[28]

In a parallel move, the Luxembourg Presidency of the European Community circulated a draft treaty 'on the Union' during the first six months of 1991. The draft treaty included a new Article 3b which provided for negotiation regarding the formulation of the principle of subsidiarity and its location within the Treaty. In particular, Article 3b of the Luxembourg draft established that:

---

[26]   See for reports of both positions, Agence Europe, No. 5514 of 17 and 18 June 1991, p. 3.

[27]   Avis de la Commission Européenne du 21 Octobre 1990 relatif au projet de révision du Traité instituant la Communauté Economique Européenne et concernant l'Union Politique, COM(90) 600 final, 23 Octobre 1990.

[28]   Report of the Commission of Institutional Affairs of the European Parliament on the Principle of Subsidiarity of 31 October 1990. Doc. A3-0267/90.

The Community shall act within the limits of the powers conferred upon it by this Treaty and of the objectives assigned to it therein. In the areas which do not fall within its exclusive jurisdiction, the Community shall only take action, in accordance with the principle of subsidiarity, if and in so far as those objectives can be better achieved by the Community than by the Member States acting separately because of the scale or effects of the proposed action.[29]

The principle of subsidiarity was eventually included in Article 3b2° of the Rome Treaty, as amended by the Maastricht reform. The final outcome resulted from a *quid pro quo* between the different camps mentioned above. On one hand, the 'legal' camp succeeded in establishing subsidiarity as a legal principle. Further, Article 3b2° adopted a stricter formulation than that established by the Luxembourg draft (Dehousse, 1993:6). In particular, the UK and Germany were responsible for the markedly negative overtone of the wording of Article 3b2° that was finally adopted[30] (Cloos *et al.*, 1993:149). In addition, Article 3b3° inserted the proportionality principle in connection with both the exclusive and concurrent Community competences. This was a concession made to the UK, unhappy with the limitation of the scope of subsidiarity to only the Community's concurrent competences (House of Commons, 1992:17[31]). Finally, the principle of attributed competences was included in the first paragraph of Article 3b, in order to underline the limited character of the transfer of sovereignty from the Member States to the European Community. The political camp succeeded both in limiting the scope of the principle to Community concurrent competences, as suggested by the European Parliament, and in saving the 'better attainment' clause of the Luxembourg draft in the last sentence of Article 3b2° (Elorza, 1992:126). However, the legal camp was able to claim victory: the thrust of its proposal was finally retained, since subsidiarity would be reviewable before the ECJ. The following words of the UK Prime Minister of the time, Mr Major, illustrate this point:

Many in this House and throughout the country have expressed anxiety that decision-making in the Community is becoming too centralised. In fact, many of the issues that

[29] Europe Documents, No. 1722/1723 of 5 July 1991, p. 4.

[30] In particular, Teasdale reports that the sentence 'the Community shall take action ... only if and in so far as the objectives of the proposed action *cannot be sufficiently* achieved by the Member States' was suggested by the UK who maintained a vision of subsidiarity as basically equivalent to a 'necessary' clause. This formulation was upheld by the German delegation in the Maastricht negotiations. See Teasdale (1993:191).

[31] House of Commons, session 1991–92, Foreign Affairs Committee, Second Report 'Europe After Maastricht', vol. II (minutes of evidence) p. 17.

are most problematic for us [. . .] are ones that arise from the application of the original Treaty of Rome, not the Maastricht Treaty. The Maastricht Treaty marks the point at which, for the first time, we have begun to reverse that centralising trend. We have moved decision taking back towards the Member States in areas where Community law need not and should not apply. Let me inform those who are unaware of the fact that we have done so in a number of ways. We have secured a legally binding text on subsidiarity . . . (House of Commons, 1992).[32]

So far, the process through which subsidiarity was incorporated within the EC Treaty has been described, and the link between the Community's federal deficit and subsidiarity has been shown. However, describing is not explaining. In order to explain the process described above, it may be useful to employ the concept of *commitment*. *Commitment* is used here not in its vulgar sense but in the more specific sense of 'a determination not to deviate from a certain course of action' (Elster, 1984). Commitment (in its more specific sense) may also be defined as 'a manipulation of the available alternatives in order to attain a specific goal which would be difficult to attain in the absence of the commitment' (Sánchez-Cuenca, 1997b:3). Though the debate on the concept of commitment has received widespread attention in political science, it is enough for my purposes to delineate two of the most important elements in this debate: *motivation* and *credibility*.

A commitment's *motivation* is the reason why one would be interested in accepting a commitment. In the original conceptualization of the idea of commitment, Elster (1984) says that the origin of any commitment is the idea of 'weakness of will' or *akrasia*. A player may be interested in 'tying his or her hands' through a commitment in order to avoid temptations. The clearest example in this regard are central banks. Politicians have an interest in delegating competences to a central bank in order to avoid the temptation to adopt decisions on monetary policy for electoral purposes and not for strictly economic or monetary ones.

In the case I am examining here, it could be argued that subsidiarity constitutes a *commitment*, in the sense that with its introduction into the EC Treaty the Member States within the Community were attempting to tie its hands to a course of action less detrimental to national sovereignty. The available alternatives would thus be restricted because Community intervention could only be used in cases of real need.

However, as suggested above, it is not enough to make a commitment in order to restrain available alternatives. In order to work, a commitment has

---

[32] *Hansard*, issue 1588 of 20 May 1992, vol. 208, col. 265.

to be *credible*. Credibility is necessary to tie the hands of a player thoroughly. There are several mechanisms which could lend credibility. One of them would be the reform of the Constitution (of the Treaties, in the Community context); another would be delegation of power to an independent agency, and in particular to a Court (judicial review). It must be clear that Constitutional (or Treaty) reform and delegation of powers to an independent agency (which includes judicial review) are not in themselves commitments, but tools intended to give credibility to commitments. In our case, the commitment would be, as suggested above, subsidiarity. Both the reform of the EC Treaty (with the purpose of introducing subsidiarity) and the conversion of the concept into a legal principle (which in turn determined that the final arbiter on the principle would be the Court of Justice) were mechanisms whose objective was to lend credibility to the commitment of subsidiarity.

After the enactment of the Treaty of Maastricht, Member States would rely on a new argument before the Court of Justice in order to annul measures adopted by a majority vote. Judicial review of the principle was intended to take the new reform seriously. That is why the position of the ECJ regarding subsidiarity is of the utmost importance for understanding the real scope of the principle. Analysis of that stance appears in Chapter V below. But before I turn to this, it is necessary to give some clues as to the legal interpretation of Article 5(2). The next section addresses this point.

D. Subsidiarity in Maastricht

The importance of Article 5(2) becomes clearer if one takes into account the idea of 'commitment' established at the end of the previous section. In effect, the idea is that only the legal shaping of subsidiarity constitutes a sufficient guarantee for Member States which are outvoted and think that the Community should not have adopted a particular measure. Therefore this section is devoted to answering the question of whether Article 5(2) has a legal scope, and if so, to what extent. The answer to this question may be anticipated: I shall show that the legal dimension of the principle is very narrow.

Let us start by recalling the intricate text of what is now Article 5(2) of the EC Treaty:

In areas which do not fall within its exclusive competence, the Community shall take action, in accordance to the principle of subsidiarity, only if and in so far as the objectives of the proposed action cannot be sufficiently achieved by the Member States and can therefore, by reason of the scale or effects of the proposed action, be better achieved by the Community.

1. *The Problem of Competence*

When interpreting Article 5(2) the first obstacle is found at the beginning of the text. In effect, Article 5(2) says that the principle will be applied 'in areas which do not fall within [the Community's] exclusive competence', which means, *a contrario*, that the principle will only be applied in areas of concurrent Community and Member State competence. The problem here is that no distinction is made in the EC Treaty between exclusive and concurrent competences. The issue is not that the distinction is unknown as a 'pure category' in the Community context, but rather that there is no legal text that explains which of the Community's competences are exclusive and which of them are concurrent. As argued below, this problem is more formal than real. However, at first glance at least, the text of Article 5(2) may surprise the reader who realizes that the Community legal order contains no express list of competences.[33]

Faced with the absence of such a list, a lawyer's logical reaction would be to turn to the case-law of the European Court of Justice. However, the search would be futile: the ECJ has only very rarely pronounced on the nature of the Community's competences.[34] The ECJ appears to be conscious that any decision on its part regarding the nature of the Community's competences could be deemed an example of judicial activism, in the absence of a list of competences. This probably explains why the ECJ has been very cautious on the issue.

Therefore, on one hand, Article 5(2) explicitly states that the principle of subsidiarity is to be applied only to concurrent competences, while on the other, there is no legally binding text defining the Community competences. The default solution is to apply subsidiarity indiscriminately to all cases in which the EC intervenes through a legally binding measure (with the exception of those cases in which the ECJ has declared that a particular Community competence is exclusive). This default solution may seem at first

[33]   See Dehousse (1996) and Dehousse (1994a). Note also that the Treaty of Nice has convoked a new Intergovernmental Conference for 2004, which will negotiate, among other issues, the insertion of a catalogue of competences within the ECT. See its 'Declaration on the Future of the Union'. On this problem, see de Witte and de Búrca (2002).

[34]   According to Alonso García (1994:563), the ECJ has only pronounced on the matter regarding the Common Commercial Policy and the Community Policy on Conservation of Maritime Biological Resources.

to contravene Article 5(2). However, the contradiction is more apparent than real if we take into account not only the text but also the spirit of Article 5(2). To substantiate this idea, it is necessary to delve into the nature of Article 5(2) ECT.

2. *The Nature of the Beast: Subsidiarity as a Principle Regulating the Exercise of Community Competences*

It must be made clear at the outset that the question which subsidiarity attempts to answer is the following: given a concrete proposal for intervention, should the Community act or not? This means that the principle of subsidiarity does not determine when the Community has competence to intervene. Rather, this question is answered by Article 5(1), which establishes the principle of attributed powers. According to this principle, the Community may act *only* when it has explicitly been granted competence (either through the Treaties or through ECJ jurisprudence on implied powers). Therefore, subsidiarity enters the scene only when it is clear that the Community has competence to act. Subsidiarity is thus a second filter which aims at determining whether, according to a number of criteria established in Article 5(2) (and now developed by the Protocol on subsidiarity) Community intervention is appropriate or not. In other words, subsidiarity is a *principle regulating the exercise, not the holding, of Community competence*. Since the enactment of the Maastricht Treaty, in order for the Community to take a particular action it must meet two tests: the (traditional) test of the principle of attributed powers and the (newer) test of subsidiarity. If the Community does not pass both tests then its action will be deemed unconstitutional and should therefore be annulled by the ECJ.

Opportunity and competence are therefore two different things, subsidiarity touching on the first but not the second. The main consequence of this conclusion is that if subsidiarity revolves around an issue of opportunity and not of competence, then the distinction between exclusive and concurrent competences becomes irrelevant for the purposes of applying the principle. In effect, the mere fact that a competence is exclusive does not imply that it will be appropriate or opportune for the Community to take a particular action which implements that competence. If this interpretation is sound, then our default solution (the application of subsidiarity to all cases) may be deemed to meet the spirit of the principle.

An example illustrates this important point. The example was widely used in the debate which took place immediately before and after the principle was incorporated into the EC constitutional order. It is that of zoo regulation (Dehousse, 1996). Imagine that the Community proposes to harmonize Member States' zoo regulation in order better to protect animals in zoos. In principle, the Community would have competence to act on the basis of its powers on animal protection, arising from the competences of the Community regarding environmental protection.[35] Let us assume for the purpose of my example that the ECJ had declared such a competence exclusive to the Community. From the angle of subsidiarity, the question would be: is it sensible to have a legally binding Community measure on the security and sanitary conditions of animals in zoos? It does not seem, at first glance, that the Community would add anything to the measures on the protection of animals in zoos adopted by individual Member States, independently of the exclusive nature of that particular competence. The exclusive nature of a particular competence does not imply, therefore, that the Community *has* to act.

The restriction established by Article 5(2) (subsidiarity is only applicable regarding concurrent competences) is, as has been shown, inconsistent with the idea of subsidiarity as a principle regulating the exercise, not the holding, of Community competences. If this is the case, then the question remains: how may one explain that restriction? To answer this question one must turn again to the negotiations which led to the incorporation of subsidiarity into the ECT. As suggested in the previous section of this Chapter, Article 5(2) resulted from a *quid pro quo* between the 'political school' and the 'legal school': the legal school obtained from the political school the legalization of the principle, but it had to grant the other camp something in return. That compensation was the restriction previously noted.

3. *Objectives*

Subsidiarity is therefore a principle regulating the exercise of Community powers, and it applies, in the absence of a clear understanding of the nature of Community competences, to any case in which the Community intervenes (with the possible exception, as noted above, of the rare cases in which the ECJ has declared a Community competence to be exclusive). The second hurdle that has to be cleared regarding Article 5(2) is that of *objectives*. In effect, as Article 5(2) indicates, the 'objectives of the proposed action' must be Community objectives. Although the presumption underlying subsidiarity

---

[35] See Title XIX ECT (ex Title XVI).

is, as shall be shown below, a preference for Member States' action, it is obvious that the objectives of the action must be Community objectives; if they were not Community objectives, then Community action would not make sense. Therefore, in the absence of a clear-cut definition of Community competences (and of their nature) the reference to 'objectives' may be seen as a supplementary guarantee for Member States opposing Community intervention. In this regard, it could be argued by the minority that the lack of clarity regarding the question of whether one particular objective must be attained by the Community is an indication that the Community should not act. However, in most cases this argument is bound to fail. First, the Community's objectives have a very wide formulation in the ECT;[36] secondly, the ECJ tends to give very broad interpretation to Community objectives in its case-law;[37] and finally, in most cases it will be possible for the Community to argue that a particular action falls within the market objective of the ECT. Therefore, although the reference to objectives seems to be a supplementary safeguard for Member States which oppose the adoption of a measure, in practice this guarantee offers only limited protection for minorities.

4. *Criteria*

The foregoing discussion provides a natural transition to the fourth issue arising from the interpretation of Article 5(2). This is the question of the criteria required in order to implement subsidiarity. The text of Article 5(2) establishes two such criteria. I refer to those criteria here as the 'sufficiency' and the 'value-added' criteria.[38] According to the sufficiency criterion, the Community shall act 'only if and so far as the objectives of the proposed action cannot be sufficiently achieved by the Member States'.[39] According to the value-added criterion, the Community shall act if 'by reason of the scale or effects of the proposed action, [the objective can] be better achieved by the Community'.[40]

The next question is whether the two criteria are mutually contradictory. On first reading it seems that the two tests establish different, even contradictory solutions. The sufficiency test requires that Member State action is justified if this would meet the objectives of the proposed action. This would

[36]   See art. 2 of the ECT and art. 2 of the EUT.

[37]   See Alonso García (1994:533–41).

[38]   Similar terminology is employed by the Commission: Communication of the Commission to the Council and the European Parliament on the Principle of Subsidiarity, SEC(92) 1990 final of 27 October 1992.

[39]   Art. 5(2) ECT.   [40]   Ibid.

be irrespective of whether Community action would meet the proposed objectives sufficiently or better than the Member States' action. The value-added test seems to require a comparison between proposed action by the Community and proposed action by the Member States. Only if it were clear that the Community's action would be better than the Member States' actions would the Community's intervention be justified according to this second criterion. Therefore, if individual Member States' proposed actions were sufficient to reach the objective, but the Community's proposal was better than those of Member States, then Member States could not act. In other words, the mechanical application of both tests could lead to contradictory outcomes in cases in which individual Member States' proposed actions were sufficient, but the Community's proposed action was better.

The explanation for this possibly contradictory outcome can also be found in the negotiation process that led to the incorporation of the principle within the ECT. In effect, the introduction of both the sufficiency test and the value-added test was also the result of a *quid pro quo* between the advocates of a 'light' version of subsidiarity (the 'political school') and the advocates of a 'strong' version of it (the 'legal school'). The former argued that the term subsidiarity should be made equivalent to a test of the value-added kind, such as was finally adopted, whereas the latter pushed for the introduction of a more restrictive test, seeking to make subsidiarity and sufficiency equivalent terms (Elorza, 1992). As agreement on this point was impossible, the Member States finally decided to incorporate both tests. However, it appears that there is a preference in favour of the value-added test, since the expression 'therefore' in Article 5(2) seems to subordinate the sufficiency test to the value-added test (Dehousse, 1993).

Is it possible to transform the results of this political bargaining into a coherent legal formula? I believe an interpretation is possible which, on one hand, co-ordinates both tests from a legal perspective, and on the other hand, respects the will of the Community's constituent power (which is, as pointed out above, to give priority to the value-added test). The following is one such interpretation. In principle, if Member States' proposed actions were sufficient to attain the objectives in question, Community action would be redundant, *unless* the Community's proposed action attains those objectives more completely, and added value is manifest. By contrast, in those cases in which the Member States' proposed actions are insufficient, the Community could not be presumed to have the freedom to act. Even in such cases, the Community would have to prove its proposal offers a substantial improvement over that of Member States for the attainment of Community objectives.

Whether or not one agrees with that legal solution, what is evident is that the discussion of the legal scope of the criteria in which subsidiarity is expressed in Article 5(2) is more theoretical than practical. Leaving aside the problems that the ECJ will encounter in seeking to implement the subsidiarity tests,[41] it is also certain that the other Community institutions, notably the Commission, will meet almost insurmountable obstacles in applying the subsidiarity criteria (*tout court*: subsidiarity) systematically. The *practical* implementation of subsidiarity is therefore the next issue discussed.

5. *Implementing Subsidiarity*

To begin with, there is the problem of how to compare two kinds of actions which only exist in theory, and not in reality. Greater certainty may perhaps be accorded to the outcome of proposed Community action, given its unity. The same cannot be said of Member States' proposed actions: by definition, we are speaking of fifteen different actions that may differ widely from each other. If the degree of certainty about Community proposals is greater than about those of Member States, this may introduce an initial bias in favour of Community intervention.

Secondly, neither the sufficiency test nor the value-added test establish objective points of comparison. In what sense are the Community institutions to understand that Community action is better than that of Member States? Article 5(2) refers to two parameters: the 'scale' and the 'effects' of the proposed action. However, both parameters are so vague and general that it is difficult to decipher any objective point of reference from them which could be relied upon by the Community institutions in order to make a decision. If no objective points of reference are established, then an examination by the Community institutions on the ground of subsidiarity can be adapted to the case at hand, and is always likely to be found to justify Community intervention.

Well aware of the difficulties that the practical implementation of subsidiarity involved, the Member States and the Community institutions focused on specifying the legal scope of the principle of subsidiarity immediately after the Treaty of Maastricht was signed on 7 February 1992. Although discussion of the texts produced with that aim was rendered almost irrelevant after the enactment of Protocol No. 30 on subsidiarity (introduced by the Amsterdam Treaty) they are still of interest since they served as a basis for the

---

[41] Analysed in Chapter V, below.

negotiation of that Protocol. Those acts had different filiations. The first was produced by the European Commission immediately after the enactment of the Maastricht Treaty: the famous *Communication of the Commission to the Council and the European Parliament on the Principle of Subsidiarity* of October 1992.[42] The response of the Member States to the Commission's position on subsidiarity came two months later, in the *Overall Approach to the Subsidiarity Principle*[43] adopted in the Conclusions of the European Council of Edinburgh (December 1992). Approximately a year later, before the enactment of the Maastricht Treaty, the Community institutions ended this debate about the principle by adopting the *Interinstitutional Agreement signed by Commission, the Council and the European Parliament on Procedures for Implementing the Subsidiarity Principle*, of 25 October 1993.[44] Since the main elements of those documents were for the most part retained in the Amsterdam Protocol on subsidiarity, they are analysed in the following Chapter, where the Amsterdam changes regarding subsidiarity are considered in detail.

E. Conclusions

This Chapter has been devoted to analysis of the subsidiarity principle as introduced by the Maastricht Treaty. To make this analysis, I discussed the foundations of the concept of subsidiarity, as opposed to the Community principle of subsidiarity. I concluded that the theoretical discussion on the principle is diffuse and ambiguous, when not incoherent. The principle seems to be used as a catch-all formula of good government and common sense, rather than a well defined political or philosophical principle, and so constitutes at most a political objective. As far as the historical dimension of the principle is concerned, the German experience is a good prima facie indicator of the legal as well as the functional limitations of the principle. As noted above, subsidiarity was never directly employed in any decision by the German Constitutional Court until the principle was introduced in the EC context. Given this historical background, it is surprising that Member States opted for this principle, rather than choosing alternative tools to correct the

---

[42] See n. 35, above.   [43] Reprinted in Bull. EC, 12–1992.

[44] The reader may find an analysis of these acts (and others of minor relevance) in Fernández Esteban (1996).

process of Community growth. Only the clear negative bias of the principle (in that it is more about preventing them fostering Community intervention may account for this).

This Chapter continued with a description of the negotiations between the Member States which ended with the incorporation of subsidiarity into the Treaties. It was shown that subsidiarity was a response by Member States to the Community's federal deficit. Beyond that description, I offered an explanation of the reasons why Member States decided to introduce subsidiarity into the *legal* part of the ECT. My account showed that Member States decided to 'tie the hands' of the EC Member States' when introducing the principle of subsidiarity into the Treaties and, above all, when providing for review of Community decisions by an independent player, the ECJ. This is an important point. From the perspective of my explanation, a key element was that the ECJ could control the way and the extent to which the principle was implemented. This was perceived by Member States as a necessary element to give credibility to the use of subsidiarity as a tool to protect minorities in the Council. It is also in this light that the analysis of the judicial implementation of the principle, to which Chapter V of this work is devoted, acquires its true relevance.

I focused next on the interpretation of Article 5(2) of the EC Treaty, which incorporates the legal principle of subsidiarity. My analysis is critical of Article 5(2). In the first place, I noted that subsidiarity is, in reality, a principle that regulates the exercise, rather than the existence, of Community competences. More simply put: the principle of subsidiarity does not indicate when the Community has or does not have competence but, assuming the Community has the competence, when it should act. Therefore the principle of subsidiarity attempts to solve a question of opportunity, but not a question of competence. It is true that both aspects seem to be inextricably linked. When the Community does not have competence, there is no way it can act; by contrast, if the Community has competence, this is a good indication that the Community should act. However, it is possible to disentangle the two dimensions of the issue. The question of competence therefore appeals strictly to the legal aspect of the problem under examination. Under subsidiarity, however, the analysis of non-legal aspects arises. This stance has further implications. To say that subsidiarity, as expressed in Article 5(2), has more to do with a meta-legal issue than with legal ones immediately casts doubt on the effectiveness of the new mechanism before the ECJ. However, from a strictly legal perspective, it is clear that subsidiarity is not a principle which attributes competence. In effect, since the question of competence seems to be solved by the principle of attribution of competences, the presence of subsidiarity must perform a different function. It would not be logical from a legal perspective to have two principles, one after the other, to perform the same function. Therefore subsidiarity is a principle regulating the exercise, and not the holding, of Community competences.

In the second place, if subsidiarity is a principle regulating the exercise of competences, then the reference to concurrent competences in Article 5(2), in the Community context, where there is no listing of competences, ceases to be a problem. In effect, if subsidiarity solves a question of opportunity, and not of competence, then the nature of the competence is deprived of interest in this regard. It may be opportune to implement a concurrent Community competence, but not to implement an exclusive Community competence. Therefore, the apparent hurdle of Article 5(2) (its reference to concurrent competences) is solved: subsidiarity, a principle regulating the exercise of Community competences, must be applied to any competence, irrespective of its nature.

Thirdly, the reference in Article 5(2) to objectives must be interpreted as a reference to Community objectives. This appears to be another brake on the Community's ability to act. However, this is again more apparent than real. The ECT is, as far as objectives are concerned, very open-ended; besides, the ECJ has given a wide interpretation to the Community's objectives. In essence, almost any kind of objective could fall within the Community's scope for action.

In the fourth place, there is the question of the criteria for implementing subsidiarity. Those criteria seem to contradict one another. However, it is possible to interpret them as not being mutually contradictory. Such an interpretation would have two rules. The first rule would be that when Member States' individual actions are sufficient to achieve the proposed objective, then the Community should not act, *unless* its action entails a very clear added value for the Community. The second rule would be that even if the Member States' individual actions are not sufficient to achieve an objective, this does not mean that the Community can act without first proving its own efficiency in achieving that objective. In other words, if both Member States' and the Community's proposed actions were inefficient, then Member States, and not the Community, would be entitled to act.

Finally, irrespective of the merits of that double formula, what is certain is that the implementation of subsidiarity is very difficult, at least according to those criteria. In other words, the discussion of the criteria established by Article 5(2) seems more an exercise in theoretical elegance than a debate with practical consequences. Member States, and the Community institutions, have attempted to approach this problem in a number of documents issued after the principle was incorporated into the ECT. However, the fact that the legal nature of those documents was uncertain prompted the Community to reopen the debate on the efficient implementation of the principle in Amsterdam. The result was a new Protocol on subsidiarity, Protocol No. 30, whose legal dimension is discussed in the next Chapter.

IV

Subsidiarity in Amsterdam

A. Introduction

This Chapter focuses on the analysis of Protocol No. 30 of the ECT, as introduced by the Amsterdam Treaty. Community institutions and Member States adopted a number of acts when subsidiarity was introduced by the Maastricht Treaty (the *Communication of the Commission to the Council and the European Parliament on the Principle of Subsidiarity* of October 1992, the *Overall Approach to the Subsidiarity Principle* of December 1992, and the *Interinstitutional Agreement signed by Commission, the Council and the European Parliament on Procedures for Implementing the Subsidiarity Principle* October 1993). The main problem posed by the three acts was their legally binding force. The ECJ case-law regarding acts such as the Commission's Communication on subsidiarity or the Edinburgh Conclusions is clear as far as their legally binding nature is concerned. Although the Court does not exclude the possibility that these kinds of acts may have *some* legal effects (for example, the ECJ may employ them in order to interpret other legal texts) it clearly denies that they are hard law (Snyder, 1994a). Community institutions and Member States are not bound to implement those acts. Things are less clear, however, regarding Interinstitutional Agreements. According to Snyder (*ibid.*) although they are not legally binding acts, in some cases the Court has confirmed their legally binding force when a number of very restrictive conditions are fulfilled.[1] Aware

---

[1] Those conditions are, according to Snyder (who draws from the ECJ case-law) (1994:15) the following: 1) such agreements must not modify the ECT or secondary legislation; 2) they must be consistent with the principle of legal certainty, and therefore expressed in sufficiently clear and unambiguous terms; 3) they must respect the principle of legitimate expectations; 4) they must respect the division of powers between the Community institutions as provided by the Treaties. Only when the four conditions are met will the ECJ be inclined to recognize the legally binding force of Interinstitutional Agreements.

of the limitations concerning their legally binding force, the Member States decided in the Amsterdam reform to include the essential elements of those acts in a protocol to be annexed to the ECT (Bribosia, 1998:26; see in general de Búrca, 1999). The aim was to reinforce the legal dimension of the principle,[2] which is acknowledged in the Protocol itself. According to its Preamble, the aim of the Protocol is to guarantee the 'strict observance' of the principle of subsidiarity and to ensure its 'consistent implementation by all Community institutions' in the Community's legal order.

The operative part of the Protocol is divided into thirteen points, which may be ordered around a number of questions with which Maastricht did not deal and which the Protocol aims to answer. These questions are: (a) which institutions are obliged to implement the principle?; (b); how does subsidiarity impinge upon the Community's constitutionalism? (c); how is subsidiarity defined?; and (d) how is the principle to be implemented? This Chapter deals with each of these questions in turn. The last section complements this discussion, which is of a functional nature, with a normative understanding of the principle. The outcome is a more sustained critique of the principle, at both the functional and the normative levels.

B. Which institutions are obliged to implement subsidiarity?

The first issue dealt with by the Protocol on subsidiarity is that of the institutions which are bound by the principle. In effect, immediately following the incorporation of subsidiarity into the ECT by the Maastricht Treaty, there was much discussion about which Community institutions were bound to observe subsidiarity.[3] Was subsidiarity addressed only to the Council and the European Parliament, or was it also addressed to other institutions such as the Commission? Since the Maastricht Treaty was silent on this point, that question was legitimate from a legal standpoint.

The first provision of the Protocol on subsidiarity addresses the question when it specifically establishes that 'each institution shall ensure that the principle of subsidiarity is complied with'. It follows that *all* Community

---

[2] According to Art. 311 ECT (ex Art. 239): 'The protocols annexed to this Treaty by common accord of the Member States shall form an integral part thereof'.

[3] That debate is reproduced in Lenaerts and Ypersele (1994).

institutions with a decisional capacity (that is, those which have powers to dictate legally binding acts), and not only the Community institutions *stricto sensu*,[4] are obliged to observe the principle of subsidiarity when they act. Thus, for example, the European Central Bank would be bound by the principle of subsidiarity regarding the acts with legally binding force that it adopts.[5]

This provision also makes clear that the ECJ has competence to review acts on the basis of subsidiarity. The last provision of the Protocol (provision no. 13) seeks to reinforce, though in an ambiguous way, this idea, when it says that 'compliance with the principle of subsidiarity shall be reviewed in accordance with the rules laid down by the Treaty'.

C. How does subsidiarity impinge upon the Community's constitutionalism?

The second issue addressed by the Protocol is that of the relationship between subsidiarity and the pillars supporting the Community's constitutional edifice. In this sense, the message sent by the Protocol is clear: the implementation of the principle of subsidiarity does not call into question any of the elements that are inseparable from the 'Community's constitutional charter', to use the words of the ECJ. This matter is resolved principally in provision 2 of the Protocol, although provisions 3 and 8 are also relevant. Provision 2 establishes that both the Community's *acquis* and the principle of institutional balance shall be respected by Community institutions when they implement subsidiarity. Furthermore, the same provision states that the implementation of subsidiarity shall not affect the principles developed by the ECJ 'regarding the relationships between national and Community law'. This clearly refers to the principles of supremacy, direct effect, Member States' liability for not implementing Community law, and legal certainty, at the very least. Finally, provision 2 indicates that the implementation of the principle of subsidiarity shall take into account the 'principle of sufficiency means', according to which 'the Union shall provide itself with the means necessary to attain its objectives and carry out its policies'. To link subsidiarity with the principle of sufficiency of means implies that the

---

[4] That is, those listed in Art. 7 ECT (ex Art. 4).

[5] In effect, Art. 110 ECT (ex Art. 108 A) establishes, for example, the possibility that the ECB dictate regulations which are of a general character and directly applicable.

Commission, when proposing the adoption of a particular measure, should take into account the means (above all the financial means) within the Community's reach. The origin of the principle of sufficiency of means may be traced back to the Reflection Group Report on the 1996 Inter-governmental Conference (Reflection Group, 1995). In that report, the Group indicated the need to establish 'consistency between the ambitions of the Union's proposals and the constraints on the Member States as provider of funds'. Lack of consistency would not only imply the violation of the principle of sufficiency of means, but would also be an indication, from the perspective of provision 2, that the Community should not act.

Provision 3 of the Protocol states that 'the principle of subsidiarity does not call into question the powers conferred on the European Community by the ECT, as interpreted by the ECJ'. This constitutes a specification of the part of provision 2 which refers to the *acquis communautaire*. Provision 8 recalls the principle of loyal co-operation (Article 10 ECT, ex Article 5) when subsidiarity is implemented. This is an important point. In those cases in which the Community considers that it should not act, the Member States will be free to do so.[6] However, the correlation between subsidiarity and loyal co-operation established by provision 8 means that Member States' intervention may not call into question the objectives of the ECT and the other obligations contracted by them with the European Community.

D. How is subsidiarity defined?

The Protocol also attempts to clarify the definition of subsidiarity, particularly in provision 3. Provision 3 states that subsidiarity is a principle regulating the exercise (as opposed to the attribution) of Community competences, since it 'provides a guide as to how [the Community's] powers are to be exercised at the Community level'. This is an Amsterdam innovation. The provision also establishes that the principle of subsidiarity is a 'dynamic' concept, which essentially means that subsidiarity allows Community action 'when the circumstances so require' and, conversely, that it allows Community action to be restricted or even 'discontinued' where it is no longer justified.

---

[6] Leaving aside the question of whether the Community's competence is exclusive or not. From a strictly legal standpoint, if we take into account the silence of the ECT in this regard, it seems more appropriate to speak here of 'pre-emption' than of exclusivity. If the field is already entirely occupied, this will hinder Member States' interventions. See Goucha Soares (1998).

To conceptualize subsidiarity as a 'face of Janus', that is, as a neutral device set towards either justifying or obstructing Community intervention, incorporates a particular vision of the principle, supported mainly by the European Commission, but also by some authors who have reacted favourably to subsidiarity (Golub, 1996). However, as examined below, it is important to note that this construction is probably contradictory to the *ethos* of the principle (which, as seen in the previous Chapter, is that of restricting and not fostering intervention by bigger units) and is certainly incoherent if measured against the *telos* of the principle, which is that of limiting the Community's intervention with the aim of protecting minorities in the Council. Furthermore, such logic also conflicts with other parts of the Protocol, for example its provision 5, which reproduces almost in its entirety Article 5(2) ECT as far as the 'sufficiency' and 'value-added' tests are concerned. If one interprets them together, as described in the previous Chapter, the only possible outcome is the more restrictive sense that has already been given to them. This more restrictive interpretation[7] implies a negative bias, in that subsidiarity is used more to prevent than to encourage Community intervention. If this interpretation of the sufficiency and value-added criteria is sound, then it is difficult to conceive of subsidiarity as a merely neutral device. I return to this point later in this Chapter.[8]

E. How is subsidiarity to be implemented?

The first thing that may be noted with respect to this question is that the Protocol on subsidiarity reiterates that the principle shall only apply to the Community's concurrent competences. However, the Protocol does not define the nature of Community competences. Neither does the ECT, nor other legally binding Community text. We therefore have here the same problem that was examined before. Amsterdam would have been a good opportunity to solve this problem, but instead the Community constituent

---

[7] According to which if Member States attain the objectives of the action sufficiently, then the Community shall not act, unless it is clear and manifest that the Community action is much better than the Member States' actions (first rule); and that when Member States' actions are insufficient, it may not be presumed that the Community's action will be, for that reason, sufficient but the latter will have to prove this (second rule). Therefore, the only possible justification on the basis of the principle would be negative: subsidiarity *does not impede* the Community from acting.

[8] See section 1 below.

opted for maintaining the *status quo*. That mistake is regrettable, if only because it fosters unnecessary legal debates on the nature of the EC competences. I have already said in a previous chapter that one of the aspects that the 2004 Intergovernmental Conference will have to deal with is the definition of the Community competences.

Secondly, the Protocol reiterates, as stated above, the sufficiency and the value-added criteria. It also develops a number of parameters which serve to specify those criteria. These parameters are directly imported from the acts produced after the introduction of subsidiarity by the Maastricht Treaty; these are examined here in detail. However, before entering into the merits of such analysis, it is important to distinguish between two separate but interrelated concepts: procedural subsidiarity and material subsidiarity.

Material subsidiarity involves a number of conditions of a substantial character which assist (or 'orientate', to use the expression employed in the Protocol) the Community institutions to answer the question of whether the Community should act or not, that is: whether the Community's intervention is appropriate. *Procedural subsidiarity* involves the establishment of a number of procedural conditions which the Community institutions must fulfil before implementing subsidiarity. Those procedural conditions are varied in character but, as shall be seen, in essence most of them point to the obligation to motivate the adoption of the Community measure from the angle of those conditions, and require such motivation to be made explicit by Community institutions. In other words, in its procedural sense subsidiarity is not aimed at solving the problem of whether the Community should act; its primary intention is that a *process* is undertaken by the Community institutions which ensures that the material side of the principle is implemented by them. It also aims to give sufficient publicity to that process.

Naturally, the line between material and procedural subsidiarity is thin. To some extent, material subsidiarity is implicit in procedural subsidiarity, the latter presupposing the former. This means that the two facets of the principle are more intertwined than the distinction set out above suggests. Therefore, if it is possible to motivate Community intervention in a certain area, this implies that, substantially speaking, the Community will be better able to act than the Member States. Therefore, although subsidiarity is not merely a formal expedient, and what really matters is that the Community is better able than the Member States to intervene, the truth of the matter is that a positive motivation will be a very strong presumption that the Community is, not only formally but also materially, better situated than the Member States to act. It follows that the distinction between material subsidiarity and procedural subsidiarity should be seen more as a heuristic device than as a clear-cut legal concept. Employed as a heuristic device, the distinction between the two sides of subsidiarity allows us to decipher more clearly the provisions of the Protocol that remain to be analysed.

1. *Material Subsidiarity*

Provision 5 of the Protocol on subsidiarity sets out a number of parameters which allow the material sense of subsidiarity to be shaped. In essence, the Protocol incorporates into provision 5 the subsidiarity tests of Article 5(2) and a synthesis of the parameters established by the Community institutions and the Member States in the acts adopted after the signing of the Maastricht Treaty, such as the Commission's communication on subsidiarity (Bribosia, 1998).

Starting with the first of those elements, provision 5 reiterates the subsidiarity tests of Article 5(2), although it introduces a slight innovation (which is unnecessary from my perspective) insofar as the sufficiency test is concerned. The innovation is that reference is made to the constitutional systems of Member States when Community institutions examine whether Member States can sufficiently attain the objectives of the proposed action. Provision 5 states that both criteria, the sufficiency and the value-added tests, must be fulfilled cumulatively. This supports my analysis in the previous Chapter, which stresses the negative bias of the principle as both criteria have to be interpreted in harmony. Provision 5 reads as follows:

For Community action to be justified, both aspects of the subsidiarity principle shall be met: the objectives of the proposed action cannot be sufficiently achieved by Member States' *action in the framework of their national constitutional system* and can therefore be better achieved by action on the part of the Community (my emphasis).

Provision 5 of the Protocol next sets out the *guidelines* (according to the expression used in the provision) which the Community institutions must follow when implementing subsidiarity. This is undoubtedly one of the most significant parts of the Protocol. In particular, provision 5 of the Protocol states that:

The following guidelines should be used [. . .]:
—the issue under consideration [must have] transnational aspects which cannot be satisfactorily regulated by action by Member States;
—actions by Member States alone or lack of Community action would conflict with

the requirement of the Treaty (such as the need to correct distortions of competition or avoid disguised restrictions on trade or strengthen economic and social cohesion) or would otherwise significantly damage Member States' interests;
—action at Community level would produce clear benefits by reason of its scale or effects compared with action at the level of the Member States.

The three guidelines can be viewed as two criteria. Thus, the first and the third guidelines can be combined to form a single criterion. In effect, the third guideline can be seen as a *genus* and the first guideline as a specification of that general proposition. In other words, the clearest cases in which the scale or the effects of particular action require Community action are those involving transnational elements. The clearest example is that of environmental pollution: a smokestack sited on the border between France and Spain will emit airborne pollution not only onto Spanish territory but also into France. The second criterion concerns the distortions that proposed action by the Member States (or, in negative terms, lack of Community action) would entail for the attainment and integrity of the single market. In the following, I will refer to those criteria as the 'transnational dimension' and the 'market distortion' criteria.

The 'transnational dimension' and 'market distortion' criteria were already present in the acts adopted by the member States and the Community institutions after the signing of the Maastricht Treaty, although with slight modifications.[9] The first problem posed by the two criteria is whether they are cumulative or not. That is, in order to justify Community action, must the Community comply with both criteria, or is it enough to comply with only one? The question is relevant if one argues that the two are cumulative: in a case of contradiction, which of them should be given more weight? In the absence of any reference to this problem in provision 5, and taking into account the *vis atractiva* of the market objectives of the Treaty, it could be argued that the second criterion should be given priority. However, this is not a very subsidiarity-prone interpretation, since it will usually be easier to justify Community action on the basis of the second than on the basis of the first criterion. The solution to this problem requires a flexible interpretation of the text of provision 5. Thus the following formula could be attempted: in principle both criteria are cumulative, except in cases in which the market distortion elements that would arise from the Community's inaction are so important as to justify the need for Community intervention.

---

[9] See in particular the *Overall Approach to the Subsidiarity Principle*, n. 41 above.

It has been forcefully argued by some authors that the two criteria might be a good basis upon which to implement the subsidiarity principle, and therefore to trace the line between actions by the Community and those of Member States. In particular, Golub has made the most serious attempt to get the best from subsidiarity: his argumentation is therefore examined here in detail. This allows me to develop my own stance on the principle, which is contrary to that maintained by Golub.

Golub (1996) starts by taking a number of examples, all from the environmental area. This choice is not random: environmental policy is one of the obvious candidates, at least in principle, for substantiating arguments in favour of subsidiarity. Using those examples as his base, Golub argues that many regulatory areas in the field of environmental protection clearly lack the required transnational dimension. For example, Golub argues that there is nothing inherently transnational about noise pollution. Thus the limitation of noise levels of lawnmowers, to cite an example discussed at length in the debate on the principle when it was introduced into the ECT, would not fall within the regulatory net of the Community, at least from a transnational perspective, due to the fact that the tolerable level of noise may vary greatly depending on factors that may be purely contingent. Another example is waste management. According to Golub, those regulations which require high levels of recycling, or which prohibit particular methods of domestic disposal, constitute restrictions of essentially national practices which have no clear adverse effects on neighbouring Member States. Another example is environmental impact assessment. According to Golub, the environmental implications of building highways, refineries, large agricultural installations, and suburban housing projects are local, or possibly regional, but certainly not transnational, except projects sited on a national border. A final example is wildlife protection, which is the subject of the clearest example of EU measures regulating what are basically national concerns. For instance, although many bird species migrate, the majority of the species targeted by the 'Birds' Directive[10] are non-migratory. Furthermore, appeals for EU competence based on the migratory character of species are, according to Golub, absurd.

Secondly, according to the 'market distortion' criterion, Golub argues that Community intervention in the field of 'process regulation' could be blocked by arguing that, in the long run, competitive strategies based on ecological dumping have negative effects for those Member States which employ them.

---

[10] Directive 79/409, OJEC L 103/1, of 25 April 1979.

The idea is that the distortion produced in Member States by the lack of Community process regulation would be offset, in the long run, by the negative economic effects which countries carrying out ecological dumping would suffer. Since Member States using ecological dumping strategies also have a price to pay, they could use this as a counter-argument against the Community argument based on the ground of market distortions.[11]

Although provocative, the difficulty with Golub's argument is that it does not get to the crux of the problem posed by the implementation of the subsidiarity principle. To begin with, good reasons may clearly be found for justifying, on the basis of the 'transnational dimensions' and 'market distortions' criteria, that the Community should act in all the cases cited by Golub. The problem is that the contrary is also true. Thus, it is clear that there is nothing *inherently* transnational about noise pollution from products such as lawnmowers. However, there are things producing noise pollution which may acquire transnational relevance: the clear example is aircraft. This example contradicts Golub's argument, according to which 'there is nothing inherently transboundary in noise pollution'. Besides, in cases such as aircraft, the transnational element would not only not stop Community intervention, but it could also be used by those interested in a Community measure on aircraft noise as a further argument in favour of it. This outcome would be paradoxical, if we take into account that the introduction of subsidiarity into the ECT was aimed at preventing new and unjustified Community intervention. It is not that without subsidiarity the argument of the transnational dimensions involved in aircraft noise regulation could not be used, but subsidiarity would clearly help to reinforce that argument.

[11] The argument is complex and needs explanation. Golub draws it from Commission attempts to convince Member States with lower process regulation standards of the benefits, in the long run, of implementing high process regulation standards. High process standards confer, according to the Commission 'in the long term, competitive advantages on firms by encouraging them to use resources more efficiently, promoting their positive public image, forcing them to develop more flexible production methods and providing "first mover" advantages by creating incentives for them to produce and sell technologically innovative remedies for environmental harms'. The implication of this stance of the Commission is, according to Golub, 'to make ... previous justifications for EU action totally untenable—if the Commission is correct, then pollution havens are a misnomer because lax environmental standards actually entail economic competitive disadvantages. States which allow lax standards do not attract foreign investment ... instead, these states are merely pursuing unwise policies which will undermine their long-term industrial competitiveness. The foolhardy decision to do this does not distort the market in their favour and does not justify harmonisation process standards at the EU level. Thus, under the subsidiarity principle, there might be no legitimate reason to set EU standards for national production processes ...' (Golub, 1996:16). Note also Commission Communication on industrial competitiveness and environmental protection, SEC(92)1986.

Secondly, in the case of waste management, another of the examples cited by Golub, a similar argument might be made. Arguments can certainly be found to support the claim that the Community should not intervene in this area (or at least in certain parts of it). However, the contrary will inevitably also be true. For instance Golub considers domestic waste disposal. It is clear that particular methods of disposal, such as disposal into sea water, may cause pollution that could affect the water not only of the Member State that produced or disposed of the waste, but also that of other Member States. If one considers other techniques of waste elimination, such as incineration, a similar argument can be made: the exact geographical impact arising from the use of that technique will always be difficult to determine in advance. It is precisely these kinds of arguments (potential transnational consequences of waste disposal into the sea and of waste incineration) that have historically been used by the Community to justify measures such as Directive 91/156,[12] establishing a general framework in the area of waste disposal (Fernández Ramos, 1997).

Thirdly, the environmental impact of the construction of refineries, highways, etc. may have, contrary to what Golub suggests, a transnational dimension. This is supported by recent data regarding the direct correlation between environmental damage and industrialization, on one hand, and global warming on the other.[13] Further, an intense debate is going on at present in the scientific world as to the existence of a causal relationship between the extinction of some animal species (even some non-migratory ones) and the global ecosystem.[14] This would justify Community intervention (even intervention beyond the Community's borders) for the protection of wildlife. In other words, the mere possibility that facts with a local dimension may have a global impact sustains the argument that the Community should intervene even in the cases discussed by Golub. And this would be possible without the need for absurd or extreme arguments, but simply by reference to the data provided by the scientific world.

We therefore see that, on the basis of the 'transnational dimension' criterion, one may obtain, even in the same regulatory ambit, radically contradictory results in most cases. At the very least, arguments will not be conclusive on the basis of this criterion because the transnational dimension (or lack of it) of a particular regulatory problem will be difficult to establish with certainty in advance in the majority of cases.

[12] OJEC L 78/32, of 26 March 1991.
[13] See issue 2 of *Revista de Gestión Ambiental*, which is entirely devoted to the analysis of the causes of global warming and climate change.
[14] Ibid.

However, the issue becomes more complicated if one turns to the second criterion of provision 5, the 'market distortion' criterion. In the absence of any reference to the relative status of the 'transnational dimension' and the 'market distortion' criteria in provision 5, it must be assumed that the two are cumulative, though with a certain primacy for the second over the first. This means that in order for the Community to act, the action has to pass both tests, *unless* the costs arising from Community action would be of such importance from a market distortion perspective that they would outweigh the benefits of preventing the Community from acting.

If the above analysis is correct, then most of the examples cited by Golub lose some of their relevance, even in those cases which had some argumentative strength from the perspective of the 'transnational dimension' criterion. Thus, even if it is obvious that there is nothing inherently transnational in regulating the noise from lawnmowers, from the perspective of the market distortion criterion the conclusion is rather the contrary. In effect, the problem with Member State regulation of lawnmower noise is that divergent legal schemes will hamper the free circulation of that product. If Germany has very high standards on noise regulation for lawnmowers and Spain very low ones, then Spanish manufacturers will be unable to export their lawnmowers to Germany. Even mutual recognition might be inadequate to pursue the objective of market integration in this case, since noise pollution might be considered an 'essential requirement' by the ECJ, therefore necessitating Community harmonization. The same principle applies to process regulation. Even if Member States opting for low process standards might suffer negative consequences in the long run, the truth of the matter is that different process regulations in Member States produce market distortions. To cite a simple example, if Italy required Italian manufacturers to use only state of the art, environmentally friendly technology to make cars, and Spain did not, then Spanish cars could not be sold it Italy. As a matter of fact, 'market distortion' has been one of the 'hard' arguments traditionally employed in order to justify Community intervention in the area of process regulation (hard in that it is difficult to contradict from the perspective of the Treaty's market objectives). However, the question here is when the market distortion elements are sufficient to justify Community action. Are they, in the cases cited by Golub, so important as to overrule the argument based on the lack of a transnational dimension? At the end of the day, the answer to this question will depend on who applies subsidiarity.

Similar problems arise in areas other than environmental protection which are close to what Member States consider to be the core of their sovereignty, for example in the field of culture. Of itself, culture clearly lacks a transnational dimension. Further, culture probably is the area which is furthest removed from the economy. However, this distance is more apparent than real. Take the example of the regulation of books or cinema. A book or a film may be seen as cultural manifestations. But both of them may also be considered as products, which are allowed to circulate freely beyond the borders of the Member State in which the book or the film is produced. Community regulation of the size of paperback books, for example, may be thought of as an illustration of Brussels' regulatory excess. However, from the perspective of books as an economic product, it is clear that the issue loses its inflammatory aspect if one acknowledges the fact that the book can only circulate freely in the Community market by size regulation. Obviously, this reasoning only applies to those authors who are interested in being read, although it may be easily assumed that this will be the case from the perspective of publishing companies.

The same can be said for cinema, as the famous example of Directive 89/552[15] (the 'directive without frontiers') illustrates. In essence, this Directive established that the Member States' public television broadcasters were obliged to include a Community quota in their programming.[16] As Herdegen (1995) reports, when the Directive was proposed, German *Länder* fiercely opposed the adoption of the measure, since they understood that the proposed directive impinged upon their *Kulturhoheit* (cultural sovereignty). *Länder* even put pressure on the German government to veto the measure. Finally, Germany (and the *Länder*) had to concede when they realized that keeping the protectionist bias of the previous German regulation would have limited German cinema to its own market. Thus the question is: what would a subsidiarity assessment recommend in all these cases? And further, would market integration have to be given more weight in all these cases?

In summary, the following points may be made. In the first place, it is obvious that from the perspective of the substantive criteria employed by provision 5 of the Protocol on subsidiarity, one may always find good reasons to block Community intervention. However, it is also certain that the reverse is true. Consequently, it will often be difficult to adopt a conclusive decision on the basis of those criteria. In the second place, although it is clear that in some cases Community intervention may be blocked on the basis of these criteria, it is not too risky to assume that, in most of them, the proposed action will pass both tests. This success will then be used by Community institutions in

---

[15]   OJEC L 298/23 of 17 October 1989.
[16]   See, in particular, Art. 4 of Directive 89/552.

order to justify the adoption of Community measures. This probable result is paradoxical: subsidiarity, a tool introduced by the Member States into the ECT to stop Community intervention, would be converted in a complementary argument to justify Community intervention. In other words, those institutions and Member States which support a proposed measure would not only have the traditional arguments in favour of it, but also their stance will be more credible than before: it would, after all, be subsidiarity which would advocate the adoption of the measure, not Member States or the Community institutions. Material subsidiarity, far from constituting an obstacle to Community intervention, may become a tool fostering it. A third problem arises from possible contradictions between the first and second criteria of provision 5. Given that they are cumulative, how does one know when the market distortion elements are more important than the transnational dimension elements (or rather: than the lack of them)?

At this point, one may ask why it is difficult to find substantive criteria to determine whether the Community or the Member States should have the power to act. To start with, it is important to emphasize that such difficulty is not due to contingent reasons, i.e. the special circumstances in which the Maastricht Treaty and ex Article 3b(2) were negotiated. That the problem is instead of a structural kind is shown by the *Report of the Centre for Economic Policy Research for 1993*. This Report is the outcome of a collaborative project between a number of well known economists whose task was to find substantive criteria for the efficient implementation of subsidiarity in the Community. The group was independent of both Community institutions and Member States. The group was also asked to make recommendations as to the best regulatory level for a number of areas ranging from environmental protection to competition law. The results of this research were somewhat deceptive with respect to the virtuosity of subsidiarity. In the words of the group,

Our illustrations of the subsidiarity principle . . . have produced recommendations that were highly dependent on the circumstances of the particular case. In many regulatory areas—with the notable exception of drinking water regulation—we see significant merit in centralised or partially centralised policies, and in many respects the Community's current practices are well thought out (CEPR, 1993:158).

The intricacies involved in defining the best regulatory level are not, as we see, co-substantial with the particular circumstances in which Maastricht was negotiated or to the specific nature of the Community. The truth of the matter is that attempting to define *ex ante* criteria of a general and abstract character for the purpose of limiting central intervention stands little hope of success. The reasons for this limitation are functional and can be found in the nature of modern regulatory problems. The functional interconnection between regulatory areas, and within the same regulatory area among different regulatory levels, makes the task of establishing clear dividing lines difficult. Even in those areas in which there seem to be clear reasons in favour of national, or even regional or local, regulation (culture is a good example, as shown above) it will always be possible to argue that due to the close relationship between these areas and the development of the single market, some Community intervention will always be necessary (Dehousse, 1992:221; Scharpf, 1978). The interdependency between regulatory areas and regulatory levels is such that the criteria of provision 5 of the Protocol on subsidiarity are of little help in preventing Community forays, at least in most cases. It is even possible to argue that the incorporation into the ECT of these substantive criteria will often have the effect contrary to that originally intended. Community intervention, far from being hindered by material subsidiarity, could even be encouraged from the optic of the criteria that the Protocol employs materially to define the principle.

2. *Procedural Subsidiarity*

Subsidiarity in its procedural sense is dealt with in various provisions throughout the Protocol: in provisions 4, 9, 10, 11, 12, and 13. Procedural subsidiarity involves the establishment of a number of procedural obligations—essentially those of motivation and publicity—on the Community institutions and even on Member States. The analysis presented below revolves around the procedural obligations imposed, in particular, on the Commission, the Council, the European Parliament, and the Member States.

(1) *Obligations on the European Commission (exclusively) and on the European Council*

Provision 9 of the Protocol on subsidiarity establishes those procedural obligations which are imposed exclusively on the European Commission. As will be seen below, other provisions of the Protocol impose further obligations on both the Commission and other institutions; those provisions are analysed elsewhere below. The obligations imposed upon the European Council are also examined in this section, since the obligations imposed on the European Council are directly linked to the fulfilment of the Commission's procedural obligations.

Provision 9 reads:

Without prejudice to its right of initiative, the Commission should:
—except in cases of particular urgency or confidentiality, consult widely before
  proposing legislation and, wherever appropriate, publish consultation documents;
—justify the relevance of its proposals with regard to the principle of subsidiarity;
  wherever necessary, the explanatory memorandum accompanying a proposal will
  give details in this respect. The financing of Community action in whole or in part
  from the Community budget shall require an explanation;
—[. . .];
—submit an annual report to the European Council, the European Parliament and
  the Council on the application of Article 3b of the Treaty. This annual report shall
  also be sent to the Committee of the Regions and to the Economic and Social
  Committee.

Provision 9 reproduces almost entirely the most relevant aspects of the
'Overall Approach' on the principle of subsidiarity that was included in the
Edinburgh Conclusions. It also includes the 'Inter-institutional Agreement'
on the principle, insofar as Commission obligations are concerned. In
essence, provision 9 imposes four kinds of obligations on this institution,
being those of consultation, motivation, information, and publication.

With respect to the first, provision 9 says that, save in exceptional cases
(according to that provision, 'urgency and confidentiality', although the
Protocol does not define them), the Commission must consult other bodies
about its legislative proposals before they are sent to the rest of the
Community institutions for approval. Provision 9 indicates that such consultation shall be 'wide', but gives no further guidance in this regard, leaving that
issue in the Commission's discretion. This is problematic, since the
Commission may manipulate that mandate in favour of Community intervention, by focusing on those public or private interests supporting the proposal. The only way to avoid the risk of such manipulation would be to spell
out in more detail who the subjects of consultation are.

As far as motivation obligations are concerned, provision 9 states that
the Commission shall show that each proposal is well founded from the
perspective of subsidiarity. The Commission must show that its proposal is
motivated by the material criteria of provision 5. The second paragraph
establishes, as was proposed by the UK (Bribosia, 1998:42) that proposals
which are to be financed by the Community budget require explanation. In
this respect, the question must be posed as to what kind of explanation the
Commission shall give. At first glance, it seems that the Commission must
explain why the cost of the Community action should be funded by the

Community budget. However, it is possible to interpret this part of provision 9 more widely, so as to reach a different conclusion. In effect, in most cases the Commission will have no problem in justifying why the cost of the Community action has to be charged to the Community's budget since, by definiton, the Commission may only make proposals within the ambit of the Community's competences. If the Community has the competence, then charging the cost of implementing that competence to the Community budget will be justified. This expedient would be easy to fulfil, and as a consequence provision 9 (second paragraph) would be greatly watered down. Yet if provision 9 (second paragraph) is linked with provision 2 *in fine*, then the outcome is a much more rigorous obligation on the Commission. Thus, as pointed out earlier in this Chapter, provision 2 *in fine* establishes the principle of 'sufficiency of means'. This principle has to be respected by the Community institutions when implementing subsidiarity. So the principle of sufficiency of means constitutes a restriction: the Community may only act when it has the means (especially the financial means) to do so. From this perspective, the Commission will have to establish when implementing provision 9 (second paragraph) that the Community has sufficient financial means to act. In order to justify this, the Commission should make an approximate estimate of the financial costs of the proposed action, and allocate that burden to a particular chapter of the Community budget. The consequence of this wide interpretation of provision 9 (second paragraph) is that, if the estimated costs of the Commission's proposed action exceeded the financial means of the Community, this would be a strong indication that the Community should not act. In other words, if from a financial perspective the Community action were not viable, this could be used by the minority in the Council as a strong argument—due to its objectivity—against Community intervention. Furthermore, such analysis might be more easily controlled by the ECJ, again due to its objective nature.

However, it is important to acknowledge that even if the wide interpretation presented above were finally accepted, the Commission's hands would not be completely tied since a major part of Community intervention is regulatory. The reason for this is precisely the limited character of the Community's budget: Community intervention through regulation has the advantage that it involves lower or no budget appropriations. This is precisely why the Commission has opted in general for regulation and not for financial-based interventions (Majone, 1993; 1994a).

Turning to the analysis of the information obligations imposed upon the Commission, provision 9 (fourth paragraph) establishes that the Commission must prepare an annual report on the implementation of the subsidiarity principle. It establishes that the Commission must present this report to the European Council, the European Parliament, and the Council of Ministers. The Commission committed itself to making and presenting that report to the Council of Ministers and the European Parliament after the signature of the Maastricht Treaty.[17] Fernández Esteban (1996:53) points out that during the negotiation of the Interinstitutional Agreement on subsidiarity, it was proposed that this report also be presented to the European Council. However, this proposal was not accepted since the European Parliament argued that it would create an unnecessary procedural burden, and that it would curtail the principle of institutional balance. However, as an informal practice the Commission ha presented this report to the European Council as well since the enactment of the Maastricht Treaty. This informal practice now forms part of the Protocol on subsidiarity.

What must the European Commission establish in these reports? Provision 9 is silent on this point. Therefore, one must turn to the informal practice that the Commission has followed. Reports usually contain the following points.[18] First, the Commission quantifies the legislative proposals that have been put forward that year and compares them with the number of proposals of previous years. Secondly, the Commission quantifies the proposals that it has withdrawn as a consequence of implementing subsidiarity. Thirdly, the Commission recommends which legislative acts should be abrogated because they are contrary to the principle of subsidiarity.

What are the consequences of the presentation of this report? Provision 10 of the Protocol gives a partial answer to this question. It states that the European Council 'shall take account of the Commission report [. . .] within the report on the progress achieved by the Union which it is required to submit to the European Parliament in accordance with Article D of the Treaty on European Union'. It seems therefore that the European Council must take into consideration the Commission's recommendations for withdrawal. If the Commission's recommendations are taken into account, then the European Council may in turn recommend to the Council of Ministers and the European Parliament the withdrawal of those legal acts. However,

---

[17] *Interinstitutional Agreement* on subsidiarity, cited above.

[18] The Commission has produced the following reports on the application of the principle of subsidiarity: 1) (COM(94) 533 final, of 25 November 1994); 2) (CSE(95) 580 final of 22 November 1995); 3) (CSE(96) 7 final of 27 November 1996); 4) (COM(97) 626 final of 6 November 1997); 5) COM(98) 345 final of 27 May 1998); 6) idem (COM(98) 715 final of 1 December 1998); 7) (COM (99) 562 final of 3 November 1999; 8) COM(2000) 772 final of 30 November 2000; 9) COM(2001) 728 final of 7 December 2001..

the European Council has no power to impose withdrawal on the Council and the European Parliament. Only the Council and the European Parliament have legislative powers to withdraw. The Protocol is silent as to the procedure to be followed by the Council and the EP for withdrawal. It is clear that, for legal acts adopted jointly by the Council and the EP, both institutions have to agree to withdraw. This may pose problems, even where both institutions are in principle in favour of withdrawal. For example, which voting procedure should be implemented when the legal act concerned was approved unanimously and now the voting procedure requires a majority vote for the same kind of legal acts? It seems that the latter should be employed. The problem here is that a Member State which approved the measure under unanimity may be against withdrawal under majority voting. Therefore, in theory, the measure could be withdrawn against its will. In this situation, Member States in the minority might claim that the former procedure should be applied. How can this dilemma be solved?[19]

My view is that the Community should opt in such cases for those procedures which best facilitate the withdrawal of the measure. In my example, majority voting should be preferred to unanimity. This interpretation is more in line with the *telos* of Article 5(2) ECT. It is important to take into account that the problem of withdrawal is not posed on its own merits, but on the basis of the implementation of the subsidiarity principle. Therefore, one may infer that withdrawal involves a sort of retroactive implementation of the principle. It is evident, however, that this way of operating has its limits, principally in order to respect the *acquis communautiare*, as provision 2 of the Protocol requires. The return to more rigorous procedures would be possible only when it was perceived that the *acquis communautaire* was in peril.

The publication obligations imposed upon the Commission can be found in the first part of provision 9, which states that 'the Commission should [. . .] wherever appropriate, publish consultation documents'. The expression 'wherever appropriate' is to be interpreted expansively. Thus, leaving aside cases of 'particular urgency or confidentiality', the rule is that they must be published. The practice of consulting and publishing the results of consultation is as old as the Community. The Commission traditionally uses the Green Papers and White Papers to present to the public the results of consultation, among other things.[20] Even if the formalization of this practice in a legal text is

---

[19] Of course, this is more a political dilemma than a legal one. In strict legal terms, the procedure to be applied should be the one that is in force.

[20] White Papers are also used to specify Commission preferences.

an improvement, it is obvious that provision 9(1) will not have a large impact in this regard, since it only juridifies the Commission's existing practice.

However, there is one context in which provision 9 may modify the Commission's practice as far as publication is concerned. Article 19 of the Commission's regulation[21] establishes what is known in Community jargon as 'inter-service consultation'. Inter-service consultation has to take place before the Commission decides to propose the adoption of a particular act. However, inter-service consultations are not made public. Provision 9 of the Protocol on subsidiarity with respect to inter-service consultation could imply that the outcome of that consultation should be made public. After all, the expression 'consult widely' in provision 9 may also be related to internal Commission consultations. The advantage would be that the public would know what the Commission really thinks about the need for a certain measure, which in turn would be an important element in attaining control over the Commission. Obviously, there would be limitations as well: confidentiality and, which is maybe more important, the Commission's expression of its true views through the inter-service consultation should not be hindered in any event. However, neither obstacle is definitive. For example, the Commission could consider publishing a summary of the inter-service consultation, and not the entire dossier.

In concluding this section it is important to stress the existence of a lacuna in provision 9. From the perspective of publication, the problem is that it does not impose on the Commission an obligation to publish the explanatory memorandum which, according to the provision, must accompany the proposals of the Commission. The silence of the Protocol on this point is unfortunate since, as provision 9(2) indicates, it is in the explanatory memorandum that the Commission has to explain its position on subsidiarity[22] in detail. The alternative solution—to impose the publication of the explanatory memorandum—would have been a complementary guarantee that the principle is truly being implemented by the European Commission.

(2) Obligations on the Council of Ministers and the European Parliament

Provision 11 of the Protocol on subsidiarity imposes on the Council of Ministers (or Council of the European Union) and the European Parliament an obligation to examine the proposals put to them by the Commission from

---

[21] Commission Rules of Procedure of 18 September 1999 (OJEC L 252/41 of 25 September 1999).

[22] It is not enough to say that the Preamble of the measure has, as provision 4 of the Protocol establishes, to include a reference to subsidiarity, as is argued later in this Chapter.

the angle of subsidiarity. It also establishes that amendments introduced by the EP or the Council to the Commission proposals must also respect the principle. Provision 11 reads as follows:

While fully observing the procedures applicable, the European Parliament and the Council shall, as an integral part of the overall examination of the Commission proposals, consider their consistency with Article 5(2) ECT. This concerns the original Commission proposal as well as amendments which the European Parliament and the Council envisage making to the proposal.

To start with, the examination of the Commission's proposals from the angle of subsidiarity is not separate from the overall examination of the measure. In other words, the proposal is not examined from the perspective of subsidiarity *prior* to the examination of the other issues posed by the proposal. Some Member States suggested, when the principle was introduced by Maastricht, a separate examination of the proposal from the perspective of subsidiarity. However, this was not accepted then, nor has it been accepted in the Protocol on subsidiarity. Since the examination of subsidiarity will be made together with the examination of the rest of the issues in the proposal, it is clear that the former will be somewhat diluted. It is also true that separating the two aspects would have placed an extra burden on the Community decision-making process. In other words, the costs in terms of efficiency of having two separate examinations would probably have been perceived to be greater than its benefits from the perspective of the protection of minorities.

Provision 11 of the Protocol establishes, as noted above, that any amendments, as well as the proposals, must be examined by the Council and the European Parliament from the perspective of subsidiarity. This is an attempt to eliminate or at least to obstruct European Parliament and Council attempts to circumvent subsidiarity through amending the Commission's proposal. Further, although provision 11 is unclear on this point, it may be that both institutions are obliged not only to implement subsidiarity when amending, but also to keep tabs on each other as far as the implementation of subsidiarity is concerned. This seems logical, taking into account that provision 11 probably intends to establish between the three institutions a system of subsidiarity 'checks and balances'. Thus, if the European Parliament proposes amendments that are not in accordance with the subsidiarity principle in the context of, say, the co-decision procedure, then the Council should be obliged to examine those amendments from the perspective of subsidiarity and to point out any breach of the principle. In theory at least, one of the arguments which could be raised by any of these institutions aggainst accepting proposed amendments would be the lack of conformity with the principle.

However, this second aspect may be more problematic. I refer in particular to the cases in which the Council introduces amendments to the Commission's proposal for subsidiarity reasons, and then the European Parliament examines and blocks them, also for subsidiarity reasons. In this case, if the Council introduces modifications to the Commission proposal, it has to do so (in principle) by unanimity, according to Article 250(1) ECT (ex Article 189a(1)). If all Member States agree that modifications should be introduced into the Commission proposal, it is not clear why the European Parliament should be able to block those amendments for subsidiarity reasons. In effect, if one considers again the *telos* of the principle, this is to protect minoritarian Member States in the Council but not the European Parliament. In other words, subsidiarity was introduced into the ECT as a guarantee of the 'statal' legitimacy on which the Community is partly based, not as a guarantee of the popular legitimacy on which it is also partly based, and which is represented by the EP. For this reason, the parallel between the Council and the European Parliament, as far as the implementation of subsidiarity is concerned, lacks solid theoretical foundations. The principle of institutional balance (which is in my view the only thing that can explain why Member States decided to introduce such parallelism into the Protocol) should not have gone so far as to allow this development.

Finally, it is evident that the day-to-day implementation of provision 11 by the Council and the European Parliament will depend on the voting procedure that applies in each case. It is not clear how a Member State opposed to the Commission proposal for reasons of subsidiarity can prevent the adoption of the measure unless the procedure to be followed is unanimity, or unless this Member State can convince a majority of the European Parliament to vote against the adoption of the measure, which in some cases only (co-decision procedure) will mean a definitive veto. In other words, provision 11 comes down in essence to a matter of procedures, as with other provisions of the Protocol on subsidiarity.

(3) Obligations on the Council of Ministers (exclusively)

Provision 12 of the Protocol on subsidiarity imposes an information obligation on the Council of Ministers. Provision 12 reads as follows:

In the course of the procedures referred to in Articles 189b and 189c of the Treaty, the European Parliament shall be informed of the Council's position on the application of Article 3b of the Treaty, by way of a statement of the reasons which led the Council to adopt its common position. The Council shall inform the European Parliament of the reasons on the basis of which all or part of a Commission proposal is deemed to be inconsistent with Article 3b of the Treaty.

The Council is obliged by provision 12 to explain its stance on subsidiarity to the European Parliament when drafting common positions (thus in the co-operation and co-decision procedures). This explanation must be incorporated in the statement of reasons which the Council must send to the European Parliament with the aim of explaining why the former adopted a common position. The Council is also obliged to explain to the European Parliament if it believes that a given Commission proposal is not in line, wholly or partly, with subsidiarity.

In order to interpret the first of the rules established by provision 12, it is necessary to recall that Articles 251 and 252 of the ECT establish that when the Council adopts a common position then it 'shall inform the European Parliament fully of the reasons which led it to adopt its common position'.[23] Provision 12 details the general requirement for information established by those ECT Articles as far as subsidiarity is concerned. Provision 12 may also be connected with provision 11, insofar as the latter complements the former. Thus the Council not only has to examine compliance with subsidiarity when it makes amendments (which, in the framework of the co-decision and co-operation procedures may amount to a common position) but, according to provision 12, it must also inform the European Parliament of such modifications if it reaches a common position. This requirement for information is, however, restricted to the co-decision and co-operation procedures, and, within these procedures, to common positions.

With this obligation to inform about common positions, it is necessary to recall that they may be adopted by either unanimity or majority vote. If a common position is adopted by unanimity this implies that all Member States think that there are no problems from the perspective of subsidiarity with proposed Community action. Articles 251 and 252 also envisage a common

---

[23] Art. 251. Art. 252 introduces a slight modification, since it says that 'the Council and the Commission shall inform the European Parliament fully of the reasons which led the Council to adopt its common position and also of the Commission's position'. However, the reference to the Commission in Art. 252 must be read in connection with the obligation of the Commission to inform the European Parliament about its own position, and not about the Council's common position. Therefore the result is that Arts. 251 and 252 say the same thing regarding the Council's obligation to explain its common position to the European Parliament.

position adopted by a qualified majority.[24] This means that some Member States opposed the adoption of the measure. In this case, those opposed to the measure will have the opportunity to explain why, from their perspective, the measure does not comply with the subsidiarity principle in the statement of reasons accompanying the common position. If the argument of the minority is well articulated, this could convince the European Parliament of the need to block the adoption of the measure for subsidiarity reasons. In other words, the European Parliament may be a good ally of those Member States in the minority, and the 'statement of reasons' included in the common position is the mechanism which can trigger that alliance.

The second rule of provision 12 is a development of what is established in provision 11 relating to the control by the Council of the Commission's proposal insofar as subsidiarity is concerned. The second rule of provision 12 imposes on the Council the obligation to inform the European Parliament when it finds that the Commission's proposal is not in line with subsidiarity. Although this part of the text is very obscure, it is possible to make the following interpretation: the second rule of provision 12 is aimed at two different cases. The first is the case in which the Council finds that the Commission's proposal is not in line with subsidiarity at all. In such a case, the Council would simply reject the Commission's proposal.

The second kind of case is that in which, although the Council thinks that the Commission's proposal is not in line with subsidiarity, it thinks that the contradiction is only partial. The Council would then modify those aspects of the Commission's proposal which are contrary to subsidiarity. The Council would adopt a common position, if it were in the framework of the co-decision and the co-operation procedure (and the second rule of provision 12 would then be saying the same thing as the first rule) or not, if it were outside the framework of the co-operation or co-decision procedures.

Therefore, the crux of the matter is that, according to the second rule of provision 12, the Council has to inform the European Parliament independently of whether or not it adopts a common position. In other words, the first rule of provision 12 would be considered in the second rule, but would also go beyond that. Thus even outside the co-operation and co-decision procedures, the Council has to inform the European Parliament of why it finds that a given Commission proposal is partially or totally contrary to subsidiarity. This is independent of the procedure in which the decision-making process takes place. The second rule of provision 12 should therefore not be linked

---

[24] Which, obviously, does not exclude the possibility that the common position be adopted by unanimity.

with the first rule of that provision. Accordingly, since the two rules do not have as their factual bases the exact same cases, it would have been much clearer to separate them in different provisions.

What is the purpose of the requirement of information to the Parliament in the second rule of provision 12? The answer depends on whether the Parliament has any decisional capacity. In cases in which the Parliament has no decisional powers, the purpose of provision 12 is merely informative. When the Parliament does have decisional capacity (especially when such decisional capacity is of a definitive character, as in co-decision and the assent procedure) and when the Council has not simply rejected the Commission's proposal, the EP may reject the Council act if it does not agree with the examination that the Council has made of the Commission proposal, as far as subsidiarity is concerned. Again, it is possible to argue that leaving the final say to the European Parliament in subsidiarity matters is contrary to the *telos* of the principle. The concerns set out above apply here as well.[25] In other words, the second rule of provision 12 would not make much sense in cases in which, as a consequence of its implementation, the EP stopped the adoption of the measure, since subsidiarity aims at protecting minoritarian Member States, not the EP powers.

(4) Obligations on Community institutions and Member States relating to their powers of legislative proposal

Provision 4 of the Protocol on subsidiarity imposes a number of procedural obligations upon those Community institutions which have the power to propose legislation.[26] It also imposes obligations on the Member States relating to their power to propose legislation.[27] Provision 4 reads as follows:

---

[25] Note section E2(2) above.

[26] Naturally, this concerns above all the European Commission, but not the Commission alone. For example, the European Central Bank has been attributed competences of decisional proposal through Art. 111(2) ECT (ex Art. 109 ECT). Independent of how one understands that decisional power (of administrative or legislative character) it is certain that, since the ECT does not differentiate between the two categories, provision 4 must be applicable here as well.

[27] Member States have the power of legislative proposal in, for example, Art. 67(1) ECT (ex Art. 73O(1)). Bribosia (1998:44) argues that the procedural obligations of provision 4 are imposed upon the European Parliament and the Council as well, on the basis of what this author calls 'the power of indirect proposal' of these institutions (Arts. 192 and 208 (ex Arts. 138b and 152, respectively)). From my perspective, Arts. 192 and 208 constitute a power of petition, and not of proposal, for the Commission. The Commission may therefore reject such petitions from the EP and the Council. Bribosia's interpretation seems to be excessive: provision 4 would not apply to the EP and the Council in these cases.

For any proposed Community legislation, the reasons on which it is based shall be stated with a view to justifying its compliance with the principle of subsidiarity [. . .]; the reasons for concluding that a Community objective can be better achieved by the Community must be substantiated by qualitative or, wherever possible, quantitative indicators.

This is one of the most important provisions of the Protocol on subsidiarity. In essence, it establishes two rules: first, it imposes the use of qualitative indicators, and wherever possible of quantitative indicators, as a method of determining when Community action is necessary; and secondly, it establishes that the reasons for the proposed act must be explained.

The first rule constitutes a major Amsterdam innovation that was not present in any of the documents which the Community institutions and Member States produced in the aftermath of the Maastricht negotiations. According to provision 4, mere rhetorical explanations will not be enough when an institution or a Member State is proposing legislation. The proposal must be supported by quantitative reasoning. Only as a second best alternative may qualitative reasoning be used.

This Amsterdam innovation raises many issues. To start with, an obvious question emerges: what will these indicators indicate? This is an important question since the recourse to indicators will be of no practical relevance if it is not known what they should indicate. Provision 4 is silent on this point. However, the probable answer to this question can be inferred from provision 5, which establishes material subsidiarity. Therefore, the indicators of provision 4 should *measure* whether and to what extent there is a 'transnational dimension' and whether and to what extent the lack of Community action will create 'market distorsions'.

The first question immediately raises a second one, on limits. The second question is at what point it can be decided whether a particular problem has a transnational dimension or when it produces market distortions. This is not clarified by the Protocol. This is because that question cannot be answered in general and abstract terms: the answer depends on each case. It is clear, however, that except in very obvious cases the ultimate solution will be contingent on the correlation of forces at Council level. This is illustrated with one simple example. Let us assume that the Commission has established that a certain industrial activity has, for example, a transnational impact equivalent to 25 per cent. It therefore proposes more stringent environmental standards for the protection of, for example, the atmosphere. Germany agrees with the Commission: for this Member State, a 25 per cent impact is important enough to justify the Community measure on transnational grounds. Say, however, that Greece opposes Community intervention: for this Member State, an impact less than 50 per cent means no impact at all. Below that percentage, the Community should therefore not act. In my example, the problem would ultimately be solved through voting. The extent of the transnational impact of the regulatory problem at hand would simply be one more aspect for convincing Member States who oppose the measure to embrace it, and vice versa. We therefore see that, in the last resort, the question of limits comes down to a question of values and interests.

In my example there is one flaw, however. It assumes that the transnational or market distortion aspects of a regulatory problem are easily measured from a quantitative perspective. This is clearly not the case. On the contrary, it will be difficult in the majority of the cases to measure impact by quantitative parameters. This is acknowledged by the Protocol itself when it says that the 'reasons for concluding that a Community objective can be better achieved by the Community must be substantiated by qualitative or, *wherever possible*, quantitative parameters'. Measuring by quantitative parameters undoubtedly leaves fewer margins for discretion. Conversely, qualitative methods leave more room for political assessment. The Community's constituent is aware of this, but is also aware that measuring by quantitative parameters is an impossible task in most cases. It is therefore probable that the Commission will opt for qualitative rather than for quantitative parameters in most cases. The result is that the innovation contained in provision 4 of the Protocol will have very limited practical impact.

Not only is it clear that the use of indicators is not an effective hindrance to the Community's impulses to act, due to the pre-eminence of qualitative measurement methods over quantitative ones, but it is also possible that the use of indicators may turn into a shelter for Community intervention. In effect, although the procedural obligations derived from Protocol 30 (the protocol on subsidiarity) apply to all Community institutions with power to propose legislation, it is clear that they are of more concern to the Commission. Thus provision 4 reinforces, for the Commission, the procedural obligations which provision 9 imposes on this institution alone.

Now, the fact that the Commission is the institution with the main duty to measure is especially problematic given that it occupies a far from neutral position in the Community's decision-making process. As I have pointed out in a different context (Estella, 1998a; Estella, 1999d) the European Commission has played an essential role as an engine of the European integration process. In fact, the activism that this institution deploys at Community level is one of the main independent variables explaining the

Community's tendency towards competential (especially regulatory) growth. Taking this into account, it is probable that the Commission will use the information arsenal it has at its disposal in order to foster European integration (giving it a veneer of objectivity) rather than to play a more neutral role in that process.

In conclusion, the use of technical and scientific knowledge is almost never a neutral device, but it serves to achieve agencies' objectives.[28] This is not to claim as the critical law school might, that everything is politics. Far from it. There are issues that are clearly outside politics and have more to do with technique. As Shapiro puts it, (quoting the so-called American Progressive movement) 'there is no Republican or Democratic way to pave a street, only the right way' (Shapiro, 1988:60). Rather, the idea is that agencies take advantage of the opportunities they have to use strategically the resources (basically information) at their disposal. Agencies are also political players, with their own agendas and policy preferences. The Commission is no exception to this rule. Therefore, the obligation to measure could be used by this institution as a way to justify the need for Community action, sheltering critics of hyper-regulation under an enormous amount of data: after all, it was the Member States themselves who decided to impose this way of operating on the Commission. In other words, it is highly likely that provision 4 will benefit the Commission in the end.

To sum up, although the first rule of provision 4 is, in principle, a further guarantee for Member States in a minority at Council level, in practice this guarantee will be ineffective. The reason is two-fold. First, it will be difficult in many cases to make quantitative analyses. Qualitative analyses will probably have pre-eminence. The problem with qualitative analyses is that they may be more easily manipulated. Secondly, even where quantitative analysis is possible, it remains problematic that the Commission (primarily) makes this analyses. It is highly likely that the Commission strategically employs information to advance its policy preferences and uphold Community intervention.

The second aspect is more problematic than the first. An example will illustrate that this problem is, far from being theoretical, a very real one. The example is taken from the Commission policy on postal liberalization. In December 1995 the European Commission proposed a draft directive on the adoption of common norms for the development of the postal sector and

---

[28]   Shapiro (1996b) also gives evidence of this for the American context.

the improvement of postal service quality.[29] The proposed measure aimed at the liberalization of Member States' postal markets and at the establishment of regulatory measures for the sector.

Apart from the political sensitivity that any Community intervention in public monopolies produces in Member States, the postal example would be less relevant if the Commission had merely proposed minimal Community involvement in the matter. However, the Commission's proposal went considerably beyond that. Besides liberalization measures,[30] the Directive established important regulatory measures such as the splitting of the commercial and regulatory functions of the national monopoly, not only for cross-border mail but for all of its activities. Further, the Commission established, in Article 16 of the Directive, a division of tasks between the Community and Member States as to the setting of quality standards (for national mail for Member States, and for cross-border mail for the Community). However, it is submitted that this division was more apparent than real. It would be naïve to think that once Community standards were implemented by the Member States they would follow different standards depending on the origin of the

[29] Proposal no. 95/C 322/10 COM(95) final-95/0221 (COD) (OJEC C 322/22 of 2 December 1995). Once the negotiation process concluded, the proposal was adopted as Directive 97/67 (OJEC L 15/14 of 21 January 1998). The Directive retains the main aspects of the Commission proposal.

[30] As far as liberalization is concerned, the proposal aimed at a smooth and gradual narrowing of national monopolies. In particular, Art. 8 of the proposal established two separate regimes, one for the letter segment and the other for incoming cross-border mail and direct mail. As far as the first is concerned, the proposal said that the collection, sorting, transport, and delivery (outward and inward activities) of items of domestic correspondence could be reserved for the Member States 'to the extent necessary to ensure the maintenance of the universal service'. The same Article limited the possibility of removing this market segment from competition through establishing a combined weight and price criteria (350g and five times the public tariff of an item of correspondence in the first weight step). This meant that those items of domestic correspondence weighing more than 350g, or costing more than five times the tariff of the first weight step, would be, according to the proposal, collected, sorted, transported, and delivered under conditions of free competition. Secondly, the proposal established a sunsetting mechanism in the third proviso of Art. 8 *juncto* Art. 23. According to both Articles, the Commission would (if applicable) propose to the European Parliament and the Council to review the extent of the reserved area (as far as the letter segment is concerned) in the first half of the year 2000 at the latest. In this re-examination process it would be assisted by a 'review' body composed of five independent experts appointed by the Commission.

Concerning incoming cross-border mail and direct mail, the proposal established, in its Art. 8 para. 2, that only the distribution would be reserved until the end of the year 2000 insofar as this was necessary for the financial equilibrium of the universal service provider. The same paragraph established a review mechanism by which the Commission would decide, on 30 June 1998 at the latest, on the convenience of maintaining the reservation of those services after 31 December 2000. As has been already pointed out, the Commission proposal was, in general, retained by the Community legislative branch.

item. The final result would be the uniformization of standards according to the standard set at Community level. In short, both aspects show the significant impact that the proposed Commission measure would have upon Member States' autonomy.

Aware of the sensitivity of the case, the Commission added a subsidiarity assessment to its directive proposal. In its explanatory memorandum, the Commission examined four points: 1) the objectives of the action envisaged; 2) the Community dimension of the problem; 3) the need for Community action; and 4) the potential benefits of a directive. Only points 1 and 2 deal directly with subsidiarity, since they entail the 'effects' and 'dimension' criteria. Points 3 and 4 deal with the proportionality principle. I therefore concentrate here on the first two points.

In the first point, the Commission stated that

the principal objective of the action envisaged is to guarantee in the whole European Union the long term provision of a good quality universal service at affordable prices, accessible to all, for which financing is assured and durable. In particular, the alignment of conditions governing the supply of postal services and the removal of legal and technical barriers to cross-border trade are obligations which are incumbent on the Community in order to attain the internal market.

In short, the argument was that there was a need for Community action not because of the merits of regulating the postal sector, but because of the *effects* that the operation of postal services could have upon the achievement of the single market. This connection between the two aspects is evident for cross-border mail: inefficient cross-border mail services would have a direct negative impact upon economic cross-border transactions. This seems clear, unless the cross-border segment of postal activity were relatively insignificant in terms of volume of mail.

That is the question that the Commission answered in its analysis in point two. As regards the Community dimension of the problem, the Commission established that 'postal traffic in the Community involves 80 billion items per year, some 3 billion of which are associated with intra-Community trade'. The words of the Commission offer some ground for confusion. One might be tempted to think that the Community dimension of the problem was important since the volume of Community traffic was 80 billion items per year, 3 billion of which consisted specifically of mail between the Member States *for trading purposes*. The question is whether the remainder of the 80 billion was mail *between* Member States for purposes different from trade, or whether it included the mail circulating *inside* each Member State. The difference is not unimportant. In the first case, the relevance of the problem in quantitative terms would be considerable. In the second case, it would clearly be unimportant, since the volume of mail circulation among Member States would be insignificant (approximately 4 per cent of the figures given by the Commission).

What the Commission was saying is clearer if one considers the Green Paper on Posts.[31] The figure of 80 billion represented, in reality, the number of mail items that circulated within the Member States, not mail circulating across the Community. The figure of 3 billion represented cross-border mail. According to Commission data established in the Green Paper on Posts, the truth of the matter was that cross-border mail amounted to only 4 per cent of the total volume of mail. This was indeed a relatively small figure to establish a 'Community dimension' of the problem. Furthermore, the Community dimension is even less significant if one considers that much cross-border mail traffic is express mail, and that express mail had already been liberalized, if not *de iure*, then *de facto*,[32] in most Member States.[33] However, these data were not clarified in the Commission's memorandum on subsidiarity.

What conclusions can be extracted from the postal case in connection to the general argument presented here? They are, at least, two-fold. On one hand, the example of posts shows that parameters (even quantitative ones) may be subject to strategic use by the Commission; on the other, it shows that, irrespective of whether data show that the Community's dimension of the problem is irrelevant, the Commission will attempt to justify Community intervention. In effect, if the Commission was objectively basing its proposals on subsidiarity, it should have proposed no intervention at all, or at least a less intensive measure, in the postal case. This was not, however, the case. In

---

[31] COM(91) 476 final, of 11 June 1992.

[32] Point 16 of the Preamble of the proposed directive.

[33] Commission Green Paper on the development of the Single Market for Postal Services, COM(91) 476 final of 11 June 1992, page 110. The figures are the following: domestic mail amounts to 93% of the volume; intra-Community cross-border mail amounts to 4% of the volume; extra-Community cross-border mail amounts to 3% of the volume. There are no figures regarding the volume of cross-border mail that may be placed in the express mail category. However, if the fact is taken into account that private operators are concentrated in the cream-skimming area of the market, which is express cross-border mail (both intra- and extra-Community), and that they control 4% of the total mail market in terms of volume, one can easily come to the conclusion that the part of Community cross-border mail that belongs to the category of express mail, being already liberalized, must be of significance. This implies that the part of cross-border mail which is not yet liberalized is almost irrelevant in terms of volume of mail. Notice that the significance of cross-border mail serves as the basis for the Commission to uphold, on the ground of subsidiarity, the need for Community action in this area.

short, the discussion on posts shows the built-in limitations of the first rule of provision 4.

Turning to the analysis of the second rule of provision 4, this establishes, as stated above, the obligation to state the reasons that justify the need for the proposal. This rule has some ambiguities. The first is that it is unclear what should be understood by the word 'state'. Should the Commission merely reveal the motives of its proposal to the Community legislator, or must it publish them? It is clear that the statement of the reasons will be included in the Commission's 'memorandum on subsidiarity' that accompanies its proposals. However, the Protocol does not oblige the Commission to publish it. In the second place, this provision does not seem to impose on the Community's legislator the obligation to state subsidiarity motives in the preamble of the definitive act (of the act eventually adopted). In effect, provision 4 refers to *proposed* legislation, not actual legislation. This is an important gap. As will be seen,[34] the ECJ has bridged this gap in its case-law on subsidiarity, by obliging the Community legislator to state subsidiarity motives in the preamble of any legal act it adopts. However, it would have been clearer if the Protocol itself had incorporated this case-law. Furthermore, as will also be seen, the ECJ case-law has not solved the problem of the extent of the obligation to state reasons in the preamble: is a mere reference to Article 5(2) enough, or must the Community legislator give detailed reasoning? Undoubtedly, the Protocol would have offered a good opportunity to resolve this matter. This opportunity has been, however, lost, since there is no reference in provision 4, or in any other part of the Protocol, to this problem.

F. Conclusions: the functional and normative limits of subsidiarity

At this juncture it is possible to summarize the points made in the previous Chapter and in this one. The first question I attempted to answer was whether, from a functional perspective, the principle of subsidiarity constitutes an effective tool to block or at least to restrain Community intervention. That is to say, if one or more Member States are in a minority at the Council level, and they raise subsidiarity as an argument against the adoption of a proposal they dislike, will this be effective for that purpose? In order to answer

---

[34] See Chapter V below.

this question, it is clear that the essential issue is the ECJ's stance on subsidiarity. This is examined in the next Chapter. However, this Chapter and the previous one have established the theoretical basis of what that answer could be. In my view there are sufficient indications in the analysis presented above to cast many doubts on the effectiveness of subsidiarity as a check on Community intervention. There are a number of arguments which justify scepticism towards subsidiarity. To start with, material subsidiarity, which is expressed as the 'transitional dimension' and the 'market distortion' criteria, is by itself incapable of offering a clear-cut answer to the question of whether the Community should or should not act. In effect, as has been examined in this Chapter, it is easy in most cases to offer arguments both for and against Community intervention from both perspectives. Furthermore, the 'transnational dimension' and the 'market distortion' criteria can be contradictory to each other. Reconciling this contradiction is not an easy task. In principle, the cumulative character of the two criteria should indicate that, in a case of conflict, the Community should not act. However, the *vis attractiva* of the market objectives of the ECT may recommend the contrary solution. In any case, it is probable that even the most detailed analysis often gives no definitive answers, or that Community intervention is finally upheld. The latter would be a paradoxical result, especially given the *telos* of the principle, which is to protect minorities in the Council.

Secondly, it is also unlikely that procedural subsidiarity will fill the lacuna left by the material side of the principle. Procedural subsidiarity has two chief aspects: the obligation to motivate and the eventual obligation to publish such motivation. There is, however, some doubt regarding both aspects. As regards motivation, it is clear that the weight of this obligation will fall upon the Commission, since it is best suited to perform that task. Yet the dominance of the Commission here is not problem-free. The Commission has a clear interest in the progress of integration, and this increases the possibility that its subsidiarity analyses will be biased towards the Community side. As regards publication obligations, this fundamental procedural safeguard is very weakly articulated in the Protocol. In effect, as this Chapter has established, the extent of this obligation is unclear on the face of the Protocol. Provision 9 also does not specify whether the Commission must publish its explanatory memorandum on subsidiarity. What is the sense of imposing extensive motivation obligations on Community institutions (in particular, on the Commission) if the obligation to publish statements of reasons is not clearly established? This undoubtedly calls into question the operation of the principle. It is probable that the *praxis* before Amsterdam, according to which the preamble of legal acts included a very general and superficial reference to the principle, has been perpetuated. This limits the ability of the ECJ to control Community intervention on the basis of subsidiarity. The only way out of this situation would be for the ECJ, through its case-law, to require a more in-depth statement of reasons in the preamble. However, as shall be seen in the next Chapter, this does not at present seem to be the intention of the ECJ.

Among the other obligations imposed on Community institutions by procedural subsidiarity, the innovations concerning the Council's obligation to inform the European Parliament of its subsidiarity stance are noteworthy. This mechanism could be used to build alliances between the minority in the Council and the European Parliament in order to stop an instance of Community intervention. However, in most cases such an alliance will be difficult to bring about, since the European Parliament generally attempts to avoid the appearance of constantly hampering Community integration. As Dehousse remarked, the reform of the co-decision procedure in Amsterdam, which eliminated the European Parliament's veto in the so-called third reading, was prompted by the EP itself, precisely to avoid projecting a negative image to European public opinion when vetoing proposals (Dehousse, 1998). This supports the theory that the EP may not be so interested in obstructing Community intervention on the ground of subsidiarity. A final point is that, despite this, from a theoretical perspective it is somewhat inconsistent that the EP becomes the final guarantor of subsidiarity. Given the *telos* of the principle, the protection of the minoritarian Member States in the Council, and not the EP, the solution of the Protocol may be deemed somewhat odd.

We therefore see that, from a functional perspective, the possibility of subsidiarity becoming an effective mechanism to protect minorities in the Council is rather slim. Even if the interpretations proposed above (which have attempted to exploit the Protocol to its fullest) were to be accepted, the outcome would be approximately the same. Therefore, the conclusion is that the Protocol on subsidiarity seems not to answer many of the questions which surfaced when Article 3(b)2, now Article 5(2), was introduced into the ECT. Certainly, the Protocol constitutes a step forward in that it resolves the problem of the legal effects of the acts that served as its basis (the Commission communication on subsidiarity and its progeny). However, it is disappointing in the sense that, except for some innovations, the Protocol merely incorporates what was already in those soft law acts. Further, the most important part of the Protocol, its procedural dimension, has so many flaws that it raises doubts about the future impact which the principle might have in effectively stopping Community intervention.

Subsidiarity is problematic not only from a functional perspective, but also from a normative one. Here we leave the relatively safe waters of analysis and enter the rougher ones of normative elucidation. This is an important point. It has been forcefully argued (see, in general, Macormick 1999, in particular Chapter 9, MacCormick, 1994; 1995) that the philosophy underlying subsidiarity could constitute a good foundation for reconstructing the relations between the Union and the Member States on a more flexible basis. The thesis of this work is the opposite one. The reasons for this are the following. To start with, it is important to go back to the basic question that subsidiarity attempts to answer: given that the Community has competence in a given area, is it appropriate that it adopt a particular act belonging to that area? The question points to a matter of opportunity, not of competence; or if one prefers, to a matter of political values, and not of legal techniques. However, it is interesting to see that subsidiarity answers a question that is political in nature with the language, and with the substance, of technique. Subsidiarity proposes two tests, the 'transnational dimension' and the 'market distortion' tests, that the Community has to pass in order to be able to answer 'yes, it is appropriate that we act'. As we have seen, subsidiarity is not an effective tool for stopping Community intervention. But imagine that subsidiarity *were* effective: then the answer to the previous question would only be contingent on a technical matter. If the dimension of a given problem was transnational, and the Community's inaction produced distortions in the market, then the Community would have to act; and conversely, if the answer was negative, then the Community would not have to act.

This outcome would be very problematic. If it is assumed that the previous question is political, and therefore its answer is a value judgement, then why should it then be resolved according to technical criteria? Why should politics depend on technique? The idea is not to deny that political questions should not take technical issues into account: that would be absurd. The problem is that the debate on subsidiarity gives the impression that the *political* space for discussion should be sacrificed on the altar of technocracy.

Subsidiarity poses a second normative problem, which points to values. Shaw (1995a; 1995b) has argued convincingly that the European construction has been traditionally guided by the 'integration' value. However, since Maastricht (if not before) there have been growing indications that the 'integration' value has started to coexist with contradictory values, such as that of diversity, in the Community context. Subsidiarity embodies the value of 'diversity'. Its introduction into the ECT as a new general principle for the

Community is the clearest symbol that the Community has become, at the level of values, a more complex, less one-sided, setting. Furthermore, given this current state of affairs at the Community level, it would be difficult to establish any hierarchy as between the two values.[35] The idea is rather that integration and diversity can coexist. In effect, whereas the value of 'integration' implies an underlying legitimate demand for more unity, the value of 'diversity' represents a correlative underlying an equally legitimate demand for more decentralization. To combine the two values (and their underlying demands) would only be possible if the Community ceased to depend, as it has been doing up to now, on a 'vertical' logic and moved instead towards a 'horizontal' one. This shift would involve the progressive abandonment of the approach to relations between the Union and the States in terms of top-down imposition and hierarchy which has so dominated the Community up to now. Here is not the place to propose solutions, but if I had to propose one I would propose the principle of reinforced co-operation.

Now, if this normative stance is sensible, then subsidiarity appears to be a very problematic instrument. We are referring now to subsidiarity not so much as a value, but as an instrument. Logically, according to the principle of subsidiarity, the question 'should we act?' can have only two possible answers: yes or no. That is, any assessment of subsidiarity may result in one of two possible alternatives, either to uphold Community intervention or to deny it.[36] This being the case, then subsidiarity as an instrument must underlie a vertical logic, rather than a horizontal one. Put more simply, it is very difficult to think of flexible solutions in which 'integration' and 'diversity' may both be accommodated, since either the Community will act, with all its consequences, or not, with all its implications. However, from the perspective of subsidiarity, intervention and non-intervention at the same time would be simply impossible. In some regards, subsidiarity shares the list of instruments of a vertical kind, such as supremacy: in reality, subsidiarity may be viewed as a sort of 'inverted supremacy'. It is interesting to note that the literature on European integration is starting to examine alternatives to (most notably) supremacy, while focusing on subsidiarity as a new panacea for the Union (see MacCormick, 1999). But subsidiarity is no panacea: it is simply a way of applying an old logic under a new label.

[35] This idea is explored in more detail in Harlow (2000).

[36] An opposing view is that of Endo (2001), who argues that '[the strength of subsidiarity] lies in the ability to moderate and contain the absolutism of any level in a multi-level and co-operative governance' (2001:10). In my opinion, it is misplaced to conceive as a technique or tool of a multi-level or cooperative mode of governance.

In conclusion, the solution that is offered by subsidiarity is problematic from a normative angle if one accepts that the Community should undertake a process of transition towards a more horizontal logic. Rather than countering integration, subsidiarity involves a very particular (vertical) view of how integration should work. Therefore, if the way to cure many Community ills is to employ mechanisms that combine integration and diversity, since they include legitimate demands for unity and heterogeneity, then subsidiarity is ill suited for that purpose.

V

Subsidiarity before the Court

A. Introduction

Courts which undertake judicial review of legislative functions may be viewed as counter-majoritarian institutions (Estella, 1999e). Although not all democratic systems incorporate judicial review of legislation as a mechanism addressed to counter-balance the majoritarian bias which is often involved therein, where review of legislation exists, the main reason for that is precisely to temper the excesses to which a strict implementation of the majoritarian principle may lead. It can therefore be said that judicial review of legislation (as a counter-majoritarian mechanism) constitutes an important part of what has been defined as the 'methodology of democracy' (La Torre, 1994).

In the European Community context, this function of judicial counter-majoritarian balancing also exists. The competence to review legislation has been granted to the European Court of Justice.[1] According to Article 230 ECT (ex Art. 173) the ECJ '. . . shall review the legality of acts adopted by the European Parliament and the Council, of acts of the Council, of the Commission and of the ECB, other than recommendations and opinions, and of acts of the European Parliament intended to produce legal effects *vis-à-vis* third parties'.

Although the text of that Article speaks of 'legality', and not of 'constitutionality', its second paragraph indicates that one reason for which the ECJ may declare a legislative act void is infringement of the ECT. If Community legislation may be annulled by the ECJ on the ground of Treaty infringement,

---

[1] For reasons of simplicity, I shall not refer here to the Court of First Instance. However, many of the points made in this Chapter apply also to the CFI.

this amounts to constitutional review of legislation, at least in national contexts.[2]

The traditional categorization of the judicial review of legislative powers that the ECT grants to the ECJ as a counter-majoritarian mechanism has been challenged, however, by Community theory and practice. The founding fathers of the Community established an institutional system which was deeply embedded in a consensual logic. Furthermore, although the Treaty itself foresaw the shift from unanimity to majority voting (and therefore a gradual change of emphasis from consensual to majoritarian logic) the Luxembourg compromise resulted in a freeze of that shift. So from 1957 to 1987 the Community's institutional system was deprived of the majoritarian trends which, in general, characterize modern democratic systems. Although consensus did not amount to a Community minoritarian bias, it undoubtedly constituted a further counter-majoritarian mechanism.

In this context, the European Court of Justice faced a paradox: its counter-majoritarian powers of judicial review were to be applied in a counter-majoritarian institutional context. To solve that paradox, it had to reinvent its powers. In so doing it changed the sense of its judicial powers of review, not to insulate a 'majoritarian bias' in the system but to facilitate the process of integration. If the ECJ had supported a majoritarian tendency in its case-law, it would have been more ready to declare void legislative decisions opposed by a majority. This has not generally been the case.[3] It can therefore be

[2] Alonso García (1994) notes that Art. 230 does not differentiate in reality between 'legality' and 'constitutional' control. This may create some confusion as to the existence of constitutional review of legislation in the EC context, at least for those lawyers educated in the continental tradition, which is in general characterized by the distinction between 'legality' and 'constitutionality' controls, each being performed by different courts.

[3] A case in point is the telecommunications case-law. Note, in particular, Cases C-202/88 [1991] ECR 3261 and Joined Cases C-271/90, 281/90, and 289/90 [1992] ECR I-5833. In both cases the ECJ supported the main aspects of Directives 88/301 (OJECL 131/72, of 27 May 1988) and Directive 90/388 (OJEC L 192/10 of 24 July 1990). These were the first liberalization measures adopted in the telecommunications sector by the Community. In particular, both Directives established the elimination of national telecommunications monopolies. Both were adopted by the Commission. The majority of Member States in the Council were against the adoption of a liberalization measure on the basis of old Art. 100a of the Treaty. Thus the Commission had to employ the normative powers that old Art. 90(3) granted it to impose both measures on Member States. Member States reacted with rage and brought actions against both measures. The attitude of Member States cannot be assessed as mere strategy: in most cases, keeping national monopolies was a policy preference. The ECJ therefore acted here in tandem with the Commission. Integration was upheld, and the majoritarian interests of Member States were overturned. One cannot argue in terms of the interests of the Member States' populace since, at best, they were indeterminate, as there was almost no experience of liberalization in Europe at the time. For a divergent view, see Poiares (1998).

argued that the ECJ has developed not a majoritarian case-law (Poiares, 1998) but rather a pro-integrationist one.

Things changed, however, after the Single European Act was enacted. It has been shown in this work that the SEA was the first step towards an ever-increasing expansion of the majoritarian features in the Community context. Further, I have given indications showing that Member States today make use of majority voting and that, consequently, some Member States are out-voted.[4] Within this new context, the Court of Justice faces a new dilemma. The 'Luxembourg dilemma' is knowing whether the time has come to become a constitutional Court in the traditional, counter-majoritarian sense, or whether, on the contrary, the consensual features of the Community system are still important enough to maintain the old line.

From this perspective, subsidiarity may be interpreted as an incentive for the Court to adopt a new track in its jurisprudence. Subsidiarity in principle gives a new argument for the Court to annul measures adopted by the Community legislature but which were opposed by a minority in the Council. Now, the question is whether the ECJ has taken this opportunity to reconcile its present powers with traditional categories.

To answer this question, this Chapter examines the Court's case-law on subsidiarity. What emerges from that analysis is that the Court has adopted a very prudent approach regarding subsidiarity. Up to now, it has never declared void a legislative measure because it contradicts subsidiarity. Thus the answer to the above question seems to be, thus far at least, negative. Beyond descriptive analysis, it is also important to understand why the Court is not implementing subsidiarity to its fullest. This Chapter develops two kinds of explanations to account for the Court's attitude. The first has to do with the legitimacy of the Court. The argument is that the Court is not currently implementing subsidiarity because, given that the principle is devoid of clear legal content, the Court could be putting its own legitimacy at risk if it decided to do so. The second explanation has to do with the Court's vision of its own role in Community integration. The argument is that the Court has its own political agenda, and that this agenda is dominated by the idea of integration. The Court's perception that subsidiarity, an anti-integration principle for the Court, puts its own integrationist agenda in real danger could also explain its prudent approach to the principle.

This Chapter's premise is linked to the discussion in Chapter III above on binding commitments. As may be recalled, subsidiarity can be conceptualized

---

[4] See Table II.1, in chapter II.

as a commitment, and review of the principle by the Court as a mechanism designed to make the 'subsidiarity commitment' credible. However, commitments may also fail. In the case of subsidiarity, it failed because of the low credibility of subsidiarity as a legal principle and because the Court had a different agenda from that of Member States. The case of subsidiarity provides further evidence, at a general level, of the conditions under which certain binding commitments will not work.

B. The ECJ case-law on subsidiarity

The European Court of Justice has taken a number of decisions on subsidiarity since its insertion into the ECT (de Búrca, 1998). Here I focus on the most relevant ones: Cases C-84/94 and C-233/94. It is notable that the cases in which the ECJ has ruled *directly* on the principle are very few.[5] The limited number of cases in which Member States have employed subsidiarity as a

[5] The principle has been invoked in other cases that have less relevance from the perspective of subsidiarity. It must be noted that the model subsidiarity case is that in which a Member State (or a number of them) is outvoted and in turn brings an action of annulment against that measure on the ground of subsidiarity. Note the following cases in which subsidiarity has been invoked: 1) Joined Cases C-430/93 and C-431/93 [1995] ECR I-4705; 2) Case C-415/93 [1995] ECR I-4921; 3) Case C-209/94 [1996] ECR I-0615; 4) Case C-192/94 [1996] ECR I-1281; 5) Case C-11/95 [1996] ECR I-4115; 6) Case C-91/95 [1996] ECR I-5547; 7) Joined Cases C-36/97 and C-37/97 [1998] ECR I-6337; 8) Case C-150/94 [1998] ECR I-7235; 9) Case T-5/93 [1995] ECR II-0185; 10) Case T-29/92 [1995] ECR II-0289; 11) Case T-224/95 [1997] ECR II-2215; 12) Case T-113/96 [1998] ECR II-125; 13) Case T-135/96 [1998] ECR II-2335.

On 5 October 2000 the Court of Justice dictated a judgment on Case C-376/98 declaring void Directive 98/43 on tobacco advertising. It was a model subsidiarity case: Germany opposed the Directive and, once the Community legislator adopted it, brought an action of annulment against the Directive. One of the motives adduced by the applicant was violation of subsidiarity. However, the Court annulled the Directive on the ground that the legal base used to adopt it had been erroneous. Therefore the Court did not analyse the rest of the arguments, including Germany's claim about subsidiarity. Thus analysis of this case is irrelevant for our present purposes. After submission of this book, the Court has ruled on case C-377/98 [2001] ECR I-7079, known as the Biotechnology case. The Netherlands brought an action for annulment of directive 98/44, of the European Parliament and the Council, on the legal protection of biotechnological inventions. It was another 'model' subsidiarity case. The Netherlands claimed that both material and procedural subsidiarity had been violated by the Community's legislature. However, none of these arguments were retained by the ECJ. Interestingly, the ECJ did not seem to give much importance to these arguments, since it rejected both of them in two rather laconic paragraphs (see paragraph no. 32 for material subsidiarity and no. 33 for procedural subsidiarity). In its conclusions, the Court discussed the Netherland's application. Therefore the Biotech case does not modify the nucleus of the argument that is presented below.

'hard' argument to annul a Community measure is also noteworthy. One would have expected that, after the interest that Member States showed in the 'juridification' of subsidiarity, they would have employed the principle more often when it was finally introduced into the ECT. Certainly, a flood of actions based on subsidiarity was not expected, but there have been only two main cases since Maastricht was enacted, undoubtedly a very low figure. It seems that Member States have been reluctant to employ subsidiarity before the ECJ, which is a paradox given the background set out above.[6]

Secondly, it is also appropriate here to comment on procedure. This aspect has been a concern for commentators since subsidiarity was inserted into the ECT (Alonso García, 1994:588). It is important to note that the most common procedural context in which the principle can be employed is an action for annulment. The model subsidiarity case is that in which a Member State which has been outvoted brings an action for annulment against the measure in question before the ECJ.[7] However, the principle can be invoked in other procedural contexts, such as preliminary rulings (on both interpretation and validity) and the illegality exception of Article 241 (ex Art. 184). It is more difficult to invoke subsidiarity within the framework of the infringement of Community obligations by Member States and failure to act, although in the latter case the Community institution which failed to act might argue that it did not act because of subsidiarity.[8]

[6] It goes without saying that this point must be taken in relative terms. In order to show that the use of subsidiarity before the ECJ has been lower than expected, one should take into account both the number of times that Member States were outvoted in the Council and the number of actions for annulment brought before the ECJ in the reference period, from the enactment of the Maastricht Treaty (November 1993) to the year 2000. Concerning the first aspect, and in the absence of more complete data, one could take into account Table II.1 above. In that Table, it was shown that Germany (one of the plaintiffs) was outvoted at least 14 times in the period from the enactment of the Maastricht Treaty to September 1995; the UK, the other plaintiff, was outvoted 16 times during the same period. Concerning the second aspect, the *Annual Report on the Activities of the ECJ* does not say how often annulment proceedings were brought by Member States, nor the kind of measure (administrative or legislative) brought against them, but it states the overall number of annulment proceedings per year. With these limitations in mind, the following data may serve, at least indirectly, for comparison purposes: in 1993, 67 actions of annulment were brought; in 1994, 33; in 1995, 30; in 1996, 35; and in 1997, 36. *Annual Reports on the Activities of the ECJ for 1992–1994; 1995; 1996; and 1997* (Luxembourg: Office for Official Publication of the EC).

[7] See n. 4 above.

[8] To rely on subsidiarity in an action for infringement would be very difficult, unless one uses a 'positive' subsidiarity argument. Accordingly, the Community institutions could argue that a particular Member State action was contrary to subsidiarity since subsidiarity justified Community action and not individual Member States action. I have, however, discarded this line of reasoning in other parts of this work (note in particular Chapters III and IV above).

Finally, the discussion among commentators when subsidiarity was inserted into the ECT concerning the direct effect of the principle has lost all its relevance today, because the Court of First Instance has not imposed this requirement on individuals.[9] I believe this stance is correct since subsidiarity is a legal principle, not a norm from which subjective rights may be derived.

1. *Case C-84/94:* United Kingdom v the Council of the European Union

Case C-84/94[10] constitutes the first important ECJ decision concerning the principle of subsidiarity. The UK asked the Court for Directive 93/104,[11] 'concerning certain aspects of the organisation of working time', to be declared void, or alternatively that a number of provisions of that Directive be annulled.

Directive 93/104 was adopted immediately after the enactment of the Maastricht Treaty. Its adoption had as its legal basis old Article 118a ECT (now Art. 138). The main aim of the Directive was, as its Preamble indicates, to establish a number of minimal dispositions concerning the organization of working time with the purpose of achieving greater protection of the health and safety of workers.[12] Articles 3, 4, 5, 6, and 7 were the most important provisions. Article 3 harmonized the minimum daily rest period;[13] Article 4, breaks;[14] Article 5 regulated the minimum weekly rest period,[15] fixing Sunday as the weekly rest day, 'in principle'. Article 6, the most significant provision of the Directive, established the maximum weekly working time of forty-eight hours.[16] Finally, Article 7 regulated annual leave.[17]

The Directive also established a number of provisions aimed at introducing an important degree of flexibility regarding the implementation of the obligations established therein. Flexibility was specified in three kinds of measures: first, those measures that were intended to lengthen the reference

---

[9] Note, in particular, Cases T-29/92 and T-5/93, cited above. Though the CFI did not directly deal with the problem of the direct effect of subsidiarity in these cases, the CFI did not reject the possibility that individuals can invoke the principle of subsidiarity for lack of direct effect.

[10] [1996] ECR I-5755.   [11] OJEC L 307/18, of 13 December 1993.

[12] Note, in particular, paragraphs 1 and 7 of the Directive's Preamble.

[13] In particular, of 11 consecutive hours per 24-hour period.

[14] Art. 4 simply imposes upon Member States the obligation to establish rest periods where the working day is longer than 6 hours.

[15] Establishing that, for each 7-day period, every worker shall be entitled to a minimum uninterrupted rest period of 24 hours, plus the 11-hour daily rest which Art. 3 refers to.

[16] With the important proviso that this period of 48 hours also included overtime.

[17] Establishing minimum paid annual leave of 4 weeks.

periods established for the application of Articles 5, 6, and 8 of the Directive;[18] secondly, those aimed at establishing derogations from the application of Articles 3, 4, 5, 6, 8, and 16;[19] and finally, measures aimed at establishing safeguard clauses and transition periods in relation to Articles 6 and 7.[20]

The negotiation process of the Directive started in 1990 (Bercusson, 1995:9) and the United Kingdom opposed the measure from the beginning. Its position was that the draft Directive regulated matters more closely related to employment and division of labour than to protection of workers' health and safety in the workplace. When the draft Directive was submitted to the Council the UK abstained and, at the same time, it announced that it would challenge the Directive before the ECJ, as it later did.

The British argument was sensible to a certain extent. Undoubtedly, the Directive's objective related to the protection of workers' health and safety in the workplace. However, its connection with employment and labour division was also evident. Thus for example Bercusson, who analysed the content of the directive in 1995, offered a review of the measure mostly from the perspective of employment and labour division. According to this author:

The working time directive imposes a 48-hour limit on the working week. The provisions of the directive will preclude employers offering work exceeding the 48 hours weekly maximum. Even in the case of countries opting to delay introduction of this provision [. . .], employees will be entitled to refuse to work more than 48 hours. This will affect case-law in the UK; for example, where an employee obliged under the terms of his employment to work overtime 'as required' was held fairly dismissed for persistently refusing to do weekend standby duty. *Not least because of high levels of unemployment, there is an argument for the re-distribution of hours, at least for those working very long hours, into shorter-time employment; in particular, more part-time jobs could be created* (Bercusson, 1995:46, my emphasis).

On the other hand, Bercusson's conclusions about whether the Directive would have an impact on UK labour legislation suggest that the UK position

---

[18] Note in particular Art. 16. For example, its second paragraph enables Member States to establish a reference period which shall not exceed 4 months, as regards Art. 6 of the Directive.

[19] Note in particular Art. 17. For example, Art. 17(1) allowed Member States to derogate from the limit of 48 hours of weekly working time for certain professional activities with specific characteristics, for example executive managers.

[20] Note, in particular, Art. 18. For example, its paragraph 1(b)(i) establishes a general safeguard for Art. 6 of the Directive. This means that, under a number of conditions, Member States may *not* apply Art. 6 of the Directive. One of these conditions is that workers may refuse to work more than 48 hours per week, and an employer cannot dismiss a worker who refuses to work more than that limit.

in the Council was not one of mere principle. On the contrary, the UK was seriously concerned with the potential impact of the Directive on its labour market. There are data confirming this point. For example, an analysis made in 1992 the *Employment Gazette*, cited by Bercusson (1995) established that, of the Member States, in the UK full-time workers worked the most hours on average.[21] Additionally, among full-time workers, a significant proportion (16 per cent) worked more than the forty-eight hours established by the Directive. This percentage was significant considering, for example, that the second Member State in that ranking was Ireland, with only 8.3 per cent of full-time workers working more than forty-eight hours.[22] It is evident from these data that the implementation of the Directive would involve a change in the UK labour market. Furthermore, the argument that the Directive was flexible enough to allow Member States not to apply it did not apply to the limit of forty-eight hours. As noted above, the Directive allowed the Member States to implement a safeguard clause in this ambit, with the proviso that workers could refuse to work more than forty-eight hours per week: this amounted to the imposition of a forty-eight-hour weekly limit.[23]

Turning now to the analysis of the Court's judgment in Case C-84/94, the UK asked the Court to annul Directive 93/104, or alternatively to declare Articles 4, 5(1), 6(2), and 7 void. The UK's arguments were the following: defective legal basis, breach of the principle of proportionality, misuse of powers, and infringement of essential procedural requirements. All these arguments were rejected by the ECJ, with the exception of the argument that the Council had failed to explain the choice of Sunday as a weekly rest day. Therefore the ECJ dismissed the applicant's action, but annulled Article 5(2) of the Directive.

Regarding subsidiarity, the principle was expressly invoked by the UK on two occasions in their application. The first mention of subsidiarity was made within the first argument (defective legal base). According to the applicant:

The Community legislature neither fully considered nor adequately demonstrated whether there were transnational aspects which could not be satisfactorily regulated by national measures, whether such measures would conflict with the requirements of the EC Treaty or significantly damage the interests of Member States or, finally, whether action at Community level would provide clear benefits compared with action at national level. In its submission, Article 118a should be interpreted in the

---

[21] This average was of 43.7 hours per week. Compare other Member States with similar economies: Italy (5.1 hours less), France (4.1 hours less), and Germany (3.8 hours less).

[22] The figures for France are 5.3%; for Germany, 4.8%; and for Italy 3.5%.

[23] Note Art. 18(1)(b)(i) of the Directive.

light of the principle of subsidiarity, which does not allow adoption of a directive in such wide and prescriptive terms as the contested Directive, given that the extent and the nature of legislative regulation of working time vary very widely between Member States. The applicant explains in this context, however, that it does not rely upon infringement of the principle of subsidiarity as a separate plea.[24]

The second UK reference to subsidiarity was made in the plea relating to the infringement of the proportionality principle. According to the UK:

a measure will be proportionate only if it is consistent with the principle of subsidiarity. The applicant argues that it is for the Community institutions to demonstrate that the aims of the directive could better be achieved at Community level than by action on the part of the Member States. There has been no such demonstration in this case.[25]

Finally, within the framework of the argument relating to the infringement of essential procedural requirements, the UK made an allegation which, albeit only implicitly, clearly concerned subsidiarity. According to the applicant, 'Nor, moreover, does the Preamble to the Directive explain why Community action was necessary'.[26]

The UK's subsidiarity arguments may be summarized by saying that the UK complained that the need for Community action was either not grounded, or that it was insufficiently grounded on the subsidiarity principle. Thus if we recall the two categories of subsidiarity established in Chapter IV above (procedural and material subsidiarity) the UK argument turned only on the first one. The UK did not reproach the Community legislature on the ground that the measure should not have been adopted because it was contrary to the principle, but only that the Preamble of the Directive had not explained, or had not sufficiently explained, why the measure should be adopted according to subsidiarity.

The Court of Justice answered the UK's arguments on subsidiarity in the following way. In the first place, the Court set out, at the beginning of its reasoning, a point which influenced the rest of its arguments on the principle: 'it is to be remembered that it is not the function of the Court to review the expediency of measures adopted by the legislature. The review exercised under Article 173 must be limited to the legality of the disputed measure'.[27]

In effect, the Court was stating its view that review of the Community legislature's discretion had to be very limited. This was the first indication from

---

[24] Case C-84/94, para. 46.   [25] Ibid., para. 54.   [26] Ibid., para. 72.
[27] Ibid., para. 23.

the Court that its control with respect to the principle was to be very restrained. Starting from that position, the Court rejected, one by one, all UK subsidiarity arguments. Thus, in paragraph 47 the Court rejected the first UK subsidiarity argument, saying that:

In that respect, it should be noted that it is the responsibility of the Council, under Article 118a, to adopt minimum requirements so as to contribute, through harmonization, to achieving the objective of raising the level of health and safety protection of workers which, in terms of Article 118a(1), is primarily the responsibility of the Member States. Once the Council has found that it is necessary to improve the existing level of protection as regards the health and safety of workers and to harmonize the conditions in this area while maintaining the improvements made, achievement of that objective through the imposition of minimum requirements necessarily presupposes Community-wide action, which otherwise, as in this case, leaves the enactment of the detailed implementing provisions required largely to the Member States. The argument that the Council could not properly adopt measures as general and mandatory as those forming the subject-matter of the Directive will be examined below in the context of the plea alleging infringement of the principle of proportionality.[28]

In relation with the second UK subsidiarity argument, the Court stated, referring to the paragraph cited above, that:

The argument of non-compliance with the principle of subsidiarity can be rejected at the outset. It is said that the Community legislature has not established that the aims of the Directive would be better served at Community level than at national level. But that argument, as so formulated, really concerns the need for Community action, which has already been examined in paragraph 47 of this judgment.[29]

Finally, in relation with the UK argument stated in paragraph 72, the Court indicated, recalling again its position in paragraph 47 that:

Nor can the argument to the effect that the Preamble to the Directive fails to explain the need for Community action be accepted as well founded. As has been pointed out in paragraphs 75 to 77 of this judgment, the Preamble to the Directive shows that the Council considered it necessary, in order to ensure an improved level of health and safety protection of workers, to take action to harmonize the national legislation of the Member States on the organization of working time. As stated in paragraph 47, the pursuit of such an objective, laid down in Article 118a itself, through harmonization by means of minimum requirements, necessarily presupposes Community-wide action.[30]

We therefore see that the ECJ employed a strictly deductive method in this case. In effect, it recalled its traditional position regarding judicial control of

---

[28] Case C-84/94, para. 47.   [29] Ibid., para. 55.   [30] Ibid., paras. 80 and 81.

the Community legislature, which strictly respects the Community's assessment of legislative opportunity.[31] From that position it derived its answers to
the UK's arguments. It is interesting to note that although the applicant only
made a procedural subsidiarity argument, the ECJ took the opportunity to
venture into the field of material subsidiarity. In effect, although the Court
answered the procedural subsidiarity argument in procedural terms, it went
well beyond, also touching on material subsidiarity. An example is found in
the following Court sentence, paragraph 47 of its ruling:

Once the Council has found that it is necessary to improve the existing level of protection as regards the health and safety of workers and to harmonize the conditions in
this area while maintaining the improvements made, achievement of that objective
through the imposition of minimum requirements necessarily presupposes
Community-wide action, which otherwise, as in this case, leaves the enactment of the
detailed implementing provisions required largely to the Member States.

The Court then went to procedural subsidiarity. For the Court, the Preamble
of the Directive did contain sufficient justification of the need for the
Community measure. However, the Court did not refer to any specific paragraph of the Preamble. In fact, the term 'subsidiarity' did not appear in the
Directive at all. This did not prevent the Court from affirming, cryptically,
that 'the Preamble to the Directive shows that the Council considered it necessary, in order to ensure an improved level of health and safety protection of
workers, to take action to harmonize the national legislation of the Member
States on the organization of working time' (paragraph 81). As shall be seen
below, the Court clarified in Case-233/94, brought by Germany, that a lack
of explicit reference to the principle of subsidiarity did not constitute an indication that the principle had been violated from a procedural viewpoint.

The Court's stance on procedural subsidiarity arose from its stance on
material subsidiarity. That is, once the Court established that subsidiarity had
not been violated from a material perspective, it seemed to concede only secondary importance to procedural subsidiarity. We therefore see that the
Court's reasoning here was based on a number of inferences, which started
from the establishment of a major premise (the Court will apply restraint
regarding the control of legislative expediency) from which it first deduced a
substantive position (material subsidiarity is deemed to be safeguarded when
the Council decides that a particular measure is necessary) and then drew a

---

[31] See, for example, Case C-341/95 [1998] ECR I-4355. Note my comments on this case in
Estella (1999b).

conclusion with respect to the specific allegations of the plaintiff. The Court followed a different approach in Case C-233/94.[32]

2. *Case C-233/94:* Germany v the Council of the European Union and the European Parliament

Case C-233/94[33] concerns an action for annulment brought by Germany against Directive 94/19[34] on 'deposit-guarantee schemes'. It is important to mention two other acts, taken before Directive 94/19 was adopted, to gain a better understanding of the case. These two acts were the 'Second Banking Directive' (Directive 89/646) and Recommendation 87/63[35] on 'the introduction of deposit-guarantee schemes in the EC'. The Second Banking Directive was adopted with the purpose of guaranteeing the freedom of establishment of credit institutions in the European Community. The main principles on which the Directive was based were three-fold: mutual recognition; supervision by the home Member State; and harmonization of minimum requirements. It is not necessary to enter into the details here of this regulation.[36] Suffice it to say that the Second Banking Directive established the so-called Community 'passport' (or licence) according to which a credit institution established in one Member State could operate in other Member States without the need for further authorization by the host Member State. Furthermore, and more importantly for my purposes, the Directive specifically excluded the implementation of the mutual recognition principle from the ambit of deposit-guarantee schemes. Therefore, before the enactment of Directive 94/19, a credit entity from one Member State wanting to establish

---

[32] As pointed out above, the Court annulled Art. 5(2) of the Directive. According to the Court, 'the fact remains that the Council has to explain why Sunday, as a weekly rest day, is more closely connected with the health and safety of workers than any other day of the week. In those circumstances, the applicant's alternative claim must be upheld and the second sentence of Article 5 (. . .) must be annulled' (para. 37). The Court's reasoning was not, however, connected to subsidiarity and in reality Member States were free to establish Sunday as a weekly rest day or not, since the directive said that Sunday was to be retained 'in principle' as a weekly rest day. It would have been interesting to see what the ECJ would have done if the Directive had not included the expression 'in principle'. Further, in this case there was no explanation at all of why the Council had chosen Sundays. Therefore the procedural 'giving reasons' requirement had not been respected. In these circumstances, it is difficult to construe a subsidiarity argument from the previous paragraph. The most that could be said, if a link between that paragraph and subsidiarity was tried, would be that subsidiarity requires that reasons be given to justify the need for Community action. But note that this is already covered by Art. 253 (ex Art. 190).

[33] [1997] ECR I-12405.   [34] OJEC L 135/5 of 31 May 1994.
[35] OJEC L 33/16 of 4 February 1987.   [36] See Ballbé and Padrós (1997).

itself in another Member State had to implement the deposit-guarantee regulations of the host Member State, when these regulations existed (Vives, 1994:9).

Recommendation 87/63 'invited' Member States lacking a deposit-guarantee system to introduce such a system into their respective legal orders. This Recommendation had, however, a very slight impact, at least according to the Commission. The latter proposed that Member States adopt a legally binding measure on the matter for that reason. After protracted negotiations, the Commission proposal became Directive 94/19.

The main purpose of Directive 94/19 was to oblige Member States to implement a system of deposit-guarantee. Another important objective was to establish a minimum level of deposit-guarantee in all Member States. There was also an underlying objective, which was to avoid competition between Member States in the banking market through their respective deposit-guarantee regulations. As far as the content of the Directive is concerned, the most important provisions were Articles 3(1), 7(1)(2), 4(1), and 4(2). Article 3(1) imposed upon Member States the obligation to introduce in their legal orders at least one deposit-guarantee system. The same provision also obliged credit institutions to implement one of the schemes provided by the Member State of origin (with one exception of a general character[37]). Article 7(1)(2) established a minimum level of guarantee of 20,000 ECUs. However, it also allowed those Member States which at the time of the implementation of the Directive had not reached the previous level, to set the minimum level at 15,000 ECUs.

The first two paragraphs of Article 4 form the legal core of the Directive. These established three rules relating to the operation of the deposit-guarantee schemes for credit institutions' branches established in another Member State. The first rule (Article 4(1), first paragraph) concerns the 'guarantee exportation'. According to this rule, the deposit-guarantee scheme of the home Member State *in principle* covered depositors of branches established in another Member State. I stress the expression 'in principle' since the second and third rules of the Directive introduced a proviso to that rule. In effect, the second rule (Article 4(1), second paragraph) established the 'prohibition against exporting the guarantee scheme', if the latter was superior to the guarantee scheme established in the host Member State. In this case, the host Member State's guarantee scheme was applicable.[38]

---

[37] Established in Art. 3(1)(2); the exception is not relevant for our purposes.
[38] Though with a time limit: the prohibition would cease on 31 December 1999.

Finally, the third rule (Article 4(2)) established the 'guarantee supplement'. According to this rule, in those cases in which the host Member State offered a deposit-guarantee scheme superior to the one offered by the home Member State, then the former should ensure that branches established therein could voluntarily join a scheme that would supplement the difference. Both the second and the third rules were intended to avoid regulatory competition through deposit-guarantee schemes between Member States.

It was precisely because of that limitation that Germany voted against the adoption of the Directive, and later brought an action for annulment before the ECJ. In effect, as Advocate General Léger indicates in his Conclusions, Germany had at the time the most efficient system of deposit-guarantee in the European Community.[39] Some data corroborate this finding. According to a study by the *Fédération Bancaire de la Communauté Européenne* of February 1992 (cited by Mckenzie and Khalidi, 1994:174) the maximum level of protection offered by the German system amounted to 30 per cent of the Bank's own resources per depositor, which meant that, as a general rule, German depositors' deposits were fully guaranteed. The well known bankruptcy case of the *Bank of Credit and Commerce International* (BCCI) illustrates the previous point: whereas British depositors received only a proportion of their deposits, German depositors obtained the whole of theirs (Mckenzie and Khalidi, 1994:177). Thus Germany, which had the most protective deposit-guarantee system in the European Community, believed that the Directive prevented its competing with this instrument, and therefore opposed the adoption of the measure.[40]

We now turn to an analysis of the Court's judgment. Germany claimed that the Directive should be declared void, or, in the alternative, that Articles 4(1)(2), 4(2), and 3(1) be annulled. The arguments adduced by Germany were the following. Regarding the first claim, Germany advanced two pleas: an erroneous legal basis and infringement of Article 190 (now Article 253). Both

---

[39] Note para. 20 of the Conclusions.

[40] One could wonder whether the German view is well founded. In effect, Art. 9(3) of the Directive prohibited advertising deposit-guarantee schemes (advertising being limited to 'a factual reference to the scheme'). Therefore if an advertisement was prohibited by the Directive, it is difficult to see how credit institutions could use deposit-guarantee schemes for competition purposes. It is also evident that in general, when customers choose a credit institution, deposit-guarantee schemes are a remote concern. This was acknowledged by Advocate General Léger in his Conclusions: 'in their choice of a credit institution, future clients are presented with many more decisive criteria, particularly when, having accepted the idea of entrusting their money to a particular bank, its future insolvency is often a distant concern and the need to belong to a guarantee scheme a superfluous precaution' (Conclusions, para. 159).

pleas were rejected by the ECJ. With regard to its second claim, Germany's arguments were the following: insufficient statement of reasons; infringement of (old) Articles 57(2)(3)(c) and 129A of the ECT; infringement of the principle of proportionality (all of them regarding Article 4(1) of the Directive); infringement of the principle of supervision by the home Member State; infringement of the proportionality principle (against Article 4(2) of the Directive); and infringement of the principle of proportionality (against Article 3(1) of the Directive). All these arguments were rejected by the Court of Justice.[41] As a result, the Court dismissed the action brought by Germany.

With regard to subsidiarity, the German claim reiterated almost in its entirety the aforementioned British one. Germany also emphasized procedural subsidiarity, rather than the material side of the principle. In effect, subsidiarity was invoked twice by the German government. The first was in its argument of infringement of Article 253 ECT (ex Article 190) that:

the Directive must be annulled because it fails to state the reasons on which it is based, as required by Article 190 of the Treaty. It does not explain how it is compatible with the principle of subsidiarity enshrined in the second paragraph of Article 3b of the Treaty. The German Government adds that, since that principle limits the powers of the Community and since the Court has power to examine whether the Community legislature has exceeded its powers, that principle must be subject to review by the Court of Justice. Moreover, the obligation under Article 190 to state the reasons on which a measure is based requires that regard be had to the essential factual and legal considerations on which a legal measure is based, which include compliance with the principle of subsidiarity.[42]

Germany continued by arguing, in the subsequent paragraph, that:

As to the precise terms of the obligation to state reasons in the light of the principle of subsidiarity, the German Government states that the Community institutions must give detailed reasons to explain why only the Community, to the exclusion of the Member States, is empowered to act in the area in question. In the present case, the Directive does not indicate in what respect its objectives could not have been sufficiently attained by action at Member State level or the grounds which militated in favour of Community action.[43]

As in the British case, Germany centred its argument not on the violation of material subsidiarity, but on the infringement of the procedural side of the principle. Thus Germany reproached the Community legislature for not stating the reasons which had led the legislature to adopt the measure in the Preamble of the Directive. One may note that the German argument was

---

[41] Ibid.: para. 86.   [42] Ibid.: para. 22.   [43] Ibid.: para. 23.

better structured than the British one. As stated above, the UK presented its allegations on subsidiarity principally within the framework of its plea relating to the infringement of proportionality and erroneous legal basis. However, Germany linked its procedural subsidiarity argument to old Article 190 (now Article 253) undoubtedly a better way to present a procedural subsidiarity argument. The ECT provision imposes a general obligation on the Community institutions to give reasons for their acts (including the Community's legislature). Furthermore, although the Court's case-law on that Article is profuse,[44] it has been interpreted as meaning that the Community institutions have to give reasons for the acts they adopt, in such a manner that those interested in the act may understand the circumstances that served as the background for its adoption. In general, the criteria that the Court uses to check whether that provision has been respected is very flexible, especially regarding legislative acts.[45]

In any case, it is clear that, from a strictly legal perspective, to link procedural subsidiarity with old Article 190 is more logical than to link it with pleas such as erroneous legal basis or infringement of proportionality. This gives more strength to the procedural subsidiarity argument, and it may explain why the Court adopted a slightly different approach when answering Germany's subsidiarity arguments in this case.

Another point (and a similarity between the German and the British cases) is that in the German case Germany did not employ material subsidiarity as an argument. This is somewhat surprising, even more so than in the British case. In effect, a material subsidiarity argument could have been used, at least in the following sense, without falling into the absurd or the extravagant. Germany could have argued that on the date in which the Directive was implemented all Member States (with the exception of Greece, which had plans to implement a deposit-guarantee system) had already implemented such a system, which proved that the Member States' actions were sufficient

---

[44] In particular, the Court has tended to be much less restrictive for legislative acts and rule-making than for adjudication. Regarding the former, the Court has been guided by an objective of transparency. Regarding the second, the Court has been guided by transparency and, more recently, by participation. This latter shift in its case-law is not, however, totally consolidated. It must also be noted that the Court has not been very strict with regard to the implementation of Art. 253 (ex Art. 190) in general terms, neither regarding legislation and rule-making nor as far as adjudication is concerned. This means that the number of cases in which the Court has annulled an act of a Community institution for violation of that provision are as yet very few. See in general Parejo, Quadra-Salcedo, Moreno, and Estella (2000).

[45] See, among many others, Case C-41/93 [1994] ECR I-1829. Note also Shapiro (1992 and 2001) and Leanerts and Vanhamme (1997).

in this field. It could also have argued that it is difficult for credit institutions to use deposit-guarantee schemes as a competitive device,[46] which suggests that lack of regulation in this sector would not distort the common market (which, as will be recalled, was one of the subsidiarity criteria).

Turning to the analysis of the Court's responses to the subsidiarity arguments raised by Germany, it must be said from the outset that the ECJ rejected them all. The Court began by clarifying that the applicant's argument was that procedural subsidiarity, and not material subsidiarity, had been violated. In the Court's own words: 'As a preliminary point, it should be pointed out that [. . .] the German Government is not claiming that the Directive infringed the principle of subsidiarity, but only that the Community legislature did not set out the grounds to substantiate the compatibility of its actions with that principle'.[47]

Once the Court had settled this point, it went on to recall the content of old Article 190. In the Court's view: 'The obligation under Article 190 to give reasons requires that the measures concerned should contain a statement of the reasons which led the institution to adopt them, so that the Court can exercise its power of review and so that the Member States and the nationals concerned may learn of the conditions under which the Community institutions have applied the Treaty'.[48]

The next point was to analyse Germany's subsidiarity arguments more specifically. The Court did so for the preamble of the measure and in two further steps. It stated that:

In the present case, the Parliament and the Council stated in the second recital in the Preamble to the Directive that 'consideration should be given to the situation which might arise if deposits in a credit institution that has branches in other Member States became unavailable' and that it was 'indispensable to ensure a harmonised minimum level of deposit protection wherever deposits are located in the Community'. This shows that, in the Community legislature's view, the aim of its action could, because of the dimensions of the intended action, be best achieved at Community level. The same reasoning appears in the third recital, from which it is clear that the decision regarding the guarantee scheme which is competent in the event of the insolvency of a branch situated in a Member State other than that in which the credit institution has its head office has repercussions which are felt outside the borders of each Member State.[49]

---

[46] This point was suggested by Advocate General Léger in his Conclusions (para. 159), as noted above.

[47] Para. 24.   [48] Para. 25.   [49] Para. 26.

In the next paragraph it stated: 'Furthermore, in the fifth recital the Parliament and the Council stated that the action taken by the Member States in response to the Commission's Recommendation has not fully achieved the desired result. The Community legislature therefore found that the objective of its action could not be achieved sufficiently by the Member States'.[50]

The Court concluded that: 'Consequently, it is apparent that, on any view, the Parliament and the Council did explain why they considered that their action was in conformity with the principle of subsidiarity and, accordingly, that they complied with the obligation to give reasons as required under Article 190 of the Treaty. An express reference to that principle cannot be required'.[51]

Let us disentangle the Court's reasoning. To start with, the Court's reasoning was more detailed in this case than in the British case. The reason for this probably lies in the way the German subsidiarity argument was structured. As has been suggested above, this was more coherent and clearer than that in the British case. Directly linking subsidiarity with old Article 190 forced the Court to study the German subsidiarity argument more carefully. Thus the Court made a more meticulous examination of whether the Preamble of the Directive justified the Community action from the perspective of subsidiarity. Secondly, the Court considered subsidiarity from the viewpoint of three criteria: dimension, effects, and sufficiency. It then went on to analyse whether the Preamble of the Directive stated the reasons for the Community legislature's intervention from the perspective of those three criteria.

Concerning the first criterion, the Court's view was that it had been retained in the second paragraph of the Directive's Preamble, where the Community's legislator established that 'consideration should be given to the situation which might arise if deposits in a credit institution that has branches in other Member States became unavailable' and that it was 'indispensable to ensure a harmonised minimum level of deposit protection wherever deposits are located in the Community'. According to the Court, this statement showed that 'in the Community legislature's view, the aim of its action could, because of the dimensions of the intended action, be best achieved at Community level'. Concerning the second criterion (effects), the Court of Justice argued that a reason had been stated in the third point of the Preamble, when the Community's legislature affirmed that 'the insolvency of a branch situated in a Member State other than that in which the credit

---

[50] Para. 27.   [51] Para. 28.

institution has its head office has repercussions which are felt outside the borders of each Member State'. According to the Court, reference to the effects in the Preamble showed that the Community legislature had taken subsidiarity into account. Finally, concerning the third criterion (sufficiency), the Court found that the Community's legislature had stated a reason in the fifth paragraph of the Preamble, in which 'the Parliament and the Council stated that the action taken by the Member States in response to the Commission's Recommendation has not fully achieved the desired result. The Community legislature therefore found that the objective of its action could not be achieved sufficiently by the Member States.'

We therefore see that the Court's reasoning was more refined here than in the British case. However, in absolute terms (that is, not in comparison with the British case) the Court's approach in the German case was still not very detailed. In effect, what the Court did to justify its stance in the German case was merely to cite the relevant parts of the Preamble. Although this was an improvement from the British case (in which the Court made only a general reference to the Preamble), the Court did not really assess whether the Preamble paragraphs cited showed irrefutably that the Community was in a better position than the Member States to intervene, nor did it establish, for example, the conditions under which a statement of reasons would be considered not to violate procedural subsidiarity. A good illustration is that the Court did not even require that subsidiarity be expressly mentioned in the Preamble. Undoubtedly, this would not have been a sufficient indication of respect for subsidiarity, but it would have obliged the Community legislature to set out subsidiarity reasons in preambles, thereby making identification of the subsidiarity arguments easier, and consequently streamlining judicial control.

On the other hand, the mixing of procedural and material subsidiarity was also present in this case. This may be less clear than in the British case, but it is still evident. In the German case the Court apparently restricted its answers to the procedural subsidiarity arguments of Germany. The allusion made by the Court in paragraph 24 that the applicant was claiming violation only of procedural subsidiarity seems to corroborate this. However, there was also spill-over into material subsidiarity. The clearest example was in paragraph 27, where the Court ended its reasoning on subsidiarity with a reference to material subsidiarity, saying the Preamble showed that the Community legislature 'found that the objective of its action could not be achieved sufficiently by the Member States'.

The approach followed by the Court in the German case was different from that followed in the British case. In the former it was also deductive, but the Court did not start by stating that it would not review the Community's discretion. On the contrary, the Court started in the German case with a reminder of the obligations derived from old Article 190. From there it reached the rest of its reasoning and the final conclusion. This methodology was logical since the German applicant linked its argument on procedural subsidiarity more clearly with old Article 190. However, the spill-over into material subsidiarity indicates that the Court did more than simply ensuring that old Article 190 was respected. In a way it does seem to have controlled the Community's discretion here—as it also did, to a certain extent, in the British case. The only difference between the two cases in this regard was that in the German case the Court avoided specifying the nature and the limits of its control. Perhaps the Court was more conscious here that the border between controlling procedural subsidiarity and the Communtiy's discretion are more blurred than is usually thought.

3. *The Court's Doctrine on Subsidiarity: A Summary*

Prudence is the word which best summarizes the Court's doctrine on the principle of subsidiarity. Prudence here means restraint on the part of the Court. The Court could have used the opportunity offered by subsidiarity to check whether the Community legislature is going astray. However, as shown above, this has not been the case, on either the material or the procedural side of the principle of subsidiarity.

Concerning the material side of the principle, the Court stance seems to be clear. This stance is that, save in cases where the Community legislature has committed a manifest error, the Court will not review a Community legislative norm on grounds of subsidiarity. This stance is, in reality, no surprise. As the Court recalls in the British case, its attitude has traditionally been not to substitute for the Community legislature's discretion its own. Therefore, the Court will generally avoid, even on grounds of the principle of subsidiarity, substituting an assessment by the Community legislature. Regarding the exceptions to that rule, it is difficult to see in which cases the Court could conclude that the Community legislature had committed a manifest error. It should be noted that the Court's case-law on manifest error is not especially clear.[52] It seems to apply a sort of rule of reason here. It therefore takes each case on its own merits, and analyses whether the Community measure is reasonable as regards the objectives pursued by the measure. In those excep-

---

[52] See Case C-34/95 [1998] ECR I-4355. See also my comments in Estella (1999g).

tional cases in which it is patently clear that the measure is not reasonable compared to the objectives, then the Court will annul it. However, it is obvious that this approach is closer to proportionality than to subsidiarity. Be that as it may, the Court seems to be sending a clear message to the Member States that it will not strongly enforce the material side of the principle.

It is important to say, however, that the way in which the British and the German subsidiarity arguments were put before the Court in the cases considered above did not pressure the Court strongly enough to take material subsidiarity seriously. In effect, as was pointed out, the Member States relied on procedural subsidiarity rather than material subsidiarity. In none of the decisions examined above did the applicants argue that the Community's legislature had violated the material side of the principle, at least explicitly. This may also explain why the Court was so superficial and flexible in its judgments.

On the other hand, as far as procedural subsidiarity is concerned, it has been shown above that the attitude of the Court is very flexible here as well. The Court is satisfied if the preamble of a measure briefly mentions the reasons why the Community legislature deemed it appropriate to act. Furthermore, the Court does not require that the Community legislature mention subsidiarity expressly. In this respect, the stance of the Court does not differ much from its stance on Article 253 ECT (ex Article 190) as far as legislative measures are concerned. In particular, the Court seems to require the Community legislature to state the reasons why, from the perspective of three standards (dimension or scale of the action, effects, and sufficiency) it considers that it is better suited to act than the Member States. However, the way in which the Court reviews the obligation to state reasons is very superficial: a mere mention of the three criteria in the measure's preamble seems to be sufficient.

Turning to the assessment of the Court's doctrine on subsidiarity, the most problematic aspect of this jurisprudence is the treatment of procedural subsidiarity, particularly in connection with Article 253 ECT (ex Article 190). It is obvious that the Protocol on subsidiarity should guide the Court towards a firmer stance in this respect. As pointed out in Chapter IV above, it is probable that, at least in the long term, the Commission will have no problem in adjusting to more stringent procedural demands of motivation. However, this observation should not prevent the Court from taking seriously the motivation obligations that subsidiarity and Article 253 ECT impose upon the Community legislature, if only for reasons of transparency. Furthermore, the Court should endeavour at the first opportunity to solve the problems of interpretation concerning the procedural side of the Protocol on subsidiarity.

It was also pointed out in Chapter IV above that there were at least three issues to be considered. The first was that the Protocol does not require the Commission to publish its explanatory memorandums (where it must include its subsidiarity assessments): the Commission itself adopted the commitment to do so.[53] However, this is clearly not enough: the Court should require the Commission to publish them. The second issue concerned paragraph 4 of the Protocol on subsidiarity. It was not clear whether that paragraph required the publication of the qualitatively or quantitatively measured reasons why the Community legislature decided to act. Although the Court has established in its case-law on Article 253 (ex Article 190) that the Community legislature must state reasons for the actions it adopts, it has been seen that the Court is very flexible in this respect. For this reason it is submitted that the Court should interpret that paragraph widely and require the publication of the data on which the Community based its decision. The third issue was that paragraph 4 also stated that the Community should use quantitative parameters to measure the need for Community action 'wherever possible'. This expression leaves a wide margin of manoeuvre for the Community's legislature. The Court should, at the very least, attempt to establish a number of criteria which the Community's legislature should follow in order to decide when to use quantitative parameters and when to employ qualitative ones. At the same time, it should make sure that the preference established by the Protocol on subsidiarity in favour of quantitative criteria is not dissipated in practice. Naturally, the Court cannot be criticized for not having adopted that course in the cases it has examined so far, since they were issued before the Protocol on subsidiarity entered in force. The point is rather that the Court's current stance on the procedural side of the principle does not allow much optimism about the future implementation of the procedural aspects of the Protocol. However, only time will tell whether the Court will take the procedural aspect of the principle more seriously. As noted above, it is unclear that minoritarian Member States will improve their situation with the shift, but at least the populace would have more information about the Community's business (Alonso García, 1994:586).

[53] See the Commission's *Communication on the Principle of Subsidiarity*, SEC (92) 1990 final, of 27 October 1992.

C. Explaining the Court's doctrine on subsidiarity

Leaving aside *ad hoc* explanations of the Court's stance towards subsidiarity, such as the way in which the applicants prepared their respective actions in the cases examined above, I now turn to the exposition of more long-term, structural reasons or the Court's current approach to subsidiarity. The Court's attitude can be explained by taking into account two main variables: the Court's own legitimacy as an institution and its political agenda. In general, the commitment to subsidiarity failed since it did not take into account the fact that counter-majoritarian institutions are also concerned about their own legitimacy and that they may develop their own agendas. Therefore, if the instruments designed for counter-majoritarian purposes lack a specific (i.e. technical) nature, the agency may not use them since their employment may put its legitimacy in question. Further, as Kiewiet and McCubbins (1991:26) indicate, agents may attempt to exploit their autonomy even against the interests of the principal. This is what those authors refer to as the 'Madison problem'. The Madison problem has also arisen, at least in part, in the ECJ. In effect, as shall be argued, the ECJ has developed its own agenda, which is dominated by the objective of integration. Although Member States also favour integration, at certain points they may prefer autonomy (i.e. national intervention) to integration. Therefore the Court's and the Member States' agendas do not entirely coincide, and may even be contradictory. The following discussion shows that both the legitimacy of the Court as an institution and the Court's integration agenda have played a role in the judicial implementation of subsidiarity.

1. *The Court's Legitimacy as an Independent Variable influencing its Doctrine on Subsidiarity*

Member States know by now that the Court of Justice has not turned subsidiarity into the counter-majoritarian totem of which they once dreamed. Recalling what has been said above on the Court's doctrine on the principle, it is clear that if a Member State is outvoted in the Council it will not be able to count on the Court to ensure that the measure is annulled on the basis of subsidiarity, as a general rule. Given the hopes that the Member States had for the legal implementation of the principle, the current state of affairs needs to be explained.

The first factor in the Court's attitude to subsidiarity is its own legitimacy as an institution. It is well known that the Court of Justice has moulded its case-law to the canons of classical legal reasoning. It could not have done otherwise. The Court wished to exercise objectivity and neutrality in its case-law, in common with courts on the continent, and beyond. Courts are not generally elected bodies, and when they are elected it is not in the same sense as politicians. Courts are essentially technical bodies. If they do not want their decisions to be challenged they must be seen to be simply interpreting and applying a technical instrument: the law. In many senses, law is for courts what a scalpel is for surgeons or a square for architects. The European Court of Justice has gained legitimacy through its insistence on appearing to legal practitioners as the *bouche qui prononce les mots de la loi*. Even the most critical observers of the Court's work acknowledge this effort (Weiler, 1991a). The Court knows that its survival as an institution, and the extent to which its decisions are accepted, depend on its continuing to convince observers that its decisions are based strictly on the interpretation and application of European Community law, and not merely a matter of preference or expediency.

Let us develop this point further. As we know, the continental and the Anglo-Saxon legal families are the legal models that the Court has used as paradigms in articulating its case-law. The first model, the continental, or Romano-Germanic model, is characterized by the idea that the legal system is complete and has no lacunas. Where no norm directly regulates a particular factual issue there appears to be a legal gap, but this is only apparent. In reality, according to the continental paradigm, the legal system is capable of absorbing those gaps, mainly through analogy. Thus, in the continental model, the judiciary must always start from the legal norm as a way to reach a decision. The link between the judicial decision and the legal norm is a real exigency of the system. The following quote, drawn from David and Brierly's analysis of the legal families of the world, is especially illuminating in this respect:

In countries of the Romano-Germanic family, the starting point for all legal reasoning is found in various forms of 'written law'. Today these textual materials consist mainly of codes, statutes and regulations whereas formerly they were made up Roman law texts and other compilations [. . .]. [Such texts] are considered to be a more or less well defined juridical framework which the work of interpretation will complete. The interpreter [. . .] has a certain latitude. But it prefers to dissimulate its creative role and give the impression that it merely applies rules drawn up by someone else. The extent to which its work is in fact creative, and the care taken to hide its creativity, vary according to the time, country, branches of law and the courts considered. It is difficult here to make comparisons, with any certainty, because the practice on this point is poorly described by doctrinal writers who are themselves often far unconscious of the way in which it operates [. . .]. However, for historical or sociological reasons, it may be that a given country is intent on preserving the appearance that statutory law is the only source in the rendering of some particular decisions—and it may be, too, that at certain times or in certain branches of law this appearance does indeed correspond to reality, because the law is satisfactory and requires no adjustment (David and Brierley, 1985:125–6).

Legal interpretation methods in the Romano-Germanic system are all of a deductive kind. The written norm is the superior premise from which, as in Kantian syllogisms, a particular answer to a given problem is derived. The Anglo-Saxon system, which has also served as a source of legal inspiration for the Court (though maybe in more recent periods, due to the late UK accession to the EC) starts from different premises than the continental model. Written law is also the main basis of the system but, especially for historical reasons, case-law has much more significance in the Anglo-Saxon model than in the continental one. This has traditionally allowed, and it still allows, a greater margin for judges' creativity. However, and this is a frequent misunderstanding, the link to the law (even if it is judge-made law) is no less strong in the Anglo-Saxon model than in the continental one. This is illustrated by the role that judicial precedent plays in the Anglo-Saxon system. Therefore the legal interpretation methods are also of a deductive kind, and they impose demands of coherence and precision similar to those in the continental system, the main difference being that the starting point is not only statute law but also case-law. As David and Brierlely point out:

English law is very clearly a product of English history when one considers particularly its categories and concepts and the prominent role played by the Courts. 'The life of the law', wrote Holmes, 'has not been logic; the life of the law has been experience'. We must however be careful not to exaggerate the difference which is sometimes said to exist between the French and English law on this point. Romanist laws are in no sense less a product of history than English law. Their history however has been different: it gave a greater place to university teaching, *la doctrine* and legislation, and the result is that Romanist law appears structurally more systematic and, perhaps, more apparently rational than English law. But is English law really less logical and more practical than the Romanist laws? This is at least doubtful. Between the practical sense dear to the English and the logic dear to the French there is a middle path, a factor that reconciles them because it is at the heart of each law: this is reason (*la raison*).

It is of course true that English law was fashioned and its legal rules enunciated only as a function of the disputes with which the royal courts chanced to deal. But when the royal courts adjudicated they were not dominated by such a sense of what was practical that they were led to render a simply equitable solution in each case. While constructing the common law system it was always necessary to seek the solution most in agreement with reason, and a deciding factor in the discovery of this solution was the desire to achieve a consistency in legal decision-making. This, necessarily, supposed recourse to logic (David and Brierley, 1985:395).

The requirement of coherency, be it in relation to a legal norm or to a judicial decision, is therefore the basis of the legal traditions on which the Court of Justice has built its own legal culture. The appearance that a court is either interpreting or applying norms has had obvious repercussions on the European Court of Justice. To keep this appearance, a court must use legal-deductive reasoning: it must show that its decisions derive, after a deductive process, from the law (in the wide sense of the term). This is the method that the European Court has used in its judgments.

The legal reasoning of the Court of Justice has been analysed in depth by Bengoetxea (1993). That analysis is especially relevant for my purposes because it argues the last point theoretically and shows empirically how the Court has endeavoured to employ a logic-deductive model of reasoning to give flesh to its decisions. According to Bengoetxea, the Court of Justice has mainly employed three kinds of 'first order interpretative criteria'[54] for justifying its decisions in 'hard cases': semiotic, systemic and dynamic. The second-order interpretative criteria show a preference for systemic-cum-dynamic criteria of interpretation (Bengoetxea, 1993:234).

Each of these criteria may be briefly analysed. With a great deal of simplification, one may say that the systemic criterion implies that legal arguments are deduced from the syntactic or semantic elements that exist in legal language. Legal criteria are also deduced from, for example, a comparison between the different official languages in which the ECT is written. Legal norms are therefore seen as 'special types of speech acts, and the semiotic criteria are drawn from the locutionary and illocutionary force of those acts in order to interpret their meaning for legal purposes' (Bengoetxea, 1993:234). 'Typical' semantic arguments used by the Court are: those that appeal to the 'literal' sense of a particular norm; those which make reference to the 'Community' meaning of a norm or principle, irrespective of the fact that the latter also exist in the national legal order with a different meaning; or the

---

[54] First-order interpretative criteria are those that serve to interpret a legal provision. Second-order criteria are those that serve to establish a hierarchy between the first-order interpretative criteria. For example, a criterion according to which 'textual' interpretation is to have preference over teleological interpretation would be a second-order interpretative criterion, and the 'textual' and 'teleological' criteria would be first-order. See Bengoetxea (1993:233).

appeal to the 'ordinary meaning' of a particular provision, in which case the method of comparing different language versions of the ECT is normally used.

Systemic criteria are those that take into account the legal context of a norm. The norm to be interpreted would make no sense if no reference to that context was made. This criterion is used by the Court particularly in cases of *stricto sensu* interpretations. Furthermore, many of the systemic arguments or criteria that the Court employs come from inferences derived from norms different to the one being interpreted. Here we have analogical arguments: *a fortiori*, *a contrario*, *lex specialis derogat generalis*, *lex posterior derogat anterior*, and so on (Bengoetxea, 1993:241).

Finally, the dynamic criteria, by far the most complex category, consist mainly of three kinds of arguments: functional arguments, teleological arguments, and consequentialist arguments. Functional arguments or criteria are those that emphasize the need to interpret Community law in such a way as to give it the fullest legal effect. Teleological arguments are those drawn from the objectives that the norms establish, either implicitly or explicitly. Consequentialist arguments point at the consequences to which a given interpretation may lead. More specifically, among the classical functional arguments that the Court employs we find the *effet utile* argument (according to which the Court opts for the interpretation that allows the norm its fullest legal effects) and arguments that refer to the fullest achievement of the competences and tasks of the Community. Further, teleological arguments refer to the objectives of a particular measure. These kinds of arguments are normally used when the Court is asked to judge whether a measure adopted by an institution is adequate. Arguments in this regard abound, since the ECT explicitly establishes a list of objectives that the Community institutions must endeavour to fulfil.[55] This led classical legal commentators to state, as Bengoetxea (1993:252) points out, that *'les Traités sont pétris de téleologie'*. A typical teleological argument is the reference to the need to achieve a single European market. Finally, regarding consequentialist arguments, typical arguments of this kind are those that refer to the legal implications of a given interpretation, or those that refer to the extra-legal repercussions (economic, for instance) that might arise from judicial decisions (Bengoetxea, 1993:256). As far as consequentialist arguments are concerned, references to the preamble and the general parts of the Treaty are very common.

---

[55] Note Art. 2 ECT (ex. Art. 2).

Bengoetxea's in-depth analysis allows us to conclude that the European Court of Justice has developed a legal infra-structure based on the logic-deductive method with the aim of offering reasoning for its decisions which correspond with a pattern of coherence, legal consistency, and predictability. The Court's legal reasoning has been the main source of its legitimacy. As a non-elected, counter-majoritarian (in principle) body, the legitimacy and acceptance of its outcomes depend upon the technical quality of its judgments. The same kind of logic applies to other technical, counter-majoritarian, institutions, such as the European Central Bank. The European Central Bank must justify its decisions according to technical criteria. Here technical means economic, and in particular monetary, criteria. It would be unacceptable for the ECB to adopt a decision according to political rather than technical criteria. In the case of the Court, technical means legal. The Court knows that its legitimacy is contingent upon the quality of its legal reasoning, and it has therefore made a considerable effort to envelop its decisions (even constitutional decisions with a big impact) in legal format.

If one accepts the foregoing, then the Court's prudence concerning subsidiarity may be accounted for. The application of Bengoetxea's scheme for subsidiarity shows that the principle adapts only partially to the parameters of legal reasoning that the Court has established over the years.

If one takes first the semiotic criterion, which attempts to reach the 'literal meaning' of a given norm on the basis of the text of that provision, it is evident that the least that can be said about Article 5(2) of the Treaty is that clarity is not its main characteristic. This has been shown elsewhere in this work and does not merit further attention here.[56] With regard to the Protocol on subsidiarity, the answer should probably be further expanded, since some provisions of the Protocol are clearer than others. But in general terms the Protocol gives a variegated and complex impression and, as noted above,[57] many of its fundamental provisions (above all as regards material subsidiarity) are unclear. Given this general obscurity, the semiotic method would not be a safe course for the Court to undertake if it wanted to make the most of the principle of subsidiarity, that is, to employ the principle to annul a Community provision against a majority in the Council.

The next criterion is the contextual criterion. This involves interpreting a legal norm by reference to the legal context surrounding that norm. From this perspective, it is difficult to see which legal norms could serve as a 'context' for subsidiarity, besides the norms contained in the Protocol on

---

[56] See, in particular, Chapter III above.   [57] See Chapter IV above.

subsidiarity. The probable exception to this is proportionality. In fact, in many analyses (and even in the British case examined above) subsidiarity is linked to proportionality. However, it must be noted that subsidiarity is not about balancing means with ends, as happens with proportionality, but about comparing potential actions *at two regulatory levels*, the national and the Community one, which further complicates assessments. Further, applying a 'proportionality' reading to the subsidiarity principle would be applying the principle of proportionality, and not strictly subsidiarity. Thus the contextual criterion must be also rejected.

Finally, the dynamic criterion includes, as stated above, functional, teleological, and consequentialist arguments. Teleological arguments would be of more interest for interpreting a principle than functional and consequentialist ones. As already noted, the objective of subsidiarity is to allow Community intervention only when it is more efficient and effective than that of Member States. The problem here is how to interpret the concepts of efficiency and effectiveness. As we know, the Protocol on subsidiarity gives a number of clues as to how to interpret those criteria: the transnational and the market distortion criteria. We would then need, as well as a teleological interpretation, a semantic-type interpretation of those parameters. However, the legal—semantic—interpretation of the transnational and market distortion criteria would not be an easy task, as has already been shown. It is therefore clear that the teleological interpretation would lead to a semantic one, which would also be very difficult to make.

Subsidiarity can thus be seen to be ill adapted to the interpretative criteria normally used by the Court. An example gives further evidence of this point. The example is extracted from the aforementioned British case.[58] Let us assume that, contrary to what the Court did in that case, the ECJ had wanted to annul the working time Directive on subsidiarity grounds. How could it have proceeded to this end?

A possible way to approach the question would be to check whether the Directive fulfils the objective of the measure (workers' health and safety protection) better than the Member States' respective regulations. To do this, however, the Court would have to make a detailed analysis of the way in which regulations of different Member States protect workers. Then it would have to compare the results of that assessment with the way in which the Directive would protect workers. It is already clear that this kind of assessment would be of great complexity. However, some authors have

---

[58] Case C-84/94 [1996] ECR I-5755.

proposed that an assessment of the ensemble could be simplified through a cost–benefit analysis (Dehousse, 1993:9). Although this kind of analysis, especially if made explicitly, is already far from being a strict legal assessment, let us see what its outcome might be.

In the first place, the Court of Justice could analyse the costs that the Community measure would impose upon the Member States' undertakings. Old Article 118A(2) (now Article 137(2)), which served as a legal basis for the working time Directive, establishes that '[directives] shall avoid imposing administrative, financial and legal constraints in a way which would hold back the creation and development of small and medium-sized undertakings'. In the second place, the Court could analyse the costs that national measures would involve for the Community, which could be determined according to the market distortion criterion. This second aspect would probably be easier for the Court to determine than the first one, since it would be difficult for the Court to ascertain the costs that a Community measure would involve for the firms of Member States. Given this problem, the Court could use the second aspect (distortion of the common market as a result of diverging working time regulations) as a *iuris tantum* presumption. The burden to prove the contrary would be on the Member States seeking to annul the measure.

The above exercise allows us to make three points. First, the complexity of the analysis that the ECJ would have to attempt is tremendous. Secondly, it should be noted that a cost–benefit analysis, as proposed, goes far beyond a mere legal analysis. Although it is true that some Court decisions (like those concerning the principle of proportionality) have been explained from the perspective of a cost–benefit analysis, it is important to note that these are post-hoc reconstructions. The Court does not usually make analysis of that kind explicit. Finally, as concluded in my example, the result of the Court's attempt would probably be to justify the Community measure. The applicant would be left with only the right to overturn the Court's presumption: but as we know, negative proof is difficult to provide, in strictly legal terms.

It can therefore be concluded that the principle of subsidiarity is difficult to handle from a legal perspective, even if dynamic criteria are employed. This difficulty explains the Court's current approach to subsidiarity—which is, as noted above, one of extreme prudence. The Court seems to have opted for preserving its own legitimacy, since this could have been questioned if the Court had systematically employed subsidiarity to annul legally binding measures.

However, the explanation is only partial. It does explain why the Court has not implemented material subsidiarity. But the 'Court's legitimacy' variable does not explain why the Court did not consider procedural subsidiarity in more depth. In effect, contrary to the case with material subsidiarity, the Court could have developed a procedural argument on subsidiarity without departing from its established mould of legal reasoning. In other words, the infringement of procedural subsidiarity is much closer to a legal argument than the violation of material subsidiarity. Why did the Court not use this second dimension of the principle to bind the Community legislature?

2. The Court's Political Agenda as an Independent Variable of its Doctrine on Subsidiarity

The terms of the problem are the following. The first independent variable (the Court's legitimacy) serves to explain one part of the Court's approach to the principle (which concerns the non-implementation of material subsidiarity) but not the other (the part that concerns the non-implementation, or lack of full implementation, of procedural subsidiarity). We need a complementary variable to explain this second aspect of the Court's attitude.

As seen earlier in this Chapter, what the Court actually does as far as procedural subsidiarity is concerned is merely to apply its case-law on Article 253 ECT (ex Article 190). That is, it exercises minimum control over the statement of reasons, or the requirement to give reasons, as far as the Community legislature is concerned. The Court is satisfied if the legislature merely makes a general statement (without the need to invoke expressly Article 5(2) or subsidiarity) of why it considered Community action to be necessary. This stance cannot be explained by the Court's legitimacy variable, since a procedural subsidiarity assessment clearly fits within a legal assessment. For example, turning again to Bengoetxea's parameters (Bengoetxea, 1993) the Court could have implemented procedural subsidiarity (especially in the German case) by using, for example, a systemic-cum-dynamic criterion, interpreting the procedural obligations to state reasons that the principle establishes from the perspective of the context and objectives of Article 253 ECT (ex Article 190).

Before discussing the merits of the analysis of the variable that could explain this stance, it is important to make two points. First, the cases examined in this Chapter were decided before the Protocol on subsidiarity was incorporated into the ECT.[59] Therefore, although unlikely, the Court might

---

[59]   The Biotech case was decided on 9 October 2001, that is, after the Amsterdam Treaty came into force, but the Netherland's application was lodged at the Court Registry on 19 October 1998, that is before Amsterdam was in force. Thus the applicant could not make use of the Protocol on subsidiarity. Therefore the Biotech case is irrelevant from this perspective.

modify its approach to procedural subsidiarity as a consequence of the Protocol. Secondly, it is important to recall a point made above in connection with the categories of 'procedural' and 'material' subsidiarity. It was stated above that in reality both categories are heuristic devices. The boundaries between procedural and material subsidiarity are more theoretical than real. The Court knows this (as its spill-overs from procedural to material subsidiarity reflect) which could explain why the Court was also reluctant to implement procedural subsidiarity. The Court may have done this in order to avoid the criticism that, through implementing procedural subsidiarity, it intended to substitute the Council's discretion with its own.

However, it is also evident that this explanation is not fully satisfactory, since the Court's implementation of procedural subsidiarity amounted only to a very superficial check. The Court could have extended its check on procedural subsidiarity and at the same time avoided criticisms of running wild. Therefore, and even assuming the link between procedural and material subsidiarity, a further explanation is still needed.

In my view there is another variable, the Court's own political agenda. In effect, as has been argued by some analysts, the Court of Justice has a political agenda, dominated by the objective of fostering European integration. For example, according to Burley and Mattli (1993:70), 'the Court's self-professed task [is] integration'. Shaw makes a similar, although less explicit, claim when she says that 'law and integration—structural and socio-economic—exist in a cosy, intimate and entirely positive relation' and that 'integration is what is natural for the EU and equally what is natural for the law' (Shaw, 1995a:7). The case-law of the European Court of Justice on constitutionalizing the ECT,[60] and some of the writings of the Court's members, seem to provide evidence of this.[61]

Assuming therefore that the Court of Justice has an agenda dominated by the objective of integration, it is possible to argue that the other factor which explains the Court's attitude towards subsidiarity is the Court's perception that the principle might go against integration, and in particular against the

---

[60] It is not possible here to develop this argument in full. One example is Case 294/83 [1986] ECR 1339, in particular para. 23, in which the Court speaks of the ECT as the fundamental constitutional charter of the Community. For an analysis of the 'constitutionalizing' case-law of the ECJ, see Weiler (1991a).

[61] Two references may illustrate this point. The first is Pescatore's *The Law of Integration* (1974) in which the former Court's judge clearly assumes that agenda on, among many others, p. 22. The second is former Court judge Mancini, in *Europe: The Case for Statehood* (1998). Mancini explicitly argued in this paper that the European Community should integrate politically and adopt the form of a state.

development of Community competences. This idea merits an explanation. In effect, as surprising as it may be, at least from a continental perspective, the European Community today has a constitution, although this has been acquired not from a constituent act but through the process of legal interpretation that the ECJ has developed. The case of *Les Verts*,[62] in which the Court referred to the ECT as the *fundamental constitutional charter* of the Community, constitutes the highest point of this case-law. In order to be able to refer to the ECT as the fundamental constitutional charter of the Community, the Court first had to develop foundations upon which that constitution could rest. One of these was its case-law on fundamental rights. The other, more important for our purposes, was its case-law on competences.

One of the most important aspects of the *constitutionalizing* jurisprudence of the Court has been its case-law on competences. As we know, the ECT does not include a list of competences,[63] unlike many national constitutions of a federal or quasi-federal character.[64] Rather, the ECT establishes material fields within which the Community may act, and it fixes objectives. This indeterminacy has allowed the Court to develop what could be termed, again using Bengoetxea's (1993) tools of analysis, a teleological reading of the issue of competence. Community competences have been interpreted primarily as a function of Community objectives, and not (or only secondarily) in *rationae materia* terms. The outcome has been a very wide interpretation of the field of Community's competences. We cannot delve into the analysis of this abundant case-law here,[65] but as evidence for this we can cite the fact that the Court has never annulled a Community legislative measure due to lack of competence (Alonso García, 1994:363).[66]

The establishment of a stable nucleus of Community competences has been an essential step in the achievement of the Court's objective of constitutionalizing the ECT. In effect, as Weiler (1997) remarks, without that competential transformation (among other things), the Court of Justice could only with

---

[62] Case 294/83 [1986] ECR 1339.

[63] But see Declaration 'on the future of the Union' of the Treaty of Nice, which has convened a new intergovernmental conference to discuss, among other things, the insertion of a catalogue of comptences within the ECT.

[64] For example the Spanish Constitution. See its Title VIII.   [65] See Weiler (1991a).

[66] It has, however, annulled legislative measures on the ground of erroneous legal basis, which admittedly is very close to lack of competence. However, note that when the Court accepts the argument that the legal base was incorrect, it is not holding that the Community totally lacks competence to intervene. What the Court is saying in these cases is that the legal basis for adopting the measure was not the correct one. In theory at least, the Court is not closing the possibility that other legal bases are used to implement a Community competence. See in this regard Case C-376/98, the co-called 'Tobacco' case, commented on in fn.4 of this chapter.

difficulty have spoken in the 1986 case of *Les Verts* of the shift from a Treaty to a constitutional charter. The connection between a wide interpretation of Community competences and the process towards the constitutionalization of the ECT, and the link between the idea of constitution and the final end of integration, which the Court has defended in its case-law, may explain the antipathy that the Court has professed towards subsidiarity. For the Court, subsidiarity threatened a hard-won achievement, since it could be used to stop the 'natural' development of Community competences towards greater integration; it could even mean that Community competences would have to be returned to the Member States. From this perspective, subsidiarity was not only very difficult to deal with in strict legal terms, but also a real danger for the fulfilment of the Court's plans for integration.

It is clear that at this point we are very close to a normative discussion, which means that evidence is difficult to obtain. I am conscious that one can either agree with this view or not. However, there is some corroboration for my thesis. Though it is true that these indications are not hard empirical evidence, at least they are clues that allow an argument to be formulated and that allow us to discount other possible explanations. On the other hand, this is a generalized problem with analysing courts' motivations. Considering that discretion is one of the main weapons of courts, one should expect these institutions to hide their real motives and preferences. Therefore the only possibility here is to rely on indirect evidence.

The indirect evidence to which I refer are the doctrinal writings of the Court's members, who write in doctrinal journals. They write a lot, and usually about the things that they know best: cases in which they have participated or might participate. This privileged source is evidence about what a judge (or a court) thinks about those things that most worry him or her. As Schepel and Wesseling suggest (1997:168), although relatively neglected, the doctrinal writings of Court members may be a useful aid to reconstructing the background to decisions.

Analysis of some European Court of Justice's members writings seem to support the idea that the Court has perceived subsidiarity to be a negative development in the Community process towards integration. Three of these pieces are, from my perspective, particularly illustrative.

The first is an article published in 1990 by Mischo, then Advocate General of the Court of Justice.[67] The article was entitled *Un rôle nouveau pour la Cour de Justice?* The Advocate General discussed whether the Court was a consti-

---

[67] Jean Mischo is again an Advocate General since 19 December 1997.

tutional court or not. It was written in the wake of a heated debate at the time of the reform of the European Court of Justice.[68] Mischo's main thesis was that discussion of whether the Court should be a constitutional court was somewhat superficial, since the Court of Justice had been implementing constitutional functions almost since its inception. For Mischo, the proof that the Court was already performing constitutional functions was three-fold: first, the control by the Court of the power conflicts among the Community institutions; secondly, the Court's check on Member States' competences; and thirdly, and conversely, the Court's check on the development of the Community's competences.

It was in the context of the last of these that the Advocate General considered it opportune to refer to subsidiarity. According to Mischo, subsidiarity was unnecessary since the mechanisms established by the Treaty for the Court's check on the development of the Community's competences were sufficient. This notwithstanding, the Advocate General was much more ambiguous when citing examples. In fact, he only cited cases in which the Court had annulled administrative, and not legislative, decisions (Mischo, 1990:682). This did not prevent the Advocate General from indicating that subsidiarity constituted a superfluous mechanism of the Community's competential control. Further, Mischo gave two complementary arguments for rejecting subsidiarity. The first was that subsidiarity was a political principle, and not a legal instrument. If the Court annulled a Community legislative measure on the ground of subsidiarity it could be accused of making politics and not law. In the Advocate General's words:

It has recently been suggested from various quarters that the possibility of granting the ECJ the competence to examine whether a particular regulation or draft directive or even an act adopted by the Community's legislature is incompatible with the subsidiarity principle. *From our perspective, we have the tendency to think* that the answer to the question of whether a particular action can be better attained at the Community level or at the Member State level can only result from an assessment of a political nature which involves taking into consideration efficiency or opportunity criteria. Judges are traditionally inclined not to judge on this kind of questions. As the former President of the Court of Justice, M. Donner, once wrote, 'to decide what, in a legal vacuum, is just and reasonable, goes beyond our capacity and engenders confusion among each of us [. . .]. The judge needs a norm, or, as happens in common law, a system of precedents, which can have as basis for delimiting the case at hand and be able to find logical motives to adopt a decision (Mischo, 1990:684; my emphasis; my translation).

---

[68]   That discussion was stimulated by a polemic article by Jacqué and Weiler (1990).

Mischo's first argument against subsidiarity is linked to what has been referred to above as the 'Court's legitimacy' variable. This was not his only argument, however. In effect, Mischo continued by saying that, at best, the principle of subsidiarity should only govern the distribution of competences between Member States and the Community in inter-governmental conferences. Therefore, each time Member States discussed whether or not to grant a new competence to the Community, the subsidiarity principle should guide them on this point. However, Mischo sounded an important warning. For him, the principle of subsidiarity should only apply to new competences, and never to old ones. Therefore the implementation of subsidiarity would make sense only in a very limited number of cases. According to the author: 'In any case, it is especially at the institutional level, and also in relation to the Monetary Union, social policy, external relations and security policy, where innovations are needed, since in relation to the other fields of Community competence, the Community has already acquired an even greater degree of integration than that obtained in the United States (Mischo, 1990:686; my translation).

Mischo concluded that subsidiarity would best be incorporated in the ECT in the Preamble (ibid.: 686).

The fear of the disintegrative potential of subsidiarity is even clearer in the two following pieces, by Kapteyn and by Lenaerts.[69]

Kapteyn expressed his view on subsidiarity in a conference in November 1990, at the annual meeting of the United Kingdom Association for European Law. Kapteyn started by acknowledging that he had chosen, 'not without hesitation' (Kapteyn, 1991:35) to lecture on the principle. Among the reasons that made Kapteyn doubt his subject choice was the idea that 'the principle of subsidiarity apparently is essentially alien to the tradition of the unitary state and to a centralised political system such as the one that exists in the United Kingdom' (ibid.: 35). For Kapteyn, as for Mischo, the principle of subsidiarity was a political guideline whose application concerns the Community legislature, not its judiciary. 'If the principle of subsidiarity' he added 'is formulated in such a way that it can be objectivised, then it is amenable to judicial review. But even this judicial control will be of a limited character and only in exceptional circumstances can lead to a negative judgement on the measures taken or to be proposed' (ibid.: 41). The reason for his scepticism is found in another paragraph. According to Kapteyn, from the perspective of the principle of integration, the principle of subsidiarity is simply a counter-intuitive term, since: 'in a system of limited powers conferred

---

[69] Kapteyn was a judge of the ECJ from 29 March 1990 to 6 October 2000. Lenaerts is a judge of the CFI at present.

on the Community for the realisation of a limited objective, namely the establishment and operation of a common market, the importation of the subsidiarity principle is redundant, confusing and dangerous because it calls in question the system laid down in the Treaty and deprives the logic of functional integration of its driving force' (ibid.: 39).

The reticence displayed by the Court of Justice concerning the principle of subsidiarity as a consequence of the contradiction between that principle and the objective of integration is even clearer in the doctrinal writings of Judge Lenaerts. This author has invested much effort, not so much in criticizing the anti-integrative potential of subsidiarity, but rather in demonstrating that subsidiarity can be interpreted in 'integration' terms, thus sending an appeal for calm to the legal world of the European Community. This is even more relevant for the purposes of my analysis. Lenaerts' efforts are a very subtle but clear way of deactivating the debate on the potential effects of subsidiarity on the Court's agenda. In effect, Lenaerts' general argument revolves around the idea that subsidiarity is, after all, not such a danger for the development of the Community, since it is a principle that could be used both for granting new competences to the Comunity and for blocking interventions. In this way it would come full circle: subsidiarity, a principle introduced into the ECT to stop Community intervention would, if properly used, serve to promote more Community interventions. This conclusion is apparently not seen as contentious or paradoxical by the Judge.

Lenaerts has written a number of articles on subsidiarity. The first article that can be cited here to substantiate my theory is an analysis published with Ypersele in 1994. In this work of almost ninety pages the authors analysed the legal implications of the principle extensively. Paradoxically, although the study acknowledged that the principle of subsidiarity was incorporated into the ECT as a tool to block 'those interventions that could be deemed to be unjustified by the Member States',[70] the authors' final conclusion was that:

In this way, the Community action is subsidiary to those of Member States, even when the Community has been attributed competence. From this perspective, the principle of subsidiarity, in itself, seems more a factor of disintegration than a factor of integration. However, this conclusion is, in reality, the result of a poorly posed question. The balance sheet that has to be drawn up, in terms of integration, is not only about Article 3B(2), but about the Treaty as a whole. Article 3B(2) is the compensation for the enlargement of Community competences, for the expansion of majority voting and for the extension of EP powers [. . .]. The combination of these transformations and of the incorporation of subsidiarity may be summarized in the

[70] My translation.

following way: more competences, even new ones, but competences whose implementation is subject to the proof of Member States' insufficiency [. . .] Conceived thus, subsidiarity should even allow for new transfers of competences to the Community (Lenaerts and Ypersele, 1994:82ff; my translation).

In a second article (1994b) Lenaerts focused on showing with a specific example (the environment) that subsidiarity was not a significant obstacle to the evolution of Community competences in that field,[71] even in those cases in which the Court implemented the principle strictly, something that the prolific Judge strongly advocates against. In effect, for Lenaerts, the Court should, at most, use self-restraint in applying the principle in its procedural dimension, but not in the material one. On the other hand, Lenaerts warned that the implementation of the principle should never call into question the *acquis communautaire*, since the principle 'does not relate to and cannot call into question the powers conferred on the European Community by the Treaty as interpreted by the Court' (1994b:893). Finally, Lenaerts concluded that the environmental example showed that the fears of the legal Community about the implementation of subsidiarity should be dissipated, since:

As we have seen, in the area of the environment, it should be easy to substantiate the reasons for Community action. As far as the need for such action is concerned, reference will be made to the several types of environmental spillovers. As to the nature and intensity of Community action, it will be sufficient to justify the division of responsibilities between the Community and the Member States for regulation, implementation, and monitoring by reference to their respective capabilities (ibid.: 895).[72]

The conclusion that can be drawn from the analysis of the doctrinal writings cited above is the following. The Court of Justice has been especially reluctant to implement material subsidiarity, but has also hesitated to implement procedural subsidiarity. Although the distance that the Court has kept from material subsidiarity can be explained by the Court's legitimacy variable, the Court's flexibility on procedural subsidiarity is hard to explain from that perspective, since the implementation of procedural subsidiarity is within the parameters of the Court's legal reasoning. Another additional explanation is therefore neces-

---

[71] It is interesting to note that environmental policy was the example used by Golub to show precisely the opposite point: that subsidiarity was useful for stopping Community intervention (see Chapter IV above). This shows the ambiguous nature of the principle.

[72] See also Lenaerts (1995). This article analyses the implementation of the principle in the field of education. It is not necessary to describe this here since Lenaerts adopts a similar approach.

sary. It has been argued above that the Court of Justice has been reticent in implementing procedural subsidiarity (but this explanation could also serve for material subsidiarity) because, in the Court's view, the principle goes against the concept of integration. Systematic implementation of subsidiarity would involve a break with the interpretative tradition of the Community competences which has been based on the idea of integration. Breaking with this expansive vision of the Community competences could, in turn, call into question the 'constitutionalizing' case-law of the Court of Justice, which depends, among other things, on the existence of an ever-growing and well settled nucleus of competences. Finally, to call into question the 'constitutionalizing' jurisprudence of the Court would go against the integrative agenda held by this institution. That the principle of subsidiarity is ill adapted to the Court's agenda is shown by three elements which can be extracted from the judges' writings on the principle: first, the Court's insistence on the idea that the principle is more political than legal; secondly, the Court's perseverance with the idea that the principle may not, in any case, call into question the *acquis communautaire*; and finally, the Court's insistence on the destructive (i.e. anti-integrationist) potential of subsidiarity, combined with the efforts of some judges to interpret the principle in integration terms. This last is the clearest indication that subsidiarity worries the Court. Considering that Member States introduced the principle in order to obstruct Community integration, an uncontested fact, even among judges, the previous interpretation is so clearly against the *telos* of the principle that it can only be explained as a strategic reaction of the Court in the face of a perceived threat.

D. Conclusions: when binding commitments fail

The introduction of subsidiarity into the Treaties has caused the ECJ to confront the dilemma of *to be or not to be* from the perspective of its view of itself as a constitutional court, in the sense of adopting a clearer counter-majoritarian role, as constitutional courts usually do. The significance of the Court's dilemma must be emphasized here. On the one side of the scale were considerations linked to the removal of protection for Council's minorities, as well as the pressure from Member States in favour of the Court adopting a clearer counter-majoritarian profile. On the other side were considerations linked to the Court's legitimacy as an institution and the potential danger that subsidiarity posed for the fulfilment of the Court's integration agenda.

I have shown above that subsidiarity could be conceptualized as a 'binding commitment' that the Member States established in order to prevent Community intervention beyond what was strictly necessary. This Chapter has provided further evidence of those cases in which binding commitments may fail. The subsidiarity case shows that commitments may fail when, technically speaking, they are not credible enough. Also, as the 'Madison problem' indicates, the 'agency' can develop agendas which may be contrary to the 'principal's' objectives. In the case of subsidiarity, the integration agenda of the Court was contrary to the contention plans of Member States; the subsidiarity commitment failed for this reason too.

That explanation still leaves a question floating in the air. This question is whether the Court of Justice was right in its approach to subsidiarity or not. As lawyers, we must also decide whether the choice adopted was just or not. As may be apparent from previous chapters, I celebrate the Court's current approach to subsidiarity: not because this will facilitate (or at least not hinder) integration, but above all because I understand that subsidiarity attempts to answer through legal technique what is, above all, a political question. The Court's stance on the principle should make Member States rethink their strategy to 'bind' the Community through subsidiarity. However, my support for the Court's stance is not without limits. Its stance on procedural subsidiarity is especially worrying, not for reasons of subsidiarity themselves, but for those of transparency. Although it is true that subsidiarity was introduced into the ECT for reasons not linked with transparency, the Court could have employed procedural subsidiarity to attempt to improve this aspect. Its current approach to procedural subsidiarity may well be a lost opportunity in this direction.

Irrespective of the positive opinion merited, in general, by the Court's current approach to subsidiarity (although our reasons are different form the Court's) it is also to be noted that the Court must start assuming a clearer counter-majoritarian role. It is evident, for the reasons stated in this work, that subsidiarity is not an adequate means of pursuing that goal. Other instruments of a more legal nature, such as proportionality, or the check of legal bases, could be used to this end. The point is not so much one of means, but rather one of objectives, of agendas. It is legitimate that the Court has its own agenda. It is also legitimate that the Court centres its agenda around the objective of integration. But the Community has changed. Other values within the ECT coexist with integration. The Court should therefore update its agenda, adapting it to the more complex valorative context that now exists in the Community. The days of integration being the only objective of the Community are simply gone with the wind; the ECJ should reflect this development in its case-law.

VI

Conclusions

This work has analysed the principle of subsidiarity and examined the judicial implementation of the principle. The aim of the first part (the analysis of subsidiarity) was to construct a more sustained legal critique of the principle. The purpose of the second part was to consider the extent to which the Court is implementing the principle and to explain the Court's current position on subsidiarity. My thesis was the following. Subsidiarity is ill adapted for use as a counter-majoritarian instrument and, more generally, for solving the federal legitimacy problems of the Community, for both functional and normative reasons. Functionally speaking, the principle seems devoid of any clear legal content, which makes its implementation, especially its legal implementation, problematic. In this I agreed with the classical legal critique of the principle. However, rather than merely assuming this point, as the latter usually does, I have attempted to demonstrate, with a detailed discussion of the different aspects of the principle, the extent to which subsidiarity is limited from a functional perspective. Further, from a normative perspective, I showed that the principle includes a kind of logic which is detrimental to the search for solutions which co-ordinate integration and diversity. In this I disagreed with the classical legal critique. In my view, subsidiarity is problematic, from a normative viewpoint, not because it runs counter to integration, but rather because it involves the continuation of an old, vertical logic in that it reduces the issue to either action by the Community or action by the Member States. This logic is probably outdated in the face of the federal legitimacy problems with which the European Community is confronted today. Solving these problems would require, in my view, a shift to a horizontally prone methodology.

Regarding the second track of this work, I showed that the Court's doctrine on the principle is extremely prudent. In particular, the Court has been very reluctant to employ subsidiarity not only to annul Community legislative measures, but also to check in depth whether the Community's legislature is respecting the new Community principle at all. This Court's stance concerns both material and procedural subsidiarity. I attempted to explain this current stance. I showed that the Court's approach to the principle may be explained by two variables: the Court's concern about its legitimacy as an institution and its integration agenda. The first variable assumes that for the Court to implement a legal instrument, it has to adapt to the classical canons of legal reasoning that the ECJ has developed over the years. If this is the case, then the Court's reluctance to implement subsidiarity fully may be explained if we take into account what was said in the first part of this book: subsidiarity is hardly a legal instrument. Therefore, one of the factors explaining the Court's attitude to the principle is that the Court does not wish to risk its own legitimacy by implementing a principle that is not clearly legal. It would have wanted to avoid, by adopting this stance, the eventual charges of being or acting politically rather than technically. The legitimacy variable does not explain everything, however. It *does* explain why the Court did not implement material subsidiarity. However, it *does not* explain, or at least not clearly, why it chose not fully to implement procedural subsidiarity. In effect, unlike material subsidiarity, procedural subsidiarity may adapt more closely to the classical canons of legal reasoning that the Court employs. This being the case, the previous explanation does not explain why the Court was also so prudent about procedural, and not only material subsidiarity. To explain this second aspect I assumed (but tried also to demonstrate) that the Court has a particular agenda which is dominated by the objective of integration. In this case, the argument was that the Court's general perception (in line with the classical critique of the principle) is that the principle of subsidiarity is a threat to integration. Thus the principle of subsidiarity would threaten the integration agenda of the Court, and this would explain why it chose not to implement the procedural dimension of the principle either. It seems, in general, that the Court dislikes the principle, and that it gives it an 'orientation' role for the Community legislature, but not a true legal dimension which could be used for enforcement purposes.

That thesis was substantiated within a more general context, by a discussion of the impact that the process of growth of the Community powers has had on Member States' sovereignty. After offering data of the growth of the Community powers, both on the expansion and implementation of competences and on the theory and reality of majority voting, I analysed such data from the perspective of a number of legitimacy models. The model I put forward was the 'federal' legitimacy model, according to which the evolution of competences in a procedural context dominated by the threat of a vote produces legitimacy tensions in those *polis* which lack the necessary degree of social cohesion. This has been the case in the European Community. The expansion of majority voting in the EC would have produced a 'federal' legitimacy crisis, since Member States perceived this development as curtailing their powers and sovereignty.

In my interpretation, the principle of subsidiarity was introduced into the ECT as a counter-majoritarian instrument. Member States attempted to 'bind' the Community through subsidiarity, mainly by making it reviewable before the Court of Justice, to a course of action more respectful of Council minorities. The 'binding commitment' of subsidiarity worked as follows: if the Community succumbed to the siren songs of intervention, then the Court would strike down those measures considered to be unacceptable. Delegation by the ECJ of the power to review legislative measures on grounds of subsidiarity was therefore the essential mechanism for making a credible commitment to subsidiarity.

However, the commitment to subsidiarity failed. It failed because the Court of Justice did not implement subsidiarity, or at least not as was expected. The Court chose not to implement subsidiarity because it was far from being a legal tool that could be implemented without risking the Court's legitimacy, and also because the perceived philosophy underlining subsidiarity was deemed to be contrary to the Court's plans. The case of subsidiarity therefore shows, on a more general level, the conditions under which binding commitments, consisting of the delegation of review powers to a Court, may not work.

BIBLIOGRAPHY

Alonso García (1994): *Derecho Comunitario: Sistema constitucional y administrativo* (Madrid Ceura)

Alter and Meunier-Aitsahalia (1994): 'Judicial Politics in the EC: European Integration and the Pathbreaking Cassis de Dijon Judgement', *Comparative Political Studies*, Vol. 26, 4, January p. 535

Althusius (1995): *Politica* (translated by Frederick S. Carney) (Indianapolis: Liberty Fund)

Amato (1995): 'Distribution of Powers' in 'A Constitution for the European Union? Proceedings of a Conference', 12–13 May 1994. Organized by the Robert Schuman Centre with the Patronage of the European Parliament, *EUI Working Paper RSC 95/9*, p. 85

Areilza (1995a): 'El principio de subsidiariedad en la construcción de la Unión Europea', *Revista Española de Derecho Constitucional*, Sep-Dec. Año 15, Número 45, p. 53

—— (1995b): 'La reforma de la Comision Europea', *Nueva Revista*, XIV, 41 Octubre-Noviembre, p. 112

Arp (1995): 'Multiple Actors and Arenas: European Community Regulation in a Polycentric System: A Case Study on Car Emission Policy' (Ph.D. thesis, Florence, EUI)

Aristotle (1944): *Politics* (Series 'Aristotles' Works' 21. London: Heinemann)

Bacigalupo (1994): 'La constitucionalidad del Tratado de la Unión Europea en Alemania (La sentencia del Tribunal Constitucional Federal de 12 de Octubre de 1993)', *Gaceta Jurídica de la CE y de la Competencia*, D-21, p. 7

Ballbé and Padrós (1997): *Estado competitivo y armonización europea* (Ariel: Barcelona)

Barón (1996): *L'Europe à l'Aube du Millenaire* (Paris: Kime)

Basabe (2000): *Problemas jurídicos en torno a la aplicación del principio de subsidiariedad en el ámbito de la Unión Europea: Justiciabilidad e intervención legislativa* (Pamplona: Universidad de Navarra)

Bellamy Bufacchi, and Castiglione (eds.) (1995): *Democracy and Constitutional Culture in the Unión of Europe* (London: Lothian Foundation)

Bengoetxea (1993): *The Legal Reasoning of the European Court of Justice* (Oxford: NY)

Bercusson (1994): 'Social Policy at the Crossroads: European Labour Law after Maastricht' in Renaud Dehousse (ed.): *Europe After Maastricht: An Ever Closer Union?* (Munich: Beck) p. 149

—— (1995): 'The Working Time Directive: A European Model of Working Time?' paper presented at the European Forum (Florence, 27, 28, 29 April 1995)

Bermann (1994): 'Taking Subsidiarity Seriously: Federalism in the EC and in the USA', *Columbia Law Review*, Vol. 94, 2, March, p. 331

Bieber *et al.* (eds.) (1988): *1992: One European Market? A Critical Analysis of the Commission's Internal Market Strategy* (Baden-Baden: Nomos)

Blair (1991): 'Federalism, Legalism and Political Reality: the Record of the Federal Constitutional Court' in Jeffery and Savigear (eds.): *German Federalism Today* (London: Leicester UP) p. 63

Botein (1987): 'Deregulation of the Electronic Media in the United States: An Overview and Status Report', in Mestmäcker (ed.): *The Law and Economics of Transborder Telecommunications* (Baden-Baden: Nomos) p. 187

Bourdieu (1991): *Language and Symbolic Power* (Cambridge: Polity Press)

Bourlanges (1996): 'Achieving a New Balance Between Large and Small States' in Philip Morris Institute for Public Policy Research (ed.): *In a Larger EU, Can All Member States Be Equal?* (Brussels: Philip Morris Institute) p. 26

Bradley (1997) 'The European Parliament and Comitology: On the Road to Nowhere?', *European Law Journal*, vol. 3, p. 230

Brent (1995): 'The Binding Leviathan? The Changing Role of the European Commission in Competition Cases', *International and Comparative Law Quarterly*, Vol. 44 2 April, p. 255

Bribosia (1992): 'Subsidiarité et répartition des compétences entre la Communauté et ses Etats Membres', *Revue du Marché Unique Européen*, 4, p. 165

——(1998): 'De la subsidiarité à la cooperation renforcée' in *Le Traité d'Amsterdam: Espoirs et Déceptions. Études coordonnnées par Yves Lejeune* (Bruxelles: Bruylant), p. 23

Bulmer (1991): 'Efficiency, Democracy and West German Federalism: A Critical Analysis' in Jeffery and Savigear (eds): *German Federalism Today* (London: Leicester UP) p. 81

Burley and Mattli (1993): 'Europe Before the Court: A Political Theory of Legal Integration', *International Organization* 47, 1, Winter, p. 41

Cass (1992): 'The Word that Saves Maastricht? The Principle of Subsidiarity and the Division of Powers within the European Community', *Common Market Law Review*, 29, p. 1107

CEPR Report (1993): *Making sense of subsidiarity: How much centralization for Europe?* (London: Centre for European Policy Research)

Charlemagne (1994): 'L'Equilibre entre les Etats Memmbres', cited by CEPS Special Report 6 (1995): *Preparing for 1996 and a Larger European Union* (Brussels: Centre for European Policy Studies)

Christiansen (1995): 'Second Thoughts: The Committee of the Regions after its First Year' in Dehousse and Christiansen (eds.): *What model for the Committee of the Regions?*, *EUI Working Paper EUF* no. 95/2 p. 34

Christophersen (1996): 'Change is inevitable, loss of influence is not' in Philip Morris Institute for Public Policy Research (ed.): *In a Larger EU, Can All Member States Be Equal?* (Brussels: Philip Morris Institute) p. 38

Chung (1995): 'The Relationship Between States Regulation and EC Competition Law: Two Proposals for a Coherent Approach', *European Competition Law Review*, vol. 16, 2 March, p. 87

Cloos, Reinesch, Vignes, and Weyland (1993): *Le Traité de Maastricht: Genèse, Analyse, Commentaires* (Bruxelles: Bruylant)

Cohen, March, and Olsen (1988): 'A Garbage Can Model of Organizational Choice' in March (ed.): *Decisions and Organizations* (Oxford: Blackwell)

Constantinesco (1974): *Compétences et pouvoirs dans les Communautés Européenes: contribution à l'étude de la nature juridique de la CE* (Paris: Pichon and Durand-Auzias)

——(1991): 'Who's Afraid of Subsidiarity?', *Yearbook of European Law*, p. 33

——(1992): 'La distribution des pouvoirs entre la Communauté et ses Etats Membres: L'equilibre mouvant de la compétence législative et le principe de subsidiarité' in Engel and Wessels (eds.): *From Luxembourg to Maastricht: Institutional change in the European Community after the SEA* (Bonn: Europa Union Verl) p. 109

Coppel and O'Neill (1992): 'The European Court of Justice: Taking Rights Seriously?', *Common Market Law Review*, vol. 29, 4, p. 668

Corbett Jacobs, and Shackleton (2000): *The European Parliament* (London: John Harper)

Cox (1994): 'Derogation, Subsidiarity and the Single Market', *Journal of Common Market Studies*, vol. 32, 2, June, p. 127

Cram (1993): 'Calling the Tune without Paying the Piper? Social Policy Regulation: The Role of the Commission in the European Community Social Policy', *Policy and Politics*, vol. 21, 2, p. 135

——(1997): Policy-Making in the EU: Conceptual Lenses and the Integration Process (London: Routledge)

Dahl (1986): *Democracy, Liberty and Equality* (Oslo: Norwegian UP)

David and Brierley (1985): *Major Legal Systems in the World Today: An Introduction to the Comparative Study of Law* (3rd edn.) (London: Stevens & Sons)

de Búrca (1998): 'The Principle of Subsidiarity and the Court of Justice as an Institutional Actor', *Journal of Common Market Studies*, p. 214

——(1999): 'Re-appraising subsidiarity's significance after Amsterdam': Harvard Jean Monnet Working Paper, no. 7/1999

Dehousse and Franklin (1990): 'La subsidiarité, fondement constitutionnel ou paravent politique de l'Union Européenne?', *Liber Amicorum E. Krings*, p. 51

——(1995): 'Les enjeux de la Conférence intergouvernementale de 1996', *Courrier hebdomadaire*, no. 1499, p. 1

Dehousse (1992): 'The Legacy of Maastricht: Emerging Institutional Issues', *Collected Courses of the Academy of European Law*, vol. III-1, p. 181

——(1988): 'Fédéralisme et relations internationales: Une réflexion comparative' (Ph.D. thesis, European University Institute, Florence)

——(1989): '1992 and Beyond: The Institutional Dimension of the Single Market Programme', *Legal Issues of European Integration*, 1, p. 109

——(1993): 'Does Subsidiarity Really Matter?', *EUI Working Paper in Law* 92/32

——(1994a): 'Community Competences: Are There Limits to Growth?' in R. Dehousse (ed.): *Europe after Maastricht: An Ever Closer Union?* (Munich: Beck) p. 103

——(1994b): *La Cour de Justice des Communautés Européennes* (Paris: Montchrestien)

——(1994c): 'Comparing National and EC Levels: The Problem of the Level of Analysis', *EUI Working Paper in Law*, 94/3

——(1995): 'Institutional Reform in the European Community: Are there Alternatives to the Majoritarian Avenue?' *EUI Working Paper RSC* 95/4

——(1996): 'Intégration ou désintégration? Cinq thèses sur l'incidence de l'intégration européenne sur les structures étatiques', *EUI Working Paper RSC* 96/4

——(1997): 'European integration and the Nation State', in Heywood, Rhodes, and Wright (eds.) *Developments in West European Politics* (London: MacMillan), p. 37.

——(1998): 'European Institutional Architecture After Amsterdam: Parliamentary system or regulatory structure?', *Common Market Law Review*, vol. 35, 3, June, pp. 595–627

——*et al.* (Club de Florence) (1996): *Europe: L'impossible statu quo* (Paris: Stock)

——Joerges, Majone, and Snyder, in collaboration with Everson (1992): 'Europe After 1992: New Regulatory Strategies', *EUI Working Paper in Law*, 92/31

——and Weiler (1992): 'The Legal Dimension' in Wallace (ed.): *The Dynamics of European Integration* (London: Pinter) p. 242

——and Majone (1994): 'The Institutional Dynamics of European Integration: From the Single Act to the Masstricht Treaty' in Stephen Martin (ed.): *The Construction of Europe: Essays in Honour of Emile Nöel* (Dordrecht: Kluwer) p. 91

——(2002): 'Un nouveau constitutionnalisme?', in Dehousse (ed.) *Une constitution pour l'Europe?* Chap. I (Paris: Presses de Sciences Po)

Delors (1991): 'Subsidiarity: Guiding Principle for Future EC Policy Responsability?', Proceedings of the Jacques Delors Colloquium Organized by the European Institute of Public Administration at Maastricht, 21–22 March 1991: *Subsidiarity: the Challenge of Change* (Maastricht: European Institute for Public Administration).

De Ruyt (1987): *L'Acte Unique Européene* (Bruxelles: Editions de l'Université de Bruxelles)

de Witte and de Búrca (2002): 'The delimitation of Powers between the European Union and its Member States', in Arnull and Winscott (eds.): *Accountability and legitimacy in the EU* (Oxford: Oxford University Press)

Dicey (1897): *The Law of the Constitution* (London: Macmillan)

Dobson (1996): 'Back to the Future: Ideas, Interests and Expertise in the Audiovisual Policy' Paper Prepared for HCM Workshop in the European University Institute, Florence, 20–22 March 1996

Dworkin (1997): *Taking Rights Seriously* (London: Duckworth)

Edwards (1996): '48–Hour Pique', *Gazzette*, 93/94 of 20 November, p. 14

Ehlermann (1984): 'How Flexible is Community Law? An Unusual Approach to the Concept of "Two-Speeds"', *Michigan Law Review*, vol. 82, April/May, p. 1274

——(1994): 'The Role of the EC Commission as regards National Energy Policies', *Journal of Energy and Natural Resources Law*, vol. 12, 3, p. 342

——(1995a): 'Harmonization Versus Competition Between Rules' *European Review*, vol. 3 4 October, p. 333

Ehlermann (1995b): 'Increased Differentiation or Stronger Uniformity', *EUI Working Paper RSC* 95/21

Eichener (1992): 'Social Dumping or Innovative Regulation? Processes and Outcomes of European Decision-Making in the Sector of Health and Safety at Work Harmonization', *EUI Working Paper SPS* 92/28

Elder and Cobb (1983): *The Political Uses of Symbols* (New York: Longman)

Elorza (1992): 'Subsidiariedad', in *Breve diccionario del Tratado de la Unión Europea, Política Exterior*, vol VI, 29 Otoño, p. 126

Elster (1984): *Ulysses and the Sirens* (Cambridge: Cambridge UP)

Emiliou (1992): 'Subsidiarity: An Effective Barrier Against "the Entreprises of Ambition"?', *European Law Review*, vol. 17, 5, October, p. 383

——(1994): 'The Principle of Subsidiarity', F.I.D.E. XVI Congress: *Le principe de subsidiarité*, (Rome: Consiglio dei Ministri) p. 113

Endo (2004): 'Subsidiarity and its enemies: to what extent is sovereignty contested in the mexed commonwealth of Europe?' Robert Schuman Centre Working Paper no. 2001/24

Erdmenger (1983): *The EC Transport Policy: Towards a Common Transport Policy* (Aldershot: Gower)

Eriksen (1994): 'Deliberative Democracy and the Politics of Pluralist Society', *ARENA Working Paper 6* (December)

Estella (1996): 'The Commission Policy for the Postal Sector', *Utilities Law Review*, vol. 7(2), p. 64

——(1997): 'The Principle of Subsidiarity and its Critique: A "Contextual" Analysis of the Principle of Subsidiarity' (Ph.D. Thesis: Florence)

——(1998a): 'La Administración de la Unión Europea, motor de integración', in AAVV: *Administraciones Públicas y Constitución. Reflexiones sobre el XX aniversario de la Constitución Española de 1978* (Madrid: INAP) p. 1063

——(1998b): 'El principio de la "alternativa menos restrictiva" en Derecho constitucional norteamericano' (Traducción), *Cuadernos de Derecho Público*, 5, p. 1

——(1999a): 'A Dissident Voice: The Spanish Constitutional Court Case Law on European Integration', *European Public Law*, vol. 5, 2, p. 269

——(1999b): 'Algo más que un simple número: La elección de la base juírica en la sentencia del Tribunal de Justicia de las Comunidades Europeas de 25 de Febrero de 1999 (Asuntos Acumulados C-164/97 y C-165/97)', *Revista de Gestión Ambiental 5*

——(1999c): '¿Integración sin ejecución? El problema de la inejecución del derecho comunitario medioambiental en la jurisprudencia del Tribunal de Justicia de las Comunidades Europeas', *Revista de Gestión Ambiental*, Año 1, 1, p. 49

——(1999d): 'El papel de la Comisión Europea como motor de integración: Análisis desde una perspectiva de "gobernación multinivel"' *Instituto Universitario Ortega y Gasset. Estudios Europeos, Papel de Trabajo* 1/99

——(1999e): 'Modelos de democracia: El modelo mayoritario y el contra-mayoritario' in Quadra-Salcedo and Estella (eds.): *Problemas de Legitimación en la Europa de la Unión* (forthcoming)

——(1999f): 'La paradoja de la subsidiariedad: Reflexiones en torno a la jurispruden-cia comunitaria relativa al art. 3 B (2) del Tratado de la Comunidad Europea', *Revista de Derecho Administrativo*, 101, p. 71

——(1999g): 'Medio ambiente y mercado: Análisis de la sentencia del Tribunal de Justicia de las Comunidades Europeas de 14 de Julio de 1998 (Asunto C-341/95), relativa a la validez del Reglamento no. 3093/94, de medidas protectoras de la capa de ozono' *Revista de Gestión Ambiental* 8, p. 59

——(1999h): 'El imparable desarrollo de la intervención de la Unión Europea en materia medioambiental', *Revista de Gestión Ambiental*, Año 1, 3, p. 1

——(2000): 'Aspectos introductorios relativos al Derecho Administrativo Comunitario' in Parejo, Quadra-Salcedo, Moreno, and Estella (eds.): *Manual de Derecho Administrativo Comunitario* (Madrid: Ceura)

Esteva Mosso (1993): 'La compatibilité des monopoles de droit du secteur des telecommunications avec les normes de concurrence du traité CEE', *Cahiers de Droit Européen* n. 29, p. 445

Everling (1984a): 'The Member States of the EC before their Court of Justice', *European Law Review*, vol. 9, 4, p. 215

——(1984b): 'Sur la jurisprudence de la Cour de Justice en matière de libre prestation des services rendus dans d'autres Étas Membres', *Cahiers de Droit Européen*, Année 20, 1–2, p. 1

——(1991): 'La extensión de la vigencia del derecho comunitario al territorio de la antigua RDA', *Revista de Instituciones Europeas*, vol. 18, 2, p. 455

——(1992): 'Reflections on the Structure of the European Union', *Common Market Law Review* vol. 29, 6, p. 1053

——(1994): 'The Maastricht Judgement of the German Federal Constitutional Court and its Significance for the Development of the European Union', *Yearbook of European Law*, 14, p. 1

——(1995): 'Independent Agencies: Hierarchy Beaters?', *European Law Journal*, vol. 1, 2, July, p. 180

——(1996): 'Will Europe Slip on Bananas? The Bananas Judgement of the Court of Justice and National Courts', *Common Market Law Review*, vol. 33, 3, p. 401

——*et al.* (1995): *The Developing Role of the European Court of Justice* (London: European Policy Forum; Frankfurt: Frankfurter Institut)

Falke (1996): 'Comitology and other Committees: a Preliminary Empirical Assessment' in Pedler and Schaefer (eds.): *Shaping European Law and Policy: The Role of Committees and Comitology in the Political Process* (Maastricht: European Institute of Public Administration)

Falkner and Nenwich (1995): *European Union: Democratic Perspectives After 1996* (Wien: Service Fachverlag)

Federal Trust Report (1995): 'Building the Union', *Federal Trust Papers* 3

——(1996): 'Enlarging the Union', *Federal Trust Papers* 5

Feral (1994): 'Les incidences de l'integration communautaire sur les collectivités territoriales françaises', *Revue du Marché Commun et de L'Union Européenne*, 374, Janvier, p. 53

——(1996): 'Le principe de subsidiarité dans l'Union Européenne', *Revue de Droit Public et de la Science Politique en France at à l'Etranger, Janvier-Fevrier*, 112–1, p. 203

Fernández Esteban (1996): *El principio de subsidiariedad en el ordenamiento europeo* (Madrid: McGraw-Hill)

Fernández Ramos (1997): 'El marco jurídico comunitario en materia de residuos', *Noticias de la Unión Europea*, vol. 13, 153, p. 37

Finer, Bogdanor, and Rudden (1995): *Comparing constitutions* (Oxford: Clarendon)

Fischer (1994): 'Federalism in the European Community and the United States: A Rose by any other Name', *Fordham International Law Journal*, vol. 17, 2, p. 389

Føllesdal (1999): 'Subsidiarity and democratic deliberation'. ARENA Working Paper no. 99/21

García de Enterría (1995): 'The System of Powers of the European Union and the Member States in the Draft Constitution' in *A Constitution for the European Union?* Proceedings of a Conference, 12–13 May 1994. Organized by the Robert Schuman Centre with the Patronage of the European Parliament. *EUI Working Paper RSC* 95/9, p. 79

Garrett (1992): 'International Cooperation and Institutional Choice: The EC's Internal Market', *International Organisation*, vol. 46 2, Spring, p. 533

——(1995): 'The Politics of Legal Integration in the European Union', *International Organisation*, vol. 49, 1, Winter, p. 171

——(1997): 'Why Power Indices Cannot Explain Decision-Making in the European Union', in Schmidtchen and Cooter (eds.) *Constitutional Law and Economics of the European Union* (Lyme: Edward Elgar)

——*et. al* (1997): 'The Politics of European Federalism', in Schmidtchen and Cooter (eds.) *Constitutional Law and Economics of the European Union* (Edward Elgar:Lyme), p. 82

Gaudissart (1993): 'La subsidiarité: facteur de (dés)integration européenne?', *Journal des Tribunaux*, 6 Mars, p. 173

Gerbert (1999): La construction de l'Europe. (Paris: Imprimerie nationale)

Giovine Di (1979): 'Seveso', *Environmental Policy and Law*, vol. 5(1), p. 38

Golub (1994): 'The Pivotal Role of British Soveregnity in EC Environmental Policy', *EUI Working Paper* RSC 94/17

——(1996) 'Sovereignty and Subsidiarity in EU Environmental Policy', *EUI Working Paper* RSC 96/2

——(1999): 'In the Shadow of the Vote? Decision-Making in the European Community', *Economic Policy*, 29, p. 289

Goucha Soares (1998): 'Pre-emption, Conflict of Powers, and Subsidiarity', *European Law Review*, vol. 23, 2, p. 132

Grimm (1995): 'Does Europe need a Constitution?', *European Law Journal*, vol. 1, 3, p. 282

Grote (1993): 'On Functional and Territorial Subsidiarity: Between Legal Discourse and Societal Needs', Paper Presented at the Annual Conference of the Italian Section of the International Regional Science Association, Bologna, (October)

Gunlicks (1995): 'The Old and the New Federalism in Germany' in Merkl (ed.): *The Federal Republic of Germany at forty-five* (London: Macmillan) p. 219

Haas (1958/1968): *The Uniting of Europe: Political, Social and Economic Forces: 1950–1957* (Stanford: Stanford UP)

——(1975): *The Obsolescence of Regional Integration Theory* (Berkeley: University of California, Institute of International Studies)

Habermas (1975): *Legitimation Crisis* (Boston: Beacon Press)

——(1984): *The Theory of Communicative Action* (Boston: Beacon Press)

——(1996): *La paix perpétuelle: Le bicentenaire d'une idée kantienne* (Paris: Éditions du cerf. Original title: *Kants Idee des Ewigen Friedens: Aus dem historischem* Abstand von 200 Jahren)

Haigh (1987): *EEC Environmental Policy and Britain* (Harlow: Longman)

Harlow (1996): 'Codification of EC Administrative Procedures? Fitting the Foot to the Shoe or the Shoe to the Foot', *European Law Journal*, vol. 2, 1, March, p. 3

——(2000): 'Voices of difference in a plural community'. Harvard Jean Monnet Working Paper no. 3/2000

Harrison (1996): 'Subsidiarity in Article 3b of the EC Treaty: Gobbledegook or Justiciable Principle?', *International and Comparative Law Quarterly*, vol. 45, April, p. 431

Hart (1961/1994): *The Concept of Law* (Oxford: Clarendon Press)

Hartley (1994): *The Foundations of EC Law: An Introduction to Constitutional and Administrative Law of the European Community* (Oxford: Clarendon Press; 3rd edition)

Herdegen (1995): 'After the TV Judgement of the German Constitutional Court: Decision-Making within the EU Council and the German Länder', *Common Market Law Review* 32, p. 1369

Héritier (1996): 'Policy-Making by Subterfuge: Interest Accommodation, Innovation and Substitute Democratic Legitimation in Europe', *Journal of European Public Policy* (1997) vol. 4(2) pp. 171–89

Hildebrand (1993): 'The European Community's Environmental Policy 1957 to 1992: From Incidental Measures to an International regime?' in David Judge (ed.): *A Green Dimension for the European Community: Political Issues and Processes* (London: Cass) p. 13

Hills (1984): *Information Technology and Industrial Policy* (London: Croom Helm)

Holm (1994): *Europe, A Political culture? Fundamental issues for the 1996 IGC* (London: Royal Institute of International Affairs)

Hoogue (1995): 'Subnational Mobilisation in the European Union', *West European Politics*. vol. 18, July, 3 p. 175

——and Marks (1995): 'Channels of Subnational Representation in the European Union' in R. Dehousse and T. Christiansen (eds.) *What Model for the Committee of the Regions? Past Experiences and Future Perspectives*, *EUI Working Paper EUF* 95/2

Hrbek (1992): 'The German Länder and EC Integration', *European Integration Journal*, vol. 15, p. 173

Hyde (1983): 'The Concept of Legitimation in the Sociology of Law', *Wisconsin Law Review*, p. 379

Ito and Iwata (1987): 'Deregulation and the Change in the Telecommunications Market in Japan', in Mestmäcker (ed.): *The Law and Economics of Transborder Telecommunications* (Baden-Baden: Nomos) p. 231

Jachtenfuchs (1995): 'Theoretical Perspectives on European Governance', *European Law Journal*, vol. 1, 2, July, p. 115

Jacqué (1994): 'Le labyrinthe décisionnel', *Pouvoirs*, 69, p. 24

——and Weiler (1990): 'On the Road to the European Union: A New Judicial Architecture', *Common Market Law Review*, 27, p. 185

Jeffery and Yates (1992): 'Unification and the Maastricht Treaty: The Response of the Länder Governments', *German Politics* vol. 1, 3, December 1992, p. 58

Joerges (1994): 'European Economic Law, the Nation-State and the Maastricht Treaty' in R. Dehousse (ed.): *Europe after Maastricht: An Ever Closer Union?* (Munich: Beck) p. 29

——(1996): 'The Emergence of Denationalized Governance Structures and the European Court of Justice', *ARENA* Working Paper 16 (October)

——and Neyer (1997) 'From Intergovernmental Bargaining to Deliberative Political Process: The Constitutionalisation of Comitology', *European Law Journal*, vol. 3, 273

——and Vos (1999): *EU Committees* (Oxford: Hart Publishing)

Justus Lipsius (1995): 'La conférence intergouvernementale de 1996', *Revue Trimestrielle de Droit Européen*, 2, p. 175

Kapteyn (1991): 'Community Law and the Principle of Subsidiarity', *Revue des Affaires Européenes*, 2, p. 35

Kellas (1991): 'European Integration and the Regions', *Parliamentary Affairs*. vol. 44, 2, April, p. 226

Kelsen (1991): *Teoría Pura del Derecho* (German translation by Roberto J. Vernengo—IXª Ed.—México: Porrúa)

Kiewiet and McCubbins (1991): *The Logic of Delegation* (Chicago: Chicago University Press)

Kingdon (1984): *Agendas, Alternatives and Public Policies* (Boston: Little, Brown)

Kokott (1998): 'Report on Germany' in Weiler *et al.* (eds.): *The European Courts and National Courts: Doctrine and Jurisprudence* (Oxford: Hart)

Komesar (1994): *Imperfect Alternatives: Choosing Institutions in Law, Economics and Public Policy* (Chicago: Chicago University Press)

Krislov, Ehlermann, and Weiler (1985): 'Political Organs and Decision Making Processes', *Integration Through Law*, vol. 1, 2, p. 3

Küster (1990): *Fondements de la Communauté Économique Européenne* (Luxembourg: Office des publications officielles de la CE)

Ladeur (1996): 'Proceduralisation and its Use in Post-Modern Legal Theory', *European University Institute Working Paper in Law*, 96/5

Lamers (1995): 'Pourquoi L'UE doit renforcer ses institutions', in Philip Morris Institute (ed.): *Quel avenir pour la Commission Européenne?* (Bruxelles: Philip Morris Institute) p. 34

Lauber (1986): 'The Political Economy of Industrial Policy in Western Europe' in Shull and Cohen (eds.): *Economics and Politics of Industrial Policy: The ESA and Western Europe* (Boulder: Westview) p. 28

Leleux (1982): 'The Role of the European Court of Justice in Protecting Individual Rights in the Context of Free Movement of Persons and Services' in Stein and Sandalow (eds.): *Courts and Free Markets* (Oxford: Clarendon Press), vol. 2, p. 363

Lenaerts (1986): 'The Application of Community Law in Belgium', *Common Market Law Review*, vol. 23, 2, p. 253

——(1988*): Le juge et la Constitution aux Etats-Unis d'Amerique et dans l'ordre juridique européen* (Bruxelles: Bruylant)

——(1990): 'Le Tribunal de Première Instance des Communautés Européennes: Genèse et premiers pas', *Journal des Tribunaux*, Année 109, 5553, p. 409

——(1991a): 'Fundamental Rights to be Included in a Community Catalogue', *European Law Review*, vol. 16, 5, p. 367

——(1991b): 'L'egalité de traitement en droit communautaire: Un principe unique aux apparences multiples', *Cahiers de droit européen*, vol. 1, 2, p. 3

——(1991c): 'Some Reflections on the Separation of Powers in the European Community', *Common Market Law Review*, vol. 28, 1, p. 11

——(1992a): 'Some Thoughts about the Interaction between Judges and Politicians in the European Community' *Yearbook of European Law*, vol. 12, p. 1

——(1992b): 'A New Institutional Equilibrium? In Search of the "Trias Politica" in the European Community' in Engel and Wessels (eds.): *From Luxembourg to Maastricht: Institutional Change in the EC after the SEA* (Bonn: Europea Union Verl) p. 139

——(1993): 'Regulating the Regulatory Process: "Delegation of Powers" in the EC', *European Law Review*, vol. 18, 1, p. 23

——(1994a): 'Education in European Community Law after Maastricht', *Common Market Law Review*, vol. 31, 1, p. 7

——(1994b): 'The Principle of Subsidiarity and the Environment in the European Union: Keeping the Balance of Federalism', *Fordham International Law Journal*, vol. 17, 4, p. 846

——(1995): 'Subsidiarity and Community Competence in the Field of Education', *Columbia Journal of European Law*, vol. 1, 1, p. 1

——(1996): 'La Conférence Intergouvernementale de 1996', *Droit Européen*, Année 4, 34, p. 217

——(1998a): 'Federalism: Essential Concepts in Evolution. The Case of the European Union', *Fordham International Law Journal*, vol. 21, 3, p. 746

——(1998b): 'Le Traité d'Amsterdam', *Journal des Tribunaux*, Année 6, 46, p. 25

Lenaerts and Ypersele (1994): 'Le principe de subsidiarité et son contexte: Etude de l'article 3B du Traité CE', *Cahiers de droit européen*, vol. 30, 1 and 2, p. 3

——and Vanhamme (1997): 'Procedural Rights of Private Parties in the Community Administrative Process' *Common Market Law Review*, 34, p. 531

Lindberg and Scheingold (1970): *Europe's Would-be Polity: Patterns of Change in the European Community* (Englewood Cliffs: Prentice-Hall)

Louis (1990): *L'ordre Juridique Communautaire* (Luxembourg: Office des Publications Officielles, 5th edn.)

MacCormick (1978): *Legal Reasoning and Legal Theory* (Oxford: Clarendon Press)

——(1991): *British Politics and the Environment* (London: Earthscan Press)

——(1993): 'Beyond the Sovereign State', *Modern Law Review*, vol. 56 1 January, p. 1

——(1994): 'Sovereignty, Democracy, Subsidiarity', *Rechtstheorie*, vol. 25, 3, p. 281

——(1995): 'The Maastricht-Urteil: Sovereignty Now', *European Law Journal*, November, 1–3, p. 259

——(1999): Questioning Sovereignty: Law, State and Nation in the European Commonwealth (Oxford: Oxford University Press)

Mackenzie and Khalidi (1994): 'The European Union Directive on Deposit Insurance: A Critical Evaluation', *Journal of Common Market Studies*, vol. 32, 2, June, p. 170

Majone (1989a): *Evidence, Argument and Persuasion in the Policy Process* (New Haven: Yale University Press)

—— (1989b): 'Regulating Europe: Problems and Prospects', *EUI Working Paper SPS* 89/405

——(1991): 'Market Integration and Regulation: Europe After 1992'. *EUI Working Paper* SPS 91/10

——(1992): 'Regulatory Federalism in the EC', *Environment and Planning C: Government and Policy*, vol. 10, p. 299

——(1993): 'The European Community Between Social Policy and Social Regulation', *EUI Working Paper* SPS 92/27

——(1994a): 'Understanding Regulatory Growth in the EC' *EUI Working Paper* SPS 94/17

——(1994b): 'Independence vs. Accountability? Non-Majoritarian Institutions and Democratic Governance in Europe', *EUI Working Paper* SPS 94/3

——(1995a): 'The Development of Social Regulation in the EC: Policy Externalities, Transaction Costs, Motivational Factors', *EUI Working Paper* SPS 95/2

——(1995b): 'Mutual Trust, Credible Commitments and the Evolution of Rules for a Single European Market', *EUI Working Paper* RSC 95/1

Mancini (1988a): 'Las instituciones comunitarias y el Acta Única Europea', *Gaceta Jurídica de la CEE*, 53, p. 2

——(1988b): 'L'incorporazione del diritto comunitario nel diritto interno degli Stati membri delle Comunità Europee', *Rivista di Diritto Europeo*, Anno 28, 2–4, p. 87

——(1989a): 'L'incidenza del diritto comunitario sul diritto del lavoro degli stati membri', *Rivista di Diritto Europeo*, Anno 29, 1–2, p. 9

——(1989b): 'The Making of a Constitution for Europe', *Common Market Law Review*, vol. 26, 4, p. 595

——(1989c): 'La tutela dei diritti dell'uomo: Il ruolo dela Corte di Giustizia delle Comunità europea', Mulino, Anno 38, 324, p. 559

——(1989d): 'Politica comunitaria e nazionale delle migrazioni nella prospettiva dell'Europa sociale', *Rivista de Diritto Europeo*, Anno 29, 3–4, p. 309

——(1990): 'Attivismo e autocontrollo nella giurisprudenza della Corte di Giustizia', *Rivista de Diritto Europeo*, Anno 30, 2, p. 229

——(1992) 'Il contributo della Corte di Giustizia allo sviluppo della democrazia', *Rivista de Diritto Europeo*, Anno 32, 4, p. 713

——(1993): 'La Corte di Giustizia: Uno strumento per la democrazia nella Comunitá Europea', *Mulino Bologna*, Anno 42, 347, p. 595

——(1998): 'Europe: The Case for Statehood', *Harvard Law School Jean Monnet Working Paper Series*, 6/98, p. 1

——and Keeling (1994): 'Democracy and the European Court of Justice', *Modern Law Review*, vol. 57, 2, p. 175

Mangas and Liñan Nogueras (1996): *Instituciones y derecho de la Unión Europea* (Madrid: McGraw-Hill)

Marks, Hoogue, and Blank (1995): 'European Integration and the State', *EUI Working Paper* RSC 95/7

Martin (1995): 'Pour être efficace, la Commission a besoin d'une grande réforme' in Philip Morris Institute (ed.): *Quel avenir pour la Commission Européenne?* (Bruxelles: Philip Morris Institute) p. 46

Mattli and Slaughter (1996): 'Constructing the European Community Legal System from the Ground Up: the Role of Individual Litigants and National Courts', Paper Presented at the Spring Term Seminar of the EUI SPS department on 'Policy Making in the European Union'

Mazey and Richardson (eds.) (1993a): *Lobbying in the European Community* (Oxford: Oxford University Press)

————(1993b): 'Environmental Groups and the EC: Challenges and Opportunities' in David Judge (ed.): *A Green Dimension for the European Community: Political Issues and Processes* (London: Cass) p. 109

Megret, Commentaire (1990): *Libre circulation des personnes, des services et des capitaux: Transports* vol. 3 (Bruxelles: Editions de l'Université de Bruxelles) p. 193

Megret and Teitgen (1987): 'La fumée de la cigarette dans la zone grise des compétences de la CEE', *Cahiers de Droit Européen*, vol. 17, p. 223

Meny and Thoening (1989): *Politiques Publiques* (Paris: Presses Universitaires de France)

Merkl (1963): *The Origin of the West German Republic* (New York: Oxford University Press)

Meyronneinc (1991): 'Le malaise des parlements devant l'union politique de l'europe: Divergences et prérogatives aux "Assises de Rome"', *Revue des Affaires Européennes*, 1, p. 67

Mill (1861/1972): *Representative Government* (London: Dent)

——(1975): *Three Essays: On Liberty. Representative Government. The Subjection of Women* (London: Oxford University Press)

Millon-Delsol (1992): *L'Etat subsidiaire: Ingèrence et non-ingèrence de l'Etat aux fonde-ments de l'histoire européenne* (Paris: Presses Universitaires de France)

——(1993): *Le principe de subsidiarité* (Paris: Presses Universitaires de France)

Mischo (1990): 'Un rôle nouveau pour la Cour de Justice?' *Revue du Marché Commun*, 342, December, p. 681

Mitrany (1943): *A Working Peace System: an Argument for the Functional Development of International Organizations* (London: Royal Institute of International Affairs)

——(1975): *The Functional Theory of Politics* (London: London School of Economics and Political Science)

Morata (1998): *La Unión Europea: Procesos, actores y políticas* (Ariel: Barcelona)

Moravscik (1991): 'Negotiating the SEA: National Interests and Conventional Statecraft in the EC', *International Organisation* 45, Winter, p. 651

——(1992): *National Preference Formation and Interstate Bargaining in the EC: 1955–1986* (Cambridge, Mass.: Harvard University Press)

——(1993): 'Preferences and Power in the European Community: A Liberal Intergovernmentalist Approach', *Journal of Common Market Studies*. vol. 31, 4. December, p. 473

——(1988): *The Choice for Europe: Social Purpose and State Power from Messina to Maastricht* (Ithaca: Cornell University Press)

Müller (1987): 'Competition in the British Telecommunications Market: The Impact of Recent Privatisation/Deregulation Decision' in Mestmäcker (ed.): *The Law and Economics of Transborder Telecommunications* (Baden-Baden: Nomos) p. 249

Nenwich and Falkner (1996): 'Intergovernmental Conference 1996: Which Constitution for the Union?', *European Law Journal*, vol. 2, 1, March, p. 83

Neunreither (1994): 'The Democratic Deficit of the European Union: Towards Closer Co-operation Between the European Union and the National Parliaments', *Government and Opposition*, vol. 29, p. 299

Niedermayer and Sinnott (eds.) (1998): *Public Opinion and Internationalized Governance* (Oxford: Oxford University Press)

Nöel (1994): 'A New Institutional Balance?' in R. Dehousse (ed.): *Europe after Maastricht: An Ever Closer Union?* (Munich: Beck) p. 16

——(1995a): 'Vers un nouvel equilibre des pouvoirs' in Philip Morris Institute (ed.): *Quel avenir pour la Commission Européenne?* (Bruxelles: Philip Morris Institute) p. 62

——(1995b): 'La conférence intergouvernementale de 1996: Vers un nouvel ordre institutionnel', *EUI Working Paper* RSC 95/22

Orsello (1993): *Il principio di sussidiarietà nella prospettiva dell'attuazzione del Trattato sull'Unione Europea* (Roma: Istituto Italiano di Studi Legislativi)

Palacio Gonzalez (1995): 'The Principle of Subsidiarity' *European Law Review*, vol. 20 4 August, p. 355

Pappalardo (1991): 'State Measures and Public Undertakings: Article 90 of the EEC Treaty Revisisted', *European Competition Law Review*, 1, p. 29

Parejo (1993): *Administrar y juzgar: Dos funciones constitucionales distintas y complementarias. Un estudio del alcance y la intensidad del control judicial a la luz de la discrecionalidad administrativa* (Madrid: Tecnos)

——*et al.* (1998): *Manual de Derecho Administrativo*, vol. 1 (Ariel: Barcelona)

——Quadra-Salcedo, Moreno, Estella (2000): *Manual de Derecho Administrativo Comunitario* (Madrid: CEURA)

Pescatore (1974): *The Law of Integration* (Leiden: Sijthoff)

——(1983): 'The Doctrine of Direct Effect: An Infant Disease of Community Law', *European Law Review*, vol. 8, p. 155

——(1985): 'Le commerce de l'art et le marché commun', *Revue Trimestrielle de droit européen*, vol. 21, 3, p. 451

——(1986): 'Il rinvio pregiudiziale di cui all'art. 177 del Tratatto CEE e la cooperazione tra la Corte de i giudici nazionali', *Foro Italiano*, Anno 111, 1, p. 26

——(1987a): 'Du droit international au droit de l'íntegration', in *Liber Amicorum Pierre Pescatore* (Baden-Baden: Nomos)

——(1987b): 'Treaty Making by the European Communities' in Jacobs and Roberts (eds.): *The Effects of Treaties in Domestic Law* (London: Sweet & Maxwell)

——(1987c): 'Some Critical remarks on the SEA', *Common Market Law Review*. vol. 24, 1, p. 9

——(1992): 'Une revolution juridique: Le rôle de la Cour de Justice européenne', *Commentaire*, vol. 15, 59, p. 569

——(1996): 'La interpretación del derecho Comunitario por el juez nacional', *Revista de Instituciones Europeas*, vol. 23, 1, p. 7

——and MacWhiney (1973): *Federalism, Supreme Courts and the Integration of Legal Systems* (Heule: UGA)

Petersmann (1995): 'Proposals for a New Constitution for the European Union: Building Blocks for a Constitutional Theory and Constitutional Law of the EU', *Common Market Law Review* 32, p. 1123

Peterson (1994): 'Subsidiarity: a Definition to Suit Any Vision?', *Parliamentary Affairs*. vol. 47 1 January, p. 116

Petite (1998): 'The Treaty of Amsterdam', *Harvard Jean Monnet Papers* 2/1998

Piris (1994): 'Après Maastricht, les institutions sont-elles plus efficaces, plus démocratiques et plus trasparentes?', *Revue Trimestrielle de Droit Européen*, 1, p. 1

Pisany-Ferry (1995): 'L'Europe à geometrie variable: Une analyse économique', *Politique Etrangère*, Année 60, 2, p. 447

Poiares (1998): *We the Court: The European Court of Justice and the European Economic Constitution. A Critical Reading of Article 30 of the EC Treaty* (Oxford: Hart)

Pollack (1994): 'Creeping Competence: the Expanding Agenda of the EC', *Journal of Public Policy* vol. 14, 2, p. 95

——(1996): *Creeping competence: The expanding agenda of the European Community* (Ann Arbor, UMI)

Predieri (1981): 'El sistema de las fuentes del derecho' in García de Enterría and Predieri (eds.): *La constitución española de 1978* (Madrid: Civitas)

Pryce (1973): *The Politics of the EC* (London: Butterworths)

Quadra Salcedo (1995): *Liberalización de las telecomunicaciones, servicio público y constitución económica europea* (Madrid: Centro de Estudios Constitucionales)

Quermone (1994): *Le système politique européen* (Paris: Montchrestien)

Rasmussen (1986): *On Law and Policy in the EC* (Dordrecht: Nijhoff)

——(1988): 'Between Self-Restraint and Activism: A Judicial Policy for the European Court', *European Law Review* 18, p. 28

Reflection Group (1995): *Reflection Group Report (and other references for documentary purposes) on the 1996 Intergovernmental Conference* (General Secretariat of the Council of the European Union. Brussels: December 1995)

Rehbinder and Stewart (1985): *Environmental Protection Policy* (Berlin: De Gruyter)

Reich (1994): 'La mise en oeuvre du Traité sur l'Union Européenne par les accors interinstitutionnels', *Revue du Marché Commun et de l'Union Européenne*. 375, Fevrier, p. 81

Rideau (1994): *Droit Institutionnel de l'Union et des Communautés Européennes* (Paris: Librarie générale de droit et de jursprudence)

Riker, William (1986): *The Art of Political Manipulation* (New Haven: Yale University Press)

Robertson (1996): 'Getting Away from an Adversarial Approach to Europe', in Philip Morris Institute for Public Policy Research (ed.): *In a Larger EU, Can All Member States Be Equal?*, p. 58

Rodríguez Iglesias (1993): 'El Tribunal de Justicia de las Comunidades Europeas' in Rodríguez Iglesias and Liñan (eds.): *El derecho comunitario europeo y su aplicación judicial* (Madrid: Civitas)

——(1996): 'Le pouvoir judiciaire de la Communauté Européenne au stade actuel de l'evolution de l'Union', *Jean Monnet Chair Papers of the Robert Schuman Center*, 41

——(1999): 'Consideraciones sobre la formación de un derecho europeo', *Gaceta Jurídica de la U.E. y de la Competencia*, 200, p. 11

——and Wölker (1987) 'Derecho comunitario, derechos fundamentales y control de la constitucionalidad: La decisión del Tribunal Constitucional federal alemán de 22 de Octubre de 1986', *Revista de Instituciones Europeas*, vol. 14, 3, p. 667

——and Valle (1997) 'El derecho comunitario y las relaciones entre el Tribunal de Justicia de las Comunidades Europeas, el Tribunal Europeo de Derechos Humanos y los Tribunales Constitucionales nacionales', *Revista de Derecho Comunitario Europeo*, vol. 1, 2, p. 329

Rubio Llorente (1999b): 'El futuro político de Europa: El déficit democrático de la Unión Europea', *Claves de Razón Práctica*, 90, p. 28

Sánchez-Cuenca (1995): *Las negociaciones agrícolas entre la Comunidad Europea y Estados Unidos en la Ronda Uruguay: Un análisis desde la lógica de la elección racional* (Madrid: CEACS)

—— (1997a): 'El déficit democrático en la Unión Europea', *Claves de Razón Práctica*, 78, Diciembre, p. 38

—— (1997b): 'Políticas económicas contra-mayoritarias y democracia. El caso de la UEM', paper presented at III Congreso Español de Ciencia Política y de la Administración, Salamanca, October

—— (1997c): 'Institutional Commitments and Democracy', *CEACS Working Paper* 1997/94

Sandholtz (1993): 'Institutions and Collective Action: The New Telecommunications in Western Europe', 45 *World Politics*, p. 242

—— and Zysman (1989): '1992: Recasting the European Bargain', *World Politics*, vol. 42, p. 95

Sauter (1995a): 'The Relationship Between Industrial and Competition Policy under the Economic Constitution of the European Union, with a Case-Study on Telecommunications', (EUI Ph.D. in Law, Florence)

—— (1995b): 'The Telecommunications Law of the European Union', *European Law Journal*, vol. 1, 1 March, p. 92

Scharpf (1978): 'Policy Effectiveness and Conflict Avoidance in Intergovernmental Policy Formation' in Hanf and Scharpf (eds.): *Interorganizational Policy-Making* (London: Sage) p. 59

—— (1994): 'Community and Autonomy: Multi-Level Policy Making in the European Union', *Journal of European Public Policy* 1:2 Autumn, p. 219

—— (1995): 'Negative and Positive Integration in the Political Economy of European Welfare States', *EUI Jean Monnet Chair Papers* 28

Schepel and Wesseling (1997): 'The Legal Community: Judges, Lawyers, Officials and Clerks in the Writing of Europe', *European Law Journal*, vol. 3, 2, p. 165

Schmidt (1995): *The Integration of the European Telecommunications and Electricity Sectors in the Light of International Relations Theories and Comparative Politics* (Köln: Max-Planck-Institut für Gesellschaftsforschung)

Schmitter (1996): 'How to Democratize the Emerging Euro-Polity: Citizenship, Representation, Decision-Making', paper presented at the Instituto Juan March de Ciencias Sociales (April)

Schwartz (1988): 'The EEC Directive on "TV without frontiers"', *Revue Belge de droit international*, vol 21 1, p. 329

Schwarze (1993): 'Le principe de subsidiarité dans la perspective du droit constitutionnel allemand', *Revue du Marché Commun et de l'Union Européenne*, 370, Juillet-Août, p. 615.

—— (1994): 'La ratification du Traité de Maastricht en Allemagne: L'arrêt de la Cour Constitutionelle de Kalsruhe', *Revue de Marché Commun et de l'Union Européenne*, 378, p. 293

Scott (1995): 'Changing Patterns of European Community Utilities Law and Policy: An Institutional Hypothesis' in Shaw and More (eds.): *New Legal Dynamics of European Union* (Oxford: Clarendon Press)

Scott *et al.* (1994): 'Subsidiarity: A Europe for the Regions v. the British Constitution?' *Journal of Common Market Studies*, vol. 32 1, March, p. 47

Seidel (1996): 'Why Only the Federal Route Offers True Equality' in Philip Morris Institute for Public Policy Research (ed.): *In a Larger EU, Can All Member States Be Equal?* (Bruxelles: Philip Morris Institute) p. 68

Seurin (1994): 'Towards a European Constitution? Problems of Political Integration', *Public Law*, p. 625

Shapiro (1964): *Law and Politics in the Supreme Court: New Approaches to Political Jurisprudence* (Glencoe: Free Press)

——(1980): 'Comparative Law and Comparative Politics', *University of Southern California Law Review* 53, p. 537

——(1981): *Courts: A Comparative and Political Analysis* (Chicago: Chicago University Press)

——(1988): *Who guards the guardians?* (Athens, Georgia: Georgia University Press)

——(1992): 'The giving-reasons requirement', *Chicago Legal Forum*, p. 180

——(1996a): 'Independent Agencies: US and EU', *EUI Jean Monnet Chair Papers* no. 34

——(1996b): 'Integrating Scientific Expertise into Regulatory Decision-Making: The "Frontiers of Science" Doctrine: American Experieces with the Judicial Control of Science Based Decision Making', *EUI Working Paper* RSC 96/11

——(1996c): 'Codification of Administrative Law: The US and the Union', *European Law Journal*, vol. 2, 1, March, p. 26

——(2001): 'The institutionalization of European Administrative Law Space', in Stone, Sandholtz and Fligstein (eds.) *The Institutionalization of Europe* (Oxford: Oxford University Press)

Shaw (1995a): 'European Union Legal Studies in Crisis? Towards a New Dynamic', *EUI Working Paper* RSC 95/23

——(1995b): 'Introduction' in Shaw and More (eds.): *New Legal Dynamics of European Union* (Oxford: Clarendon Press)

Siebert and Koop (1993): *Institutional Competition v. Centralization: Quo Vadis, Europe?* (Kiel: Universitaet Kiel, Institut für Weltwirtschaft)

Sinn (1994): 'How much Europe? Subsidiarity, Centralization and Fiscal Competition', *Scottish Journal of Political Economy*, vol. 41, 1, February, p. 85

Sked and Cook (1990): *Post-War Britain* (London: Penguin)

Slaughter (1995): 'International Law in a World of Liberal States', *European Journal of International Law*, 6, p. 503

Snyder (1990): *New Directions in European Community Law* (London: Weidenfeld and Nicolson)

——(1993): 'Soft-Law and Institutional Practice in the EC', *EUI Working Paper in Law* 93/5

——(1994a): 'Interinstitutional Agreements: Forms and Constitutional Limitations', *EUI Working Paper in Law* 95/4

——(1994b): 'Out on the Weekend: Reflections on European Union Law in Context', *EUI Working Paper in Law* 94/11

——(1995): 'The Taxonomy of Law in EC Agricultural Policy: A Case Study of the Dairy Sector', *EUI Working Paper in Law* 95/3

Stone (1997): 'Constitutional Dialogues in the European Community' in *The European Court and the National Courts—Doctrine and Jurisprudence: Legal Change in its Social Context*, Co-edited with A-M. Slaughter and J. Weiler (Oxford: Hart)

——and Caporaso (1998a): 'La Cour européenne et l'intégration', *Revue francaise de science politique*, vol. 48, 2, p. 195

——and Brunnell (1998a): 'The European Courts and the National Courts: A Statistical Analysis of Preliminary References, 1961–95', *Journal of European Public Policy*, vol. 5, 1, p. 66

——and Caporaso (1998b): 'From Free Trade to Supranational Polity: The European Court and Integration' in W. Sandholtz and A. Stone Sweet (eds.), *European Integration and Supranational Governance* (Oxford: Oxford University Press)

——and Brunell (1998b): 'Constructing a Supranational Constitution: Dispute Resolution and Governance in the European Community' *American Political Science Review*, vol. 92, 1, p. 63

Strozzi (1994): 'Le principe de subsidiarité dans la perspective de l'intégration européenne: Une enigme et beaucoup d'attentes', *Revue Trimestrielle de Droit Européen*, Année 30, Juillet-Septembre, p. 373

Sun and Pelkmans (1995a): 'Regulatory Competition in the Single Market', *Journal of Common Market Studies*, vol. 33, 1, March, p. 67

————(1995b): 'Why Liberalisation Needs Centralisation: Subsidiarity and EU Telecommunications', *World Economy*. vol. 18, 5, September, p. 635

Teasdale (1993): 'Subsidiarity in Post-Maastricht Europe', *Political Quarterly*, p. 191

Temple Lang and Gallagher (1995): 'The Role of the Commission and Majority Voting: A Unique Relationship with the Council', *IEA Occasional Paper* no. 7

Teubner (1993): *Law as an Autopoietic System* (Oxford: Blackwell)

Tizzano (1987): 'The Powers of the Community' in Commission of the European Communities (ed.): *Thirty Years of Community Law* (Luxembourg: Office for Official Publications of the EC)

Tomás de Aquino (1978): *The Summa Theologica* (Chicago: *Encyclopaedia Brittanica*)

Torre, La (1994): 'Democracy and Tensions: Representation, Majority Principle, Fundamental Rights', *EUI Working Paper in Law* 95/5

Torres Simó (1995): 'Cambio en la política de telecomunicaciones: Aspectos jurídicos y económicos', *Información Comercial Española*, Abril, 740, p. 63

Toth (1992): 'The Principle of Subsidiarity in the Maastricht Treaty' *Common Market Law Review*, 29, p. 1079

——(1994a): 'Is Subsidiarity Justiciable?', *European Law Review*, vol. 19, 3, June, p. 268

——(1994b) 'A Legal Analysis of Subsidiarity' in O'Keefe and Twomey (eds.): *Legal Issues of the Maastricht Treaty* (London: Chancery Law Publishing)

Toulemonde (1996): 'Peut-on évaluer la subsidiarité? Eléments de réponse inspirés de la pratique européenne', *Revue Internationale des Sciences Administratives*, vol. 62, 1, Mars, p. 59

Ungerer and Costello (1990): *Telecommunications in Europe: Free Choice for the User in Europe's 1992 Market. The Challenge for the European Community* (Luxembourg: Office for Official Publications of the EC)

Utz (1976): *Entre le néo-liberalisme et le néo-marxisme: Recherche philosophique d'une troisième voie* (Paris: Beauchesne)

Van der Knaap (1996): 'Government by Committee: Legal Typology, Quantitative Assessment and Institutional Repercussions of Committees in the EU' in Pedler and Schaefer (eds.): *Shaping European Law and Policy: The Role of Committees and Comitology in the Political Process* (Maastricht: European Institute of Public Administration)

Vandersanden (1992): 'Considérations sur le principe de subsidiarité' in *Présence du droit public et des droits de l'homme: Mélanges offerts à Jacques Velu*, vol. 1 (Bruxelles: Bruylant) p. 193

Verbeek (1994): 'The Politics of Subsidiarity in the European Union', *Journal of Common Market Studies*, vol. 32, 2, June, p. 215

Vibert (1995a): 'Plaidoyer pour un demantelement de la Commission' in Philip Morris Institute (ed.): *Quel avenir pour la Commission Européenne?* (Bruxelles: Philip Morris Institute) p. 72

——(1995b): *A Core Agenda for the 1996 Inter-Governmental Conference* (London: European Policy Forum)

Vives (1994): 'Desregulación y reforma regulatoria en el sector bancario' *Papeles de Economía Española*, 58, p. 9

Vogel (1986): *National Styles of Regulation. Environmental Policy in Great Britain and The United States* (Ithaca: Cornell University Press)

Von Beyme (1983): *The Political System of the Federal Republic of Germany* (Aldershot: Gower)

Vos (1997): 'The Rise of Committees'. *European Law Journal*, vol. 3, p. 210

Wallace and Golberg (1989): 'Television Broadcasting: The Community's Response', *Common Market Law Review*, 26 p. 717

Wallace and Wallace (1995): *Flying Together in a Larger and More Diverse European Union* (The Hague: SDU Uitgeverig)

Weiler (1981): 'The Community System: The Dual Character of Supranationalism', *Yearbook of European Law* 1, p. 257

——(1982): 'Community, Member States and European Integration: Is the Law Relevant?' *Journal of Common Market Studies*, 25, p. 39

——(1991a): 'The Transformation of Europe', *Yale Law Journal*, vol. 100. p. 2403

——(1991b): 'Problems of Legitimacy in Post 1992 Europe', *Aussenwirtschaft*, 46 Jahrgang, p. 179

——(1994): 'Fin-de-Siècle Europe' in R. Dehousse (ed.): *Europe after Maastricht: An Ever Closer Union?* (Munich: Beck) p. 203

——(1995): 'European Democracy and its Critique: Five Uneasy Pieces', *EUI Working Paper* RSC 95/11

——(1996): 'Legitimacy and Democracy of Union Governance: The 1996 Intergovernmental Agenda and Beyond', *ARENA* Working Paper, no. 22 (November)

——(1997): 'The Reformation of European Constitutionalism', *Journal of Common Market Studies*, vol. 35, 1

——(1998): 'Europe: The Case against the Case for Statehood', *Harvard Jean Monnet Working Paper Series*, 6/98.

——(1999): *The Constitution of Europe. Do the new clothes have an emperor? And other essays on European integration* (Cambridge: Cambridge University Press)

——and Lockhart (1995): '"Taking Rights Seriously" Seriously: The European Court and its Fundamental Rights Jurisprudence' (Part I), *Common Market Law Review*, vol. 32, 1, p. 51; (Part II), *Common Market Law Review*, vol. 32, 2, p. 579

——(2002): 'Fédéralisme et Constitutionalisme: Le Sonderweg de l'Europe', in Dehousse (ed.): *Une Constitution pour l'Europe?* (Paris: Presses de Sciences Po)

Weizsäcker (1989): *Erdpolitik. Oekologische Realpolitik an der Schwelle zum Jahrhundert der Umwelt* (Darmstadt: Wissenschaftliche Buchgesellschaft)

Whitelegg (1988): *Transport Policy in the EC* (London: Routledge)

Wilke and Wallace (1990): 'Subsidiarity: Approaches to Power Sharing in the EC', *RIIA Discussion Paper* no. 27

Winscott (1995): 'Political Theory, Law and European Union' in Shaw and More (eds.): *New Legal Dynamics of European Union* (Oxford: Clarendon Press) p. 293

Wyplosz (1994): 'Le principe de subsidiarité', *Economie Intenationale: La Revue du CEPII*, 58, Avril-Juin, pp. 131–48

Zuleeg (1997a): 'A Community of Law: Legal Cohesion in the EU', *Fordham International Law Journal*, vol. 20, 3, p. 623

——(1997b): 'The European Constitution under Constitutional Constraints: The German Scenario', *European Law Review*, vol. 22, 1, p. 192

INDEX